101 Forgotten Pop Hits of the 1980s

Nick Parkhouse

authorHOUSE®

AuthorHouse™ UK Ltd.
500 Avebury Boulevard
Central Milton Keynes, MK9 2BE
www.authorhouse.co.uk
Phone: 08001974150

© 2010 Nick Parkhouse. All rights reserved.

No part of this book may be reproduced, stored in a retrieval system, or transmitted by any means without the written permission of the author.

First published by AuthorHouse   4/26/2010

ISBN: 978-1-4490-9847-6 (sc)

This book is printed on acid-free paper.

For my dad

He hated most of this pop rubbish, to be honest. However, without his and my mum's love of music, there'd be no way I feel as passionately about this pop nonsense as I do today.

I do have to thank him for chapter 15, though. He made a detour to the big HMV store on Oxford Street on the way to work one day to buy this for me, in order that I'd get a free poster....

And to Maddie:

I know you only know *Mickey* and *Ghostbusters* now, but give it ten years....

Acknowledgements

I'd like to thank the following musicians, producers, vocalists, writers and general Eighties legends without whose help this book would never have become a reality:

Angry Anderson, Neil Arthur, Toni Basil, Robin Beck, Nick Beggs, Gary Clark, Sara Dallin, Simon Climie, Peter Cox, Phil Creswick, Richard Darbyshire, Hazell Dean, Elisa Fiorillo, Bobby Gee, Boon Gould, Graham Gouldman, Calvin Hayes, Michael Jay, Holly Johnson, Pat Kane, Nik Kershaw, Mark King, Limahl, David MacKay, Mark Moore, Nathan Moore, Mike Nocito, Rick Nowels, Charlene Oliver, Doris Pearson, Su Pollard, Danny Saxon, Sinitta, Curt Smith, Greedy Smith, Tiffany, Simon Toulson-Clarke, Ben Volpeliere-Pierrot, Martyn Ware, Walter Werzowa, Kim Wilde and Keren Woodward.

To Tony Hadley – thanks for not only unknowingly politely posing for a photo when I performed as Elton John on the same bill as you - but for your help with *Gold* and for reforming my favourite 80s band of them all. Truly you are the nicest man in pop.

To George Merrill and Shannon Rubicam – thank you for your enthusiasm and willingness to help, at a stage where I wasn't sure I was going to be able to finish this book. The help that the two of you gave made me believe I could do it.

To Pal Waaktaar – discussing a Bond theme with one of a-Ha? How much better can it get?

I'd also like to thank Caitlin Sorrell, Tom Coupe, Sarah Richardson and my family - my sister Abby, brother Matt and my mum – for having to put up with this endeavour from start to finish. And there's a bottle of wine waiting for you, Paul Adams – thanks for helping me compile the initial list.

Huge thanks also to my great friend Tim Sorrell without whose support, advice and careful grammatical knowhow, this would be just a shambolic collection of badly apostrophised drivel.

Finally, thanks to my wife, Di. This is despite cruelly vetoing Angry Anderson's *Suddenly* as a wedding choice and not understanding the appeal of Stefan Dennis. She's wrong on both counts, obviously.

Foreword

I've often found it strange how frequently the term 'pop music' is used in a negative sense. Somehow the notion that a record is categorised as 'pop' means it is looked down on as a poor relation with the intimation that there will be an absence of quality and/or talent involved.

Frankly, I think this is poppycock. The enduring success over recent decades of artists like Kylie, Take That, Westlife, Will Young, the Spice Girls and Madonna, and (I hate to use the term) 'revival' of pop music recently with the likes of Mika, Leona Lewis, Britney Spears, Lily Allen and Lady GaGa means the genre has never been more popular or successful.

It's easy to be snobby about three minute pop records, particularly those by artists that are deemed 'manufactured'. I don't see the need. Weren't the Monkees manufactured? Didn't the Beatles and Slade write catchy three minute pop records? Didn't the Blur and Oasis genre have 'pop' in its name?

The purpose of this book is to celebrate some of those pop records from a great decade that have been buried in the great landfill of time.

When presenting on University radio in the late 1990s, and on the odd occasion someone has been daft enough to invite me to DJ a function or pub/club night, my aim has always been one thing: I have always wanted to play records that make people stop, however briefly, before their brain searches its filing system in an often futile attempt at recollection. I love the phrase "God, I haven't heard this for **ages**!"

I have been to plenty of Eighties nights and clubs in my time. Many of my friends would tell you the number is unhealthy for a man of my years, but I'll leave that open to interpretation.

My biggest gripe with them is that there seems to be a rigid 80s playlist developing of songs that attending punters are expecting to hear. And, more worryingly, there doesn't seem to be any significant deviation from this list. There are a dozen or so songs that a DJ might as well tick off as they are played.

The 80s was a fantastic decade for pop music with hundreds of memorable songs. This book is intended as testament to the 'forgotten' songs of that era. That is why you won't find *Tainted Love* in here, or *Wake Me Up Before You Go-Go* or *Don't You Want Me?* Neither will you find *The Reflex*, *Relax* or *Karma Chameleon*. Don't get me wrong, these records are superb pop singles in their own right but overexposure and their already-secured spot in the public consciousness eliminates them.

So what is included? I'll be honest – it's shamelessly arbitrary. Firstly, I have tried to ignore any record which I consider is already part of the 80s furniture. That doesn't mean I have avoided big hits – there are twelve number One records included – but I have tried to avoid the giant behemoth 80s records played week in, week out at weddings and birthday parties up and down the land.

Secondly, I have tried to exclude anything I don't consider pure 'pop' music. This was more difficult to define. It's easy to take out 'rock' music and so, for example, Van Halen's *Jump*, Huey Lewis' *The Power Of Love* and John Farnham's *You're The Voice* – all great records – were eliminated. I also excluded 'dance/rap/hip-hop' music (ignorantly lumping together three utterly discrete genres) and that did for M/A/R/R/S *Pump Up The Volume*, Grandmaster Flash's *White Lines* and Soul II Soul's *Back To Life*.

I then tried to omit anything which had a purely novelty feel about it, even if it were a decent enough record. I couldn't therefore find a place for Russ Abbott's *Atmosphere*, Anita Dobson's *Anyone Can Fall In Love* or the Firm's *Star Trekkin'* (all brilliantly kitsch records in their own way).

Finally, I tried to avoid anything that was too obscure. Whilst I love the phrase "I haven't heard this for **ages**!", I hate the phrase "what on **earth** is this?". I therefore owe 'sorries' to many, including Westworld for their great *Sonic Boom Boy*, to Dream Academy for *Life In A Northern Town* and to Robbie Nevil for *C'est La Vie*.

My biggest problem, and I don't mind admitting this, was whether to include Dennis Waterman's *I Could Be So Good For You*. The original 'write the feem choon, sing the feem choon', it's a great single from, let's be fair, a great TV series. I agonised over it, and decided it probably wasn't quite 'pop' in its truest sense. Sorry, Dennis, it didn't make the cut.

So, what's left is a selection of 101 of the finest pop singles of the decade: some might be staples in your house and not 'forgotten' at all; some you will no doubt have no recollection of whatsoever and wonder whether you were living in a parallel universe. You will no doubt clamour for the inclusion of omitted tracks and question my inclusion of others. And so it always will be – pop music will divide, but it will ultimately rule.

1 Brother Beyond
The Harder I Try

Released: 20 July 1988 **Parlophone R 6184**
Highest UK Chart Position: #2

"My A&R man said to me once that the difference between a number One record and a number Two record was huge. It's only now I realise why that is. When radio stations do their 'on this day' feature, they'll play whatever was number One twenty years ago, but not what was number Two…"

Nathan Moore, the eternally youthful lead singer of Brother Beyond, concisely explains the problem that many of the songs in this book have experienced. They may have sold hundreds of thousands of singles, but they are passed over twenty years hence because they didn't quite make that coveted number One spot.

Brother Beyond have Phil Collins to blame for denying them their number One record. Despite selling 400,000 copies and being number One in the midweek charts right up until Friday afternoon, *The Harder I Try* ended up being outsold by a mere two hundred panel sales over the course of seven days and *A Groovy Kind Of Love* claimed the coveted number One position on 10 September 1988.

Brothers Dave and Eg White, Carl Fysh and singer Nathan Moore had worked tirelessly to no avail through 1986 and 1987 to launch their chart career. Despite some reasonable airplay and publicity, their first four singles had failed to trouble the top Forty and they were in danger of being dropped by their record label.

In early 1988, the multi-million selling songwriting team of Stock, Aitken and Waterman decided to auction their services for charity. EMI won the auction (for the princely sum of £20,000) and asked the team to write a song for their band the Belle Stars.

Pete Waterman had previously met Brother Beyond on several occasions (often in their local pub), and asked EMI if he could write a song for Brother Beyond instead of the all-girl band. The record company agreed and some weeks later *The Harder I Try* was born.

Just as the single came about, drummer and songwriter Eg White decided he was unhappy with the direction of the group and left to be replaced by the band's live drummer Steve Alexander. Despite missing out on their success, White continued to write great music for the likes of Joss Stone, James Morrison, Adele and James Blunt and won a coveted Ivor Novello award in 2004 for writing Will Young's chart-topping single *Leave Right Now*.

It took about three hours for Moore to record the vocals for the single under the careful eye of producer Mike Stock. A video shot in Milan involving Nathan sprinting around the old town ("…the director filmed each sequence about six times and so I basically spent my day running around the city!") helped promote the single and on 30 July 1988 it began its slow climb up the charts, peaking at number Two for two weeks in September 1988.

Despite being written at the peak of their popularity, it is by no means a formulaic S/A/W record. Waterman wanted the song to have a Motown feel and, by sampling the drum introduction of the Isley Brothers *This Old Heart Of Mine*, they created a more soulful, crafted pop record. There is less of the standard synthesised PWL sound in evidence – indeed many people were surprised it was a S/A/W record at all. Even though it was not the producers' biggest hit, many think it is the finest record the threesome ever wrote.

Brother Beyond followed up this single with another S/A/W penned single, the number Six hit *He Ain't No Competition* (Pete Waterman called this "their message to Matt Goss") and the top Twenty hit *Be My Twin*. They were also on the receiving end of one of the multitude of gaffes at the infamous 1989 Brit awards when Samantha Fox and Mick Fleetwood failed to announce their nomination in the 'Best New Band' category.

Despite their success with the Hit Factory, guitarist David White was overheard by Waterman making disparaging remarks about the songwriters during an interview on Radio 1 and their relationship was effectively ended. When the Hit Factory decided to remake *Do They Know It's Christmas?* in 1989, Brother Beyond were conspicuous by their absence, a disappointment compounded only by the invitation extended to their bitter rivals Bros to appear on the record.

Without the S/A/W input, their second album *Trust* barely made the top Seventy-Five and the band split soon after. Nathan achieved significant further success in continental Europe with his band Worlds Apart and, despite an offer to reform for the ITV series *Baby One More Time*, the band have yet to appear together again. Shame, really, as *The Harder I Try* remains one of the most recognisable and loved singles of its time.

2 Climie Fisher
Love Changes (Everything)

Released: 12 March 1988 **EMI EM47**
Highest UK Chart Position: #2

Reaching number Sixty-Seven in September 1987 on its original release, *Love Changes (Everything)* was nearly the best record of the 80s never to be a hit. As it was, a successful remix and reissue propelled it into the top Ten and gave the duo a well deserved top Three smash.

Songwriter Simon Climie had already tasted chart success by the time he met with Naked Eyes keyboardist Rob Fisher at the bar of the Abbey Road studios where both were working as session musicians. His composition *I Knew You Were Waiting (For Me)* had been a 1987 UK number One for George Michael and Aretha Franklin and his songs had also been recorded by the likes of Jeff Beck and Smokey Robinson. Fisher had achieved significant success in the US and Canada with his band Naked Eyes but was perhaps most famous in the UK for the insidious bassline he provided on Billy Ocean's hit *When The Going Gets Tough* in 1986.

There is an urban myth that Climie originally offered *Love Changes (Everything)* to Rod Stewart and when he declined, Climie sang the vocals himself in a Stewart-esque style. Whilst Climie had submitted songs to Stewart in the past (his song *My Heart Can't Tell Me No* appeared on Rod's 1988 album *Out Of Order*) *Love Changes (Everything)* was never actually intended for Stewart. It had actually been sent to Robert Palmer (who Climie was a huge fan of at the time) but had been passed over.

After Palmer declined the song, legendary producer Steve Lillywhite encouraged Climie to record *Love Changes (Everything)* alongside more of his own material, and the duo commenced the recording of their debut album as the band Climie Fisher. Most of the writing took place at Fisher's Richmond home and Simon often arrived to find that Rob had the basic components of a song (the drumbeat or a basic melody) already written. The verse of *Time Changes Everything* (as it was originally to be called) came pretty quickly and the whole song took the duo under two hours to pen. The album itself took eighteen months to write and record (partly due to producer Lillywhite having to leave the album half way through the recording process to work on another project) and included several collaborations with American songwriter Denis Morgan.

Eventually, the lyrics and title of the debut single were changed to *Love Changes Everything* (the duo believed it sounded better) and it was released in September 1987. Without much backing from their record company EMI the single barely scraped the top 75. On the brink of being dropped by the label, EMI asked Climie's advice as to what to do next and he suggested they release the song *Rise To The Occasion*. A hip-hop mix of the record (rather than the lush ballad originally recorded) became a big hit across Europe and spent three weeks inside the UK top Ten.

On the back of this success, *Love Changes (Everything)* started getting significant airplay in Germany (where it became a hit) and it was decided to re-release the song in the UK. Accompanied by a stylish black and white video, the song climbed to number Two in the spring of 1988, only kept off the top of the charts by the Pet Shop Boys' third number One single *Heart*. It went on to be a huge hit worldwide including reaching number Twenty-Three on the US Billboard singles chart and winning the Ivor Novello award in 1989 for 'best pop song'.

Clime Fisher's subsequent releases failed to scale the heights of *Love Changes (Everything)* and despite further top 40 hits (including the stunning *Love Like A River*) the duo split in the early 1990s. Simon Climie continues to be a successful producer for the likes of Eric Clapton and Michael MacDonald and Fisher also continued in the industry, co-writing Rick Astley's superb 'comeback' single *Cry For Help* in 1991. Sadly, however, Rob Fisher died in August 1999 during surgery for bowel cancer. He was just 39 years old.

Love Changes (Everything) (the brackets were included deliberately as it was Climie and Denis Morgan's desire "to say something that someone has said before in a brand new way") is, in my opinion, quite simply the finest pop record of the 1980's. Andy Gill in *The Independent* once said that Climie's voice "simultaneously soothes and suggests heartbreak" and this description can also be applied to this song. Both mournful and optimistic, its magical mixture of melody, bittersweet lyrics and superb vocals have rarely (if ever) been bettered, and if any record of the decade deserved to be a number One hit, this was it.

3 Owen Paul
My Favourite Waste Of Time

Released: 31 May 1986   Epic A 7125
Highest UK Chart Position: #3

The 1980s saw its fair share of 'one hit wonders', defined as those artists who had one single chart success. Indeed, the Eighties saw a number of number One wonders – chart-topping songs which were a particular artists sole chart success. From the likes of Fern Kinney (*Together We Are Beautiful*) through Steve "Silk" Hurley (*Jack Your Body*) to The Timelords (*Doctorin' The Tardis*), the decade was littered with acts who appeared, had one smash hit and then disappeared down the Dumper (as *Smash Hits* would have said) as quickly as they arrived.

One such one-hit wonder, although largely by choice, was Scottish singer-songwriter Owen Paul McGee. Born in Glasgow in May 1962, McGee was actually a promising footballer in his teenage years and was an apprentice with Celtic when he decided to pursue a career in music. He was 'roped in' to a band at the height of the punk boom (even though he couldn't play an instrument) and, inspired by the punk movement, McGee decided that he wanted to be a singer and musician rather than a footballer.

McGee's elder brother Brian was also a guitarist who, in the same year Owen left Celtic, formed the band Johnny and the Self Abusers alongside school friends Jim Kerr, Charlie Burchill and Tony Donald. They later became the hugely successful rock band Simple Minds and McGee remained a member of Simple Minds for four albums before leaving in 1981.

Changing his name to Owen Paul, the singer moved to London and was involved with a number of lesser known punk and New Romantic bands before his big break came on the BBC's *Oxford Roadshow* in the mid 1980s. Although his first single *Pleased To Meet You* failed to chart, it was his follow-up release that would become Paul's one chart success.

My Favourite Waste Of Time was not an original song but a cover of a track written by the American singer-songwriter Marshall Crenshaw. Crenshaw first shot to fame after playing John Lennon in the off-Broadway musical *Beatlemania* and, whilst not an internationally successful artist commercially, Crenshaw has a deserved reputation as a talented songwriter. He has released a number of critically acclaimed albums since his self-titled debut in 1982 and appeared as Buddy Holly in the 1987 film *La Bamba*. Crenshaw also co-wrote the title track to the 2008 film *Walk Hard: The Dewey Cox Story* for which he was nominated for both a Grammy and a Golden Globe.

Paul's version of *My Favourite Waste Of Time* (featuring future Thunder bassist Mark Luckhurst) was a summer hit in 1986 spending fourteen weeks on the chart on its way to peaking at number Three in July. As well as Paul's version the song has also been covered by artists as diverse as Bette Midler and New York singer-songwriter Freedy Johnston. In 2009, Paul's version was also used in a Kellogg's cereal commercial.

During the song's climb up the UK top Forty, Paul was invited to appear on the BBC's popular lunchtime magazine show *Pebble Mill*. The result was one of the most embarrassing television appearances of the decade as when the presenter introduced Paul and his band and the backing track began playing, neither the musicians nor the singer realised the song had begun. Whilst the music played happily for the viewing public Paul leant nonchalantly on a railing failing to mime along to the music for a full minute before the programme cut back to the studio.

Although *My Favourite Waste Of Time* was a huge success for Paul, it became obvious that everything was not well with the singer. Feeling he was going in a musical direction that he wasn't comfortable with, Paul engaged in an increasingly bitter fight with Sony Records, arguing that they were 'killing' what he had to offer. His follow-up singles all failed to chart, and, disillusioned with the music industry Paul turned his back on music at the end of 1986.

Paul's second unfortunate TV appearance occurred in 2002 during the first season of the reality sitcom *The Osbournes*. Upset with the noise being made by their next door neighbours the dysfunctional family protested by throwing food into the adjoining garden. Sharon Osbourne even lobbed a leg of ham in an attempt to persuade the neighbour – later revealed as Owen Paul – to quieten down.

Paul did return with the album *About Time* in 2002 although it is likely he will just be remembered for his one UK hit. *My Favourite Waste Of Time* is a superb, chirpy pop song although ironically its commercial nature ended up turning Paul away from the music business and the chance of further success.

4 Holly Johnson
Americanos

Released: 1 April 1989   MCA MCA1323
Highest UK Chart Position: #4

It would be fair to say that every teenager goes through at least one phase when an obsession takes over their life. From Tom Cruise to *Twilight*, the Beatles to Boyzone, every child encounters something in their formative years that completely takes over their life (temporarily of course, or at least until something else comes along and supplants it).

I'm not embarrassed to confess that for a few months in early 1989 I was a little bit obsessed with Holly Johnson (for the record: shortly after Martika, shortly before Tears for Fears). I had not even been that big a fan of Frankie Goes To Hollywood, if I am honest, although oddly I did like their least successful and little remembered final single *Watching the Wildlife*.

Johnson had spent years at the top of the music industry with Frankie. They became only the second act in history to have their first three singles go to number One in the charts (fellow Liverpudlians Gerry and the Pacemakers were the first) and their mammoth hits *Two Tribes* and *Relax* remain two of the UK's top Thirty best selling singles of all time. *Relax*, of course, was also famously banned by the BBC after Radio One DJ Mike Read branded the record 'disgusting' on his show (ironically, of course, sending the record immediately to the top of the charts on the back of the publicity this generated.)

Despite Frankie Goes To Hollywood's success the group split in 1987 as a result of increasing differences between Johnson and the rest of the band. Wanting to embark on a solo career, Johnson became embroiled in a bitter (and ultimately groundbreaking) High Court case with Frankie's record label ZTT who insisted that Johnson record his solo material through them.

After a hearing lasting a fortnight, the court found in Johnson's favour, holding that the restrictive nature of his ZTT contract constituted a 'restraint of trade'. The singer was then free to sign a solo recording deal with MCA Records and released his first solo single *Love Train* in 1989. Featuring a Brian May guitar solo the single was well received and it reached the top Five in February of that year.

The roots to Johnson's follow up single *Americanos* can be traced back several years to the end of 1986. Johnson and his partner Wolfgang had decided to spend the Christmas of that year in Pittsburgh with Wolfgang's sister Brigitte Rossi and her family. Johnson loved the American culture and admitted to enjoying walking round the supermarkets seeing an array of unusual and exotic groceries (including, of course, Oreos, to which the song refers repeatedly.) The term 'Americanos' also stems from that visit as it was a word that popped up regularly on a Radio Pittsburgh feature about the increasing Spanish population in the US and how Spanish had become America's second most spoken language. The lyrics are actually a clever satire of the late 80s American culture – a country where a penniless child can grow up to be President is one of America's great lies – particularly for the Latino community.

A demo of the song was recorded in 1987, produced by Johnson's friend Steve Lovell and with a string arrangement by World Party's Guy Chambers (who would later achieve significant success as co-writer and producer of many of Robbie Williams' early hits). Johnson convinced MCA to allow Lovell and Andy Richards to produce two songs from his debut album although the first efforts at *Americanos* weren't promising. Johnson felt the slow R&B bassline didn't fit the song (and sounded too much like Bruce Springsteen's *Hungry Heart*) and so, with the help of American producer Dan Hartman, he came up with a Latino bassline. PWL mixers Ian Curnow and Phil Harding had also come up with a very commercial version of *Americanos* (which Johnson found 'too Kylie and Jason') and so the single ended up being a combination of the best bits of these two versions.

Accompanied by a John Waters inspired video, *Americanos* gave Johnson his second top Five hit, reaching number Four in the UK for two weeks in April 1989. This was followed by the release of the number One platinum album *Blast* and further hits *Atomic City* and *Heaven's Here*. It was to be the end of Johnson's chart career, however, as disagreements with record company MCA over the promotional budget for the follow-up album *Dreams That Money Can't Buy* meant the singer had left the label by the time of release.

It is a real shame that Johnson's solo work tends to be overlooked in favour of the Frankie Goes To Hollywood output when *Blast* and its singles, particularly *Americanos*, are at least as good as anything that band ever produced.

5 Olivia Newton-John
Physical

Released: 10 October 1981   **EMI 5234**
Highest UK Chart Position: #7

Olivia Neutron-Bomb (as she became less than affectionately known in the 1970's) first hit the big time in the UK back in the early 1970's. Born in Cambridge but brought up in the Australian city of Melbourne from the age of five, Newton-John returned to the UK in the mid 1960s having won a trip to England on the popular Aussie talent show *Sing, Sing, Sing*.

Her first hit in the UK was a cover of the Bob Dylan song *If Not For You* which reached number Seven in the summer of 1971. Her success spread to America when her 1973 album *Let Me Be There* reached the top Ten in the US as well as earning Newton-John two Grammy awards. In 1974, Newton-John represented the United Kingdom at the Eurovision Song Contest, but her song *Long Live Love* finished fourth behind the eventual winners – Abba with their career-launching *Waterloo*.

Newton-John's career continued to develop until a chance meeting with film producer Allan Carr at a Hollywood party led to her being cast in his upcoming movie adaptation of the Broadway musical *Grease*. Insisting on a screen test with  the film's male lead, John Travolta (amid concerns that at the age of 29 she was too old to play a High School senior) Newton-John secured the part of Sandy and the script was re-written to explain her Australian accent and to 'toughen up' her character.

Grease was the biggest box office hit of 1978 and the soundtrack spawned a number of huge singles. Duetting with Travolta, both *Summer*

Nights and *You're The One That I Want* made number One in the UK, the latter selling almost two million copies and becoming one of the top Ten selling singles in UK chart history. Newton-John also had a solo hit with the ballad *Hopelessly Devoted To You* which reached number Two in November 1978.

Following her success in Grease, Newton-John re-launched her music career by moving from the more country sound of the early 70s to more contemporary pop. Further hits *A Little More Love* and *Xanadu* (her number One collaboration with the Electric Light Orchestra) followed before she returned to the studio with long-time collaborator John Farrar to record her next album.

The previous year, American musician Steve Kipner had teamed up with English songwriter Terry Shaddick to write a song focusing on the physical (rather than the emotional) side of love called, appropriately, *Let's Get Physical*. Newton-John's manager Lee Kramer overheard the song being played to a record company executive and thought it would be suitable for his client. It was re-titled *Physical* and recorded in early 1981.

Newton-John was initially concerned about recording *Physical* because of its sexual innuendo and felt that it would damage her clean-cut image. To mask the sexual content, the video featured Newton-John working out in a gym with several overweight men who eventually turn into thin, muscular guys. It is also revealed at the end of the video that the men are gay, which resulted in MTV often cutting the end of the video to eliminate this scene. The sensuous video was also banned by some Western broadcasters (even though it won the Grammy award for 'Video Of The Year') and the song itself was banned in certain conservative communities for its sexual content.

Physical was released in the US in the autumn of 1981 and it became the most successful Billboard Hot 100 single of the 1980's, spending an unprecedented ten weeks at the top of the singles chart, selling over two million copies. The song also made the top Ten in the UK, peaking at number Seven on the same day it hit the top of the American chart.

The timing of *Physical* couldn't have been better as it coincided with the start of the home exercise video phenomenon. Mirroring Newton-John's video for the single, *The Jane Fonda Workout* (released in 1982) became one of the best-selling home movies of all time and is credited with helping to launch the VCR market in America. The song was even included in an episode of the popular children's series *Sesame Street*, renamed *Let's All Exercise* and featuring Grover and Prairie Dawn amongst other Muppets.

Whilst Newton-John never had another hit on the scale of *Physical*, she continues to release albums as well as being a vocal health advocate having survived breast cancer in the early 1990s. She also sang at the opening ceremony of the Sydney Olympic Games in 2000.

6 Reynolds Girls
I'd Rather Jack

Released: 25 February 1989 **PWL PWL25**
Highest UK Chart Position: #8

Stock, Aitken and Waterman didn't have very many 'one hit wonders' and most of their protégés ended up having a reasonable string of decent sized hits. The Reynolds Girls, however, are probably the most famous exception.

Even during the Hit Factory's huge success of the late 80s Pete Waterman continued to present a weekly radio show in Liverpool. It was during one of his visits to the studio in the city that he was pestered by two young sisters wanting him to listen to their demo tape. Linda, an eighteen year old blonde and Aisling, her sixteen year old brunette sister were from a Liverpool family of nine siblings – three brothers and six sisters. Determined to be pop stars, they spent hours sitting outside Waterman's office trying, without success, to get the writer and producer to listen to their tape. Eventually, Waterman put the cassette on in his car ("by accident, really!") and liked what he heard. He played the tape to colleague Mike Stock, who also liked the girls' vocals, and they were duly signed to the PWL label. Linda left her job in a hairdressing salon and Aisling dropped out of studying for her "A" levels to pursue their singing careers.

With a contract with PWL secured, the girls needed a song to record. The idea for what turned out to be their only hit came from a chance remark made by Aitken some months before. The producers were unhappy that the PWL stable (and other similar pop acts) had been overlooked at the Brit Awards in favour of artists such as Steve Winwood, Enya and Tanita Tikaram.

As Waterman said "Fleetwood Mac are the typical example of your boring old farts that are always on the radio. We just wanted to say to the DJ's "Excuse me guys, but just remember now and again that you are 40 year old blokes with CDs in your cars and there is actually a whole big generation of teenagers out there who want to hear the latest dance stuff, the latest hits, and need encouragement. So it's time the old codgers moved over – don't let the music industry evolve around a few select 40 year olds' personal musical taste.""

Complaining one day about how hopeless they thought Fleetwood Mac were, Matt Aitken grumbled "…hmmmm. I'd rather jack" and so the idea for the song was born. The hit featured lyrics about how the radio was eschewing newer talent in favour of older, more established acts (Pink Floyd, the Rolling Stones and Dire Straits are namechecked in the song) although the catchy *I'd Rather Jack* made little sense considering no-one was quite sure what 'to Fleetwood Mac' meant.

The girls were slightly unsure at the unusual lyrics at first but soon came round. As Aisling argued "we love the House stuff and Yazz and Bros and Bananarama – they're all great to sing along to and that's good. Cos that's what kids want – they don't want to hear about problems of the world, they want to go out and have a good time, listen to really good fun records. And that's what ours is, it's fun. It's not about nuclear waste, it's got a great beat, there's humour in it and it's now, it's today…."

The video for the single featured the girls prancing about in their home city of Liverpool and featured some awful 80s dancing that made Rick Astley look like Fred Astaire (the video also featured members of the girls' family as extras). The song itself was released in February 1989 and climbed to number Eight in the UK.

The girls also embarked on the Hitman Roadshow tour with the likes of Big Fun, Jason Donovan and Shooting Party to a rapturous reception. Smash Hits Australia called them 'the new Mel and Kim' and it appeared the world was at their feet. However, when the girls went into PWL to record their debut album, some 'creative differences' quickly arose. Waterman claimed that the girls had become "too big for their boots" (he stated that the girls' failure to cancel a pre-booked holiday to record and promote their second single was arrogant) and was also critical of the girls' TV appearance ("the record went flying up the charts but when the Reynolds Girls appeared on *Top of the Pops* they killed it stone dead"). The duo split from PWL after just one single.

The girls argued that they only ever had a one-record deal and that they wanted to pursue their own careers. With the backing of their father the pair recorded the follow-up single *Get Real* but without the Stock, Aitken and Waterman backing the song failed to chart and that was the last anyone ever saw of the duo.

I'd Rather Jack has been rather tarnished by time and is widely used by anti-Hit Factory types who hold it up as everything that was wrong with their manufactured sound. However, the song was intended to make a point (which it clumsily did) and if you strip out the terrible clichéd late 80s image the girls created, it's nowhere near as bad a song as you'd presume. I still don't know how you 'Fleetwood Mac', though.

7 Johnny Hates Jazz
I Don't Want To Be A Hero

Released: 29 August 1987   **Virgin VS948**
Highest UK Chart Position: #11

For thousands of people turning up at the Nottingham Ice Arena on the evening of the 9th May 2008, very few of them would have been aware that they were about to witness a music first. For, at around 8pm that evening, Johnny Hates Jazz took the stage for their first ever live arena performance since their debut on the charts over twenty years earlier.

Johnny Hates Jazz were formed in 1986 by friends Phil Thornalley, Mike Nocito and Calvin Hayes and the name came very literally from Nocito's brother in law Johnny's dislike of jazz. When Thornalley had to withdraw as vocalist due to the production commitments he had with American singer Robbie Nevil (he co-produced Nevil's top three hit *C'est La Vie*), the band enlisted Clark Datchler to front the project. Their first single *Me And My Foolish Heart* was released on Hayes' father (the legendary producer Mickie Most)'s RAK Records label in late 1986 and when the single failed to chart, the trio went in search of a major label contract.

The band arranged a showcase for their music ("to fool labels into thinking we were a live group") and this was, ironically, held at Ronnie Scott's jazz club in London. Virgin signed the band after this performance and their first single *Shattered Dreams* was released in March 1987. The song was a huge success on both sides of the Atlantic, reaching number Five in the UK and number Two in the American Billboard chart.

The band then went into the studio to begin the meticulous process of recording their debut album. The trio wanted to ensure that everything on the record was perfect and would take days to ensure that all the sequencing, programming and production was correct. Hayes recalled how *Turn Back The Clock* was recorded in the studio adjacent to that in which the Pogues were recording their 1988 album *If I Should Fall From Grace With God*. Whilst Johnny Hates Jazz's studio looked like a science lab, the Pogues' looked like a pub as the band shambled through the recording of their most successful record (the two albums were eventually released just a week apart).

With great pressure on the band to follow up *Shattered Dreams*, the catchy chorus of *I Don't Want To Be A Hero* led to it being chosen as the follow-up single. The demo of the record was slower and darker than the eventual single release which was also improved by a great Julian Mendelssohn remix. The great strength of *I Don't Want To Be A Hero* lies in its poignant lyrics which tell the tale of a soldier questioning his participation in a war he considers unjust (and which remain as relevant in the 21st century as they were in 1988).

I Don't Want To Be A Hero was released in August 1987 and eventually peaked just outside the UK top Ten, reaching number Eleven in September. However, the head of Virgin Records in America, Jordan Harris, was unhappy with the choice of …*Hero* as the follow-up single because of its anti-war sentiment. When the video was reworked with clips of Vietnam and similar MTV wouldn't touch it. This lack of exposure and its difficult subject matter meant it only reached number Thirty-One in the US charts.

Johnny Hates Jazz's next single, the laid-back *Turn Back The Clock* reached the top Twenty before the album of the same name debuted at number One in January 1988. The further single *Heart of Gold* followed (featuring a video directed by acclaimed American director David Fincher, responsible for *Se7en* and *Fight Club*) but this continued success was masking the fact that the band had already split. Datchler had already informed his bandmates after a TV show in Finland that he wasn't planning to make another Johnny Hates Jazz record and whilst he remained "officially" in the band throughout most of 1988, he undertook little promotional work and their world tour had to be shelved.

The remaining due rehired Phil Thornalley as vocalist for their second album *Tall Stories* released in 1991 but the momentum was lost and the record failed to chart. As of course did Datchler's solo work and, despite being the writer of most of the bands biggest hits, he couldn't translate this into a successful solo career. Thornalley became a successful writer, penning hits for artists as varied as Bryan Adams, Natalie Imbruglia and Pixie Lott.

Johnny Hates Jazz split in 1992 and it took fifteen years for the name to reappear when Hayes, Nocito and new vocalist Danny Saxon agreed to perform four nights at a 1980's reunion show at Butlins, Minehead in late 2007. The success of these gigs prompted the trio to agree to more shows and they embarked on a nationwide tour alongside the likes of Rick Astley and Paul Young in May 2008.

8 Kim Wilde
Kids In America

Released: 21 Feb 1981 **RAK327**
Highest UK Chart Position: #2

One of the most recognisable voices and faces of the decade, Kim Wilde (born Kim Smith) was the highest selling and most charted British female soloist of the 1980s. Despite never achieving a number One single in the UK, Wilde had a string of top Twenty hits between 1981 and 1993 and spent almost three and a half years on the singles chart during that period.

Her story began in 1980 after she had finished an Art and Design course at St Albans College. Her brother, Ricky, had taken a number of songs to legendary producer RAK Records boss Mickie Most who had agreed to let him record them. A 20 year old Kim was invited to the studio as a backing vocalist for Ricky's recordings, believing she would be able to earn her living as a session singer.

Whilst working on Ricky's album, Most saw and heard Kim, and immediately expressed an interest in working with her, believing he had found a 'ready-made pop star'. Ricky (and Kim's father Marty, himself a successful singer in the 1950s and 1960s) were determined to be involved with Kim's career, and so wrote several songs for her to record.

In a gothic recording studio in Hereford (owned by prog-rock band Enid) Kim Wilde recorded some of her early songs, including a high-energy pop number called *Kids In America*. On hearing the demo tape, Most remixed the song himself, although the single release ended up being very similar to the demo recording.

Released in February 1981, *Kids In America* was Wilde's debut single and an instant success, selling between thirty thousand and forty thousand copies a day at its height. It climbed to number Two on the UK top Forty by the end of March 1981 and it took the biggest selling British male soloist of the 1980s (Shakin' Stevens) to keep *Kids In America* off the top of the charts.

Many people assumed Wilde was American simply due to the content of the lyrics and her tomboy-ish looks (she wore her dad's dinner jacket in the video for this single) which were inspired by the likes of Chrissie Hynde and Debbie Harry. Questions were asked as to what a white middle-class girl from Hertfordshire was doing singing about New York and East California, but the lyrics of the song reflected her father's formative years growing up in the 1950s. All the cool things that were happening in popular and youth culture in that immediate post-war era were happening in America (and to the kids thereof).

Kids In America sold over a million copies worldwide and was, for years, Kim's biggest hit (later to be equalled by her cover of the Supremes *You Keep Me Hangin' On* which made number Two in the UK and number One in the US in 1986). Whilst not everybody's personal Wilde favourite (who could ignore the pop perfection of *You Came?*) *Kids In America* remains arguably Wilde's most popular and most well-known single. On her return to the pop music scene in recent years, Wilde re-recorded *Kids In America* with ex-Ash guitarist Charlotte Hatherley and this new version appeared on her 2006 album *Never Say Never*.

Kids In America also launched Wilde's quarter of a century long career which incorporated collaborations with the likes of Junior and TV comic Mel Smith, a near year-long chart run with her fantastic album *Close* and a Brit award for 'Best Female Artist' in 1983.

On her effective retirement from the music business in the mid 1990's, Kim embarked on her second successful career as a horticulturalist. In 2000, Wilde became involved with the Channel 4 series *Better Gardens* and the BBC show *Garden Invaders* and has subsequently written two books on the subject. She also won a Gold award at the Royal Horticultural Society (RHS) Chelsea Flower show in 2005 for her 'Cumbrian Fellside' garden.

As well as holding the record for the biggest selling British female artist on the 1980's, Wilde (with fellow horticulturalist Dave Fountain) also holds an entry in the *Guinness Book of Records* for moving and transplanting the world's largest tree. Rather unfortunately, it blew over in a storm in January 2007.

9 Spandau Ballet
Gold

Released: 13 August 1983 **Reformation SPAN2**
Highest UK Chart Position: #2

Whilst it might be the least forgotten of these songs, and might be wheeled out during every Olympic Games from now until time immemorial, there can be no denying the majesty of this record: one of the decade's finest.

They say that the artists who enjoy long and successful careers are those who change, and adapt to the prevailing musical environment. Singers such as Madonna and Kylie have managed to sustain lengthy chart lives thanks to their ability to evolve in terms of their style, sound and appearance. In 1983, Spandau Ballet's gradual evolution from electronic New Romantic trendsetters into sophisticated, soulful pop was complete, and no record epitomised this transformation more than *Gold*.

Brothers Gary and Martin Kemp, drummer John Keeble, guitarist Steve Norman and singer Tony Hadley had become Spandau Ballet (the term referring to the spasms of Nazi war criminals hanged at Berlin's infamous Spandau prison) at their Islington school during the latter part of the 1970s. As the quintet spent more time in the trendy London nightclubs of the late Seventies, their musical style transformed from a standard sixties-inspired R&B into cutting edge electronica.

Signed to Chrysalis Records in 1980, there was already a huge buzz around the band that led to their debut single *To Cut A Long Story Short* being released a mere ten days after recording. Spandau became instantly popular and their debut album *Journeys to Glory* and the follow-up *Diamond* were spiky, funk-inspired records which cemented Spandau's position at the forefront of the New Romantic movement. Further hit singles followed including *Musclebound*, *Instinction* and the top three smash *Chant No 1*.

The evolution from New Romantic electronica into an internationally recognised adult contemporary band began with the recording of their third album *True* in 1983. Eschewing the 'tea towels on the head' and kilts in favour of sharp 1940's suits, the band shook off their cold electronic sound in favour of a record inspired by soul and R&B and featuring the saxophone talents of guitarist Steve Norman. The band decamped to the exotic Compass Point Studios in the Bahamas and, under the guidance of producers Steve Jolley and Tony Swain, came up with an album designed to appeal to the mainstream market.

Whilst the *True* album was just eight songs and thirty-five minutes long, it was a massive international success on its release in March 1983. The lead single *Lifeline* made the UK top Ten swiftly followed by top Twenty hit *Communication* but it was the release of the album's title track that catapulted Spandau to major international success.

True was the band's first and only UK number One single and also reached number Four in the USA. A six minute love song that pays tribute to Motown legend Marvin Gaye, it is one of the defining and best-selling singles of the 1980s as well as being one of the most sampled songs from that era (acts including PM Dawn, Z-Ro and Nelly have used the track).

In the summer of 1983 Spandau Ballet were the biggest band around and followed up the massive success of *True* with another slice of clever, stylish pop - the catchy and slick *Gold*. *Gold* was inspired by the James Bond themes that Kemp had grown up with and whilst rivals Duran Duran recorded the theme to 1985's *A View To A Kill*, *Gold* was the theme song a James Bond film never had.

Steadfastly following the fashion for music videos of the day to be set in warm, exotic locations, *Gold* was widely expected to be the band's second consecutive chart topper on its release in August 1983. However, despite storming to number Two within a fortnight it failed to dislodge

KC and the Sunshine Band's *Give It Up* peaking just off the top spot. It also made the US top Thirty.

The song re-appeared the following year when the BBC elected to use it as the theme song for their coverage of the 1984 Los Angeles Olympic Games. Despite not having any sporting context whatsoever, the mere title of the song has made it a favourite choice of anyone needing to make a gold medal montage.

Spandau continued to have huge success with their albums *Parade* and *Through the Barricades* before splitting after the release of their sixth studio album in 1990. A lengthy and costly court case in the 1990s saw Hadley, Norman and Keeble unsuccessfully sue Gary Kemp for a share of the band's songwriting royalties, and whilst the Kemp's launched moderately successful acting careers, Hadley enjoyed something of a renaissance when he won the ITV show *Reborn in the USA* in 2003.

Incredibly, and just a few months after Hadley told me in early 2008 that 'hell would freeze over' before Spandau Ballet got back together, the quintet announced their reformation. A successful European tour and top Ten album, *Once More*, followed in 2009.

Spandau Ballet remain one of the 1980's most recognisable and successful acts selling over twenty million albums and spending over four hundred weeks on the UK charts. Whilst *Gold* might not have been their biggest selling single, I would argue that it is their finest.

10 Glenn and Chris
Diamond Lights

Released: 18 April 1987 **Record Shack KICK1**
Highest UK Chart Position: #12

The 1980s saw all manner of weird and wonderful chart acts from comedians to cartoon characters. Whilst not the only footballers to hit the top Twenty over the course of the decade, this pair of ex-Tottenham Hotspur midfielders were different in so much as they made the charts with what you would consider a 'traditional' pop record, not an FA Cup Final anthem.

Several football club songs did sell well during the decade. The most successful (and ridiculous) was probably Liverpool FC's daft *Anfield Rap* which introduced the world to the rapping talents of winger John Barnes (and his ability to rhyme "Barnes" with "Bananas") and reached number Three in May 1988. Everton also made the top Twenty (terrace favourite *Here We Go* reached number Fourteen in 1985) as did Manchester United who made number Thirteen with *Glory Glory Man United* in 1983 and number Ten with *We All Follow Man United* in 1985.

Despite being by no means the finest team of the decade (and ably assisted by the loveable Cockney duo Chas'n'Dave) Tottenham Hotspur managed three chart hits in the 1980s. After their huge 1981 hit *Spurs Are On Their Way To Wembley* (inspired by their Argentinean international Ossie Ardiles) they made number Nineteen the following year with *Tottenham, Tottenham* and number Eighteen in 1987 with *Hot Shot Tottenham*. Hiding in the 1987 squad line-up were two of Spurs' most talented players, number 9 Chris Waddle and number 10 Glenn Hoddle.

Hoddle had been a fixture in the Tottenham side since 1976 and was described by Arsene Wenger as 'the most skilful player I have ever worked with'. He was supremely talented and although he won 53 caps for England he was generally seen as a 'luxury' player and regularly omitted for England in favour of more combative, typically English players of his era.

Chris Waddle was one of the country's most gifted wingers. He was plucked from his job in a sausage factory in 1980 by his hometown club Newcastle United where he became a huge star. He made his England debut in 1985, the same year he joined Tottenham for a fee of £590,000.

In 1987 songwriter Bob Puzey teamed up with the duo to record a single. Puzey had already written and produced several other artists including the Dooleys, the Nolans (he co-wrote their smash hit *I'm In The Mood For Dancing*) and Russ Abbott (co-writing his top Ten hit *Atmosphere*.) The song *Diamond Lights* featured Puzey on keyboards and the pair (called "Glenn and Chris") sang harmony in the verses before Hoddle took the higher part of the chorus.

As two of the most recognizable English players of their time, the novelty value of the song created a lot of media attention. The fact that the song was released a month before they both represented their club side in the FA Cup Final also helped sales. The pair appeared on *Top of the Pops* in April 1987 with the song and that performance has become somewhat legendary. Their late 80s footballer fashions (*Miami Vice*-esque jacket, buttoned up shirt and jeans) barely camouflaged their terror and whilst Waddle was 'petrified', Hoddle took it is his confident stride (even if he did forget to mime a bit of the song towards the end). Their pair of almost matching wondrous Eighties mullets are also a joy to behold.

Despite the lack of much singing ability, *Diamond Lights* spent eight weeks in the chart and reached number Twelve in May of 1987. It's easy to see it as a novelty record, although the truth is that it's a pretty reasonable song, if a little bit heavy on the synth, drum machine and bassline. It's also true that Hoddle can sing a bit (although quite how much vocal talent Chris Waddle has is a matter of some conjecture).

The pair did follow up *Diamond Lights* with a number 92 'hit' *It's Goodbye* which rather concisely and accurately described their pop career. A twenty-six year old Waddle continued a glittering football career with

Spurs, Marseille and Sheffield Wednesday winning 62 England caps and a host of titles. Most famously of course, he blazed England's fifth and final penalty over the crossbar in the 1990 World Cup semi-final costing his country the chance of a place in the final.

Hoddle went on to manage Swindon Town, Chelsea and the England national team before becoming something of a figure of fun for his belief in faith-healing and his views on reincarnation (which cost him the England job). He subsequently managed Spurs, Southampton and Wolverhampton Wanderers and now runs a football academy in Spain.

11 Toni Basil
Mickey

Released: 6 February 1982 **TIC4**
Highest UK Chart Position: #2

Back in the Seventies, the glam-rock equivalent of Stock, Aitken and Waterman was a duo comprising of Londoner Nicky Chinn and Aussie Mike Chapman. Whilst they may not be as famous as the Hit Factory trio, Chinn and Chapman wrote a string of hugely successful records throughout the 1970's after a chance meeting in a restaurant that Chinn frequented.

Joining up with Mickie Most's RAK label, Chinn and Chapman began writing for a new band called the Sweet and over the course of the next few years wrote classic glam-rock hits for the band including *Blockbuster!*, *Wig-Wam Bam*, *Little Willy* and *Ballroom Blitz*.

The duo then turned their attention to young rocker Suzi Quatro, writing her number One singles *Can the Can* and *Devil Gate Drive*. They also wrote most of Mud's biggest hits including their two number One singles *Tiger Feet* and the festive standard *Lonely This Christmas* as well as penning Smokie's hits including *Livin' Next Door To Alice*. (Yes, that's the one that Chubby Brown effed and blinded all over.)

Chinn and Chapman also wrote RAK Records biggest selling single *Lay All Your Love On Me* for the band Racey, which reached number Two in 1978. Racey were a British pop group from Weston-super-Mare and whilst they are perhaps not as well-known as some of the other mid 70s acts, in 1979 they did originally record a Chinn/Chapman composition about a girl named Kitty.

The song made it to America where it was heard by the singer/dancer Antonia Christina Basilotta. Toni Basil, as she was known, had been a multi-talented performer since the mid Sixties having released solo singles, acted in movies such as *Easy Rider* and *Five Easy Pieces* and choreographed films and concert tours for the likes of David Bowie.

She was signed to Chrysalis Records as a solo performer and during the recording of her album *Word Of Mouth*, she decided to re-work the Racey song from a woman's perspective, changing the lyrics to 'Mickey'. The 'Mickey' in question was the Monkees Mickey Dolenz with whom Basil had worked on the 1968 movie *Head*.

By the time the record company had released the album in 1982, Basil was reluctant to release *Mickey* as a single, believing that it already sounded dated (having been recorded some time before.) The song picked up airplay in the UK first - partly thanks to two self-penned, directed and choreographed BBC "specials" - and reached number Two in the UK charts in March 1982 (it was held off the top spot by Tight Fit's *The Lion Sleeps Tonight*).

The record took longer to be a hit in America, but it eventually reached number One on the Billboard chart in December 1982 where it stayed for one week.

The repetitive melody and the shouts of "Hey Mickey!" also turned the song into a cheerleading favourite (Basil was a cheerleader herself). Its popularity with the cheerleading fraternity was established by its groundbreaking video which was one of the most popular in the early MTV era. It featured Basil in her own Las Vegas High cheerleading outfit dancing against a bright white background. Its imagery makes it one of the most recognisable videos of the era, and it actually resides in the permanent collection of the Museum of Modern Art.

Whilst her career in choreography may be long and distinguished, Toni Basil is generally considered a 'one hit wonder'. Her follow-up single *Nobody* reached number Fifty-Two in the UK and subsequent releases failed to make an impact in either the UK or USA. Her recording career ended after just two albums.

Mickey has become ubiquitous over the intervening quarter century and a number of cover versions and parodies of the song have been recorded.

The UK singer Lolly took a cover of *Mickey* to number Four in the charts in 1999 and there have been alternative versions with names as diverse as Weird Al Yankovic's *Ricky*, Nitty's *Hey Bitty* and Draco and the Malfoy's *Hey Neville*. It was also used in the hit 1992 film *Wayne's World*.

Whether you love it or hate it, *Mickey* remains one of the catchiest songs of the decade. Whilst its frothy cheerleader-themed video may make it seem like it is a throwaway pop record, it has been suggested that the lyrics of the song (about a woman trying to 'turn' a gay man by offering him anal sex) are altogether darker. Considering it was originally written from a male perspective, though, and the name changed because of a crush on one of the Monkees, most of us would prefer to remember it as the cheerleader inspired silliness that it was.

12 Kajagoogoo
Too Shy

Released: 22 January 1983 **EMI 5359**
Highest UK Chart Position: #1

There are many defining fashion styles of the 1980s – shoulderpads, pop socks and ra-ra skirts to name but three. Hair-wise, mind, there was one particular style that straddled the decade, and one of the most famous proponents of the much-seen mullet was a young singer from Wigan.

Having held down several theatre jobs, providing vocals for three bands and writing and recording several demos, Chris Hamill answered a 1981 advert in *Melody Maker* for a lead singer for an up and coming electro-pop band. He was successful at the audition, and got the job as the lead vocalist with the band Kajagoogoo (a name taken from a list of phonetic baby sounds written out by bassist Nick Beggs).

The band, including Beggs, Steve Askew, Stuart Neale and Jez Strode had already written the demo of a song about a boy imploring a girl to open up to him. Entitled *Too Shy*, the newly renamed Limahl (an anagram of Chris' surname) recorded a vocal for the song as well as writing some lyrics for a second verse and chorus. The song was then taken back into the studio where their friend Thomas Dolby was working and a second demo was recorded.

At the time, the band had been unsuccessful in obtaining a record deal despite a number of well-received gigs. Singer Limahl was supplementing his income from the band by working as a barman and waiter in London's trendy Embassy Club, an exclusive venue frequented by the music glitterati of the time. Whilst working at the club, Limahl had a chance meeting with Duran Duran keyboardist Nick Rhodes who was charmed by the young singer and promised to listen to their demo tape. At Rhodes' recommendation, EMI signed Kajagoogoo just six weeks after turning them down.

The debut album *White Feathers* was recorded in Chipping Norton during 1982 with Rhodes as producer. Once completed, it was decided that *Too Shy* should be the band's debut single. EMI liked the track, but were concerned about the length of the introduction to the song (it was almost a minute long). Thinking that the radio stations wouldn't play it, four bars were cut from the intro to shorten it before it was sent to the stations. Once it began to appear on playlists, disc-jockeys actually loved the song as the long introduction provided them with an opportunity to introduce the record before Limahl's vocals kicked in.

Too Shy was an immediate hit and reached number One in the UK just three weeks after release where it stayed for two weeks (only the might of Michael Jackson's *Billie Jean* prevented a longer number One run). It was also a huge hit worldwide, spending a mammoth ten weeks at the top of the German charts as well as being number One in Japan and seven European countries. It also reached number Five in the US Billboard charts.

At one point, the demand for the song was so great that EMI were struggling to manufacture enough copies to keep up with the demand estimated at thirty thousand copies per day. The single sold a million copies in France alone, and between four and five million copies worldwide. It also won countless awards including an American Society for Composers, Authors and Publishers (ASCAP) award which was presented to the band by legendary songwriter Hal David.

Kajagoogoo (and Limahl in particular) were an overnight sensation and became huge instant global stars. The main focus of adulation was reserved for the singer and his blond mullet which has entered Eighties folklore as a defining style of the era. "Blame the Seventies", said Limahl. "Bowie, Abba and Slade all had outrageously ambiguous hair before the punk era of the late 70s made everyone cut it short again. Then there was the three day week, and the strikes and everything became a bit dull – and I was just trying to make everything a bit more colourful again." Still, today, if you wandered into your local hair salon and asked for a 'Limahl' they'd know exactly what you were after.

The band followed up *Too Shy* with the top 5 single *Ooh to be Aah* before amazingly, in August 1983 (after just eight months of success), Limahl was 'fired' from the band, being told that the group were going to carry on without him. Vocal duties were assumed by bassist Nick Beggs on their future releases (including hit single *Big Apple*) and Limahl went on to have a moderately successful solo career. Still performing *Too Shy* today, Limahl jokingly claims the song "has created its own groove in his vocal cord" considering the number of times he has performed it.

13 Heaven 17
Temptation

Released: 16 April 1983   **Virgin VS570**
Highest UK Chart Position: #2

Of all the British cities that produced talented musicians and songwriters of the early 1980s, Sheffield is perhaps the most celebrated. Three of the early decade's finest bands came from the 'Steel City' – the superb ABC, the Human League and, born from the League themselves, Heaven 17.

Martyn Ware and Ian Craig split from the Human League in 1980 before forming the band British Electric Foundation (BEF). Recruiting vocalist Glenn Gregory they renamed their band Heaven 17 after the fictional pop group in Anthony Burgess' novel *A Clockwork Orange* and set about recording their debut album.

Having experienced the album-making process with the Human League, Heaven 17 found the creation of their debut album straightforward. Written in three months, *Penthouse and Pavement* was recorded at the same time and in the same studio as the Human League's seminal album *Dare*. The bands co-owned the studio - the Human League would record in the day, and Heaven 17 in the evening – and both records were a critical and commercial success, Heaven 17's spawning their first single *(We Don't Need This) Fascist Groove Thang*.

Following their success, the band moved to London and continued their writing at Gregory's London flat, nicknamed the 'Sheffield Embassy'. Basic chords for songs including *Come Live With Me*, *Let Me Go* and *Temptation* were written on a home keyboard at the Embassy, whilst the rest of the album took shape at the London studio.

The aim with *Temptation* was to create a pastiche of a grand disco record (which were often about sex) and the band thought this hilarious as they had never written a song on that topic before. The sexual tension of the lyric matches the structure of the song, as the chords gradually build throughout the entire song until the 'climax' of the end chord.

Whilst *Penthouse and Pavement* might have been influenced by the early 1980s electronic sound, the second album *The Luxury Gap* was much less so. *Temptation* was a case in point, as during the writing of the song, Ware came up with the idea of using a large orchestra on the record. Having spoken to an arranger, the band came to the conclusion that the song had to sound epic and so a fifty piece orchestra was hired to give the song the sound of a 'giant optimistic American soundtrack'. At some expense (the Air Studios cost £1,500 per day) and with a big string and brass section the orchestra created the perfect sound for *Temptation*, which was then mixed with the rhythmic electronic programming.

Once the backing track was recorded, it became apparent to the band that they needed a big female vocal performance with a high range to complete the song. Gregory had recorded the main male vocals on *Temptation* but the band went in search of a female lead. Primarily known as a session-backing singer (having appeared on albums such as Dexy's Midnight Runners' *Too-Rye-Ay*), Carol Kenyon was invited to provide the lead vocals for Temptation. (Kenyon, incidentally, continued to provide lead and backing vocals for many artists and appeared with Pink Floyd at 2005's Live 8 concert.)

Once *The Luxury Gap* was complete, it was played to Virgin Records who adored the album although they did have some reservations about releasing *Temptation* as a single because of the fact that Kenyon's was almost the lead vocal on the record, and she wasn't even part of the band or in the contract. The band was convinced *Temptation* would be a hit, however, and set about recording a German expressionism inspired video with acclaimed director Steve Barron (who had recorded Michael Jackson's famous *Billie Jean* video).

The song was a major hit, reaching number Two in May 1983 (held off number One by Spandau Ballet's *True*) and becoming the 32nd biggest selling single of that year. In 1992, a Brothers In Rhythm remixed version of the song was released and this again was a major hit, reaching number Four in November of that year.

At the end of 1983 and after the success of *Temptation*, the band (under their BEF guise) helped launch the solo career of Tina Turner by producing and providing the backing vocals for her 'comeback' hit *Let's Stay Together*.

After three further albums in the 1980's, the band had a hiatus until the 1996 when the album *Bigger Than America* was released and they embarked on their first ever tour. A further nine year absence followed, ended by the 2005 album *Before After*.

14 Fun Boy Three
Our Lips Are Sealed

Released: 30 April 1983   **Chrysalis FUNB1**
Highest UK Chart Position: #7

Once described in a *Q* magazine review as a man 'with more bands than a short wave radio', Terry Hall was one of the most recognisable frontmen of the early 1980s. His biggest chart success came as part of the ska band The Coventry Automatics, better known as the Special AKA and later The Specials. Their hits, *Too Much Too Young* (1980) and *Ghost Town* (1981), were both UK number One singles and they scored several other top Forty hits in their short-lived but influential chart career.

Shortly after the success of *Ghost Town*, Hall, Neville Staple and Lynval Golding left the Specials to form the new band Fun Boy Three. They retained Hall's emotionless frontman persona and the wit and political content of their lyrics but added a much breezier, poppier sound. The trio had an instant top twenty hit with *The Lunatics (Have Taken Over The Asylum)* before launching the career of fellow threesome Bananarama when they teamed up with the girl band to record the 1982 top Five hit *T'Ain't What You Do (It's The Way That You Do It)*.

Bananarama then returned the favour by asking Fun Boy Three to feature on another top Five hit – the poppy *Really Sayin' Something* - and a further top Twenty hit *The Telephone Always Rings* followed from their debut album *Fun Boy Three*.

Meanwhile, on the west coast of the USA another girl group had been experiencing success thanks to Terry Hall's influence. Four piece guitar band the Go-Gos had built up a cult following in their home city of Los Angeles before travelling to the UK where they released their first single *We Got The Beat* on the Stiff label. Featuring the future stars Jane Wiedlin and Belinda Carlisle, the Go-Gos supported UK hit makers Madness in both England and America where they came to the attention of Hall. The Specials also attended a Go-Gos show at the Whiskey Club on Sunset Strip in 1980.

Hall invited the Go-Gos to be the opening act on their upcoming tour and when Hall met guitarist Jane Weidlin, they ended up having a brief relationship. Hall had a girlfriend in the UK at the time so after he returned to the UK he mailed a set of lyrics to Weidlin called *Our Lips Are Sealed* about their 'forbidden' romance. Weidlin liked the lyrics and wrote a melody for the tune which she was initially afraid to show to the rest of the band in case they didn't like it. Eventually the Go-Go's recorded *Our Lips Are Sealed* and it became their debut US single reaching the Billboard top Twenty in 1982. It narrowly failed to reach the top Forty in the UK, peaking at number Forty-Seven in June 1982.

Our Lips Are Sealed also opened the Go-Go's debut album, *Beauty and the Beat,* which was a surprise US chart topper, spending six consecutive weeks at number One on the way to selling over three million copies.

Fun Boy Three returned to the charts in 1982 with a cover of the George Gershwin song *Summertime* before the recording of their acclaimed second album *Waiting,* released in early 1983 and produced by Talking Heads' David Byrne. Singles *The More I See (The Less I Believe)* and the Top ten hit *The Tunnel Of Love* were released from *Waiting* before the trio released their own version of the Go-Go's hit. With Weidlin and Hall credited as co-writers, the Fun Boy Three version of *Our Lips Are Sealed* is more downbeat and, as Weidlin says, 'gloomier' than the Go-Go's version but it became the bands' biggest 'non-Bananarama' hit single when it reached number Seven in the UK singles chart in May 1983.

Our Lips Are Sealed proved to be Fun Boy Three's final single as Hall's change in musical direction led him to team up with Toby Lyons and Karl Shale to form the Colourfield who made the UK top Twenty in 1984 with their great single *Thinking Of You.* Hall has subsequently worked with the likes of Dave Stewart (the duo formed the band Vegas), Ian Broudie of the Lightning Seeds and more recently with Damon Albarn and his Gorillaz project. His career has also come full circle with the recent reformation of The Specials.

The Go-Gos went from strength to strength in the USA after the success of *Our Lips Are Sealed* and *Beauty and the Beat*, scoring two further top twenty albums. Their success also launched the solo careers of not only Weidlin (whose terrific pop single *Rush Hour* was a top Twenty hit on both sides of the Atlantic in the summer of 1988) but also fellow vocalist Belinda Carlisle.

15 Level 42
Lessons In Love

Released: 26 April 1986   **Polydor POSP790**
Highest UK Chart Position: #3

It took Level 42 six years to score their first and only top Five hit in the UK but when it arrived, it completed their transformation from cult disco-funk band into global chart megastars. It also led to funk-pop based graffiti being daubed on car parks up and down the land....

Brothers Phil and Rowland (better known as 'Boon') Gould and Mark King grew up on the Isle of Wight and had played together in various bands during their teenage years. In late 1979, King was introduced to keyboard player Mike Lindup, a friend Phil Gould had met whilst studying at London's Guildhall School of Music and Drama. The band were formed in early 1980 and their rehearsal sessions led to the foursome determining the musical responsibilities for the band as each of them were competent on multiple instruments.

Boon Gould took the main guitar role with brother Phil on drums. Whilst also primarily a drummer, King volunteered to learn the bass guitar and developed his famous 'thumb slap' style having watched American funk guitarists play in the London music store where he worked. Lindup was studying piano at the Guildhall School and so took on keyboard duties.

King and Boon Gould wanted the band to have a name that was simply a number and initially they chose '88' – the number of the bus they caught to the recording studio. However, after Lindup had seen a poster for a band named Rocket 88, they were forced to rethink. Boon Gould, King and the band's early producer Andy Sojka had been reading Douglas Adams' sci-fi classic *The Hitch-Hikers Guide To The Galaxy* in which the answer to 'life, the Universe and Everything' was the number

42 and so they settled on this number with the appendage 'level' added shortly after.

Sojka signed the band to his Elite Records label in 1980 and their debut single *Love Meeting Love* was released in July of that year. The song reached the UK funk/disco charts and brought them to the attention of Polydor Records who signed them. Although their first three albums all reached the UK top Twenty, it wasn't until 1983 that the foursome scored their first top Forty UK single success with the number Twenty-Four hit *The Chinese Way*.

The band were now becoming increasingly successful worldwide and subsequent singles *The Sun Goes Down (Living It Up)* and *Hot Water* were top Twenty hits, as were the albums *Standing In The Light* and *True Colours*. In 1983, the band also embarked on an extensive world and European tour.

It was to be the release of their fifth studio album that would catapult Level 42 into the mainstream. Moving away from their disco/funk sound into mainstream adult orientated pop, the album *World Machine* was released in 1985. It featured the hit singles *Something About You* and *Leaving Me Now* which both reached the UK top Twenty as well as giving the band their first chart success in the USA and Canada.

In January 1986 the record company wanted to give the *World Machine* album a sales boost and so the band commenced the writing of some new material. With the initial elements of a song written at King's Streatham home – with the main section laid down by King and long-time collaborator Wally Badarou – *Lessons In Love* was created. Boon Gould contributed the lyrics which were 'upbeat in a downbeat kind of way' – most of the band's lyrics were slightly doleful in nature to match the melancholic note in King's voice. The lyrical message of 'if we learn our lessons, everything will be OK' seemed to fit the song, and the band immediately recorded the track in London's Maison Rouge studios.

Lessons In Love was released as a single in April 1986 and became the band's biggest UK chart success, spending three weeks at number Three in May of that year. It reached number One in Denmark, Germany and Switzerland as well as the top Twenty in countries as far afield as the USA, South Africa and Norway.

The success of the single had the desired effect, propelling the *World Machine* album back into the UK top Ten (despite *Lessons In Love* not featuring on the record). It is a terrific pop single, perfectly combining King's signature bassline, Boon Gould's downbeat lyrics, brother Phil's great guitar solo and Lindup's clever and engaging middle eight vocals. It was a huge hit and was only kept from being a deserved number One by a combination of Spitting Image's novelty *Chicken Song*, Falco's *Rock Me Amadeus* and Patti Labelle and Michael McDonald's *On My Own*.

I asked bassist and lead singer Mark King if the rumour was true that at the height of their success his thumb had been insured for £1million. "No," he laughed, "that's rubbish. It was £3million."

16 Thompson Twins
Hold Me Now

Released: 19 November 1983 **Arista TWINS2**
Highest UK Chart Position: #4

Neither related, nor a duo, the Thompson Twins were formed in Sheffield as early as 1977 when friends Tom Bailey, Pete Dodd, John Roog and Jon Podgorski combined, taking the band name from the bumbling detectives from the *TinTin* series of books.

Moving to London in 1977, the band line-up changed regularly until the release of their first single *Squares and Triangles* in 1979. They were a six-piece at the time of the release of their debut album *A Product Of.... (Participation)* and a septet (not including the contribution of Thomas Dolby) by the time of second album *Set* in 1982. Whilst UK chart success eluded them, single *In The Name Of Love* reached number One on the US dance chart featuring a sound that was a significant departure from their previous work.

Band members Bailey, Joe Leeway and Alannah Currie had considered starting a side project to continue recording with a more synthesised sound along the lines of *In The Name Of Love*. Planning to call themselves *The Bermuda Triangle*, the trio were instead persuaded by their manager John Hade to whittle the Thompson Twins down to three members. The remaining band members were paid £500 and allowed to keep their instruments and the trio that remained headed abroad to start the writing and recording of their first album as a three-piece.

Having recorded at the famous Compass Point studios in the Bahamas with Grace Jones' producer Alex Sadkin, their first single as a trio, *Lies*, failed to reach the UK top Forty. However, follow-up single *Love On Your Side* became the band's first UK top Ten single reaching number Nine in March 1983. Their album *Quick Step and Side Kicks* reached number

Two in the UK album chart and further singles *We Are Detective* (featuring Currie's vocals for the first time) and *Watching* followed. The group also scored some success in the USA with both the singles and album and supported the Police on their American tour in 1983.

The band's popularity quickly grew thanks to their catchy new-wave songs and striking images of Bailey's flame red hair and Currie's unusual xylophone playing style. After their breakthrough success, the band returned to the Bahamas to work with Sadkin once more on their follow-up album *Into the Gap*.

The lead single from this number One album was a heartbreaking song in which Bailey attempted to repair a fractured relationship with his girlfriend by imploring her to work through their problems. *Hold Me Now* is an interesting song – ostensibly a ballad, but one that uses new-wave instruments such as synthesizers, piano and latin percussion. Variously praised (compared to Spandau Ballet's *True*) and criticised (its repetitive choruses at the end go on for a third of the length of the whole song) *Rolling Stone* said the record had a 'hypnotic, swaying groove that suggests reserves of pastoral contentment even in the wake of the storm'. *Hold Me Now* became a major international hit reaching number Four in the UK in December 1983 and number Three in the USA six months later.

The song pushed the Thompson Twins firmly into the pop mainstream and their follow-up single *Doctor! Doctor!* reached the UK top Three. Album *Into the Gap* was a number One hit (selling five million copies worldwide) and the band almost repeated this success with single *Love On Your Side* which tantalisingly fell short of the number One spot in April 1984 (held off the top by Lionel Richie's *Hello*). Further singles *Sister of Mercy* and *Lay Your Hands On Me* followed as well as an appearance at the American Live Aid concert (joined on stage by a just-famous Madonna) before Bailey fell ill from exhaustion during the recording of their follow-up album *Here's To Future Days*.

A delay in the album's release led to a loss of momentum and whilst single *Don't Mess With Doctor Dream* reached the UK top Twenty the band's success had peaked. Leeway left the band in 1986 and Currie and

Bailey continued for a further seven years (they married in 1991) until formally dropping the Thompson Twins name in 1993.

In an era where music critics were sceptical that good music could me made with electronic instruments, the Thompson Twins proved that it was possible to make quality commercial pop music using modern technology. Whilst most of their singles were more up-tempo pop or dance numbers, *Hold Me Now* remains the band's biggest selling and most enduring single.

17

Joe Fagin
That's Livin' Alright

Released: 7 January 1984   Towerbell TOW46
Highest UK Chart Position: #3

Whilst the majority of the great music in this book was produced in the UK it could be argued that most of the iconic television of the 1980s was born in the USA. *Knight Rider, the A-Team, Dallas, Airwolf* et al were all very American productions.

That's not to say that some of the best television of the decade didn't come from the UK, though, and it would be accurate to say that one of the most fondly remembered series of the 80s was British through and through.

Auf Wiedersehen, Pet told the story of a septet of itinerant British construction workers living and working, initially, on a Dusseldorf building site. The show, first broadcast in 1983, was immensely popular thanks to its blend of humour and gritty drama and ran for two Eighties series' as well as a successful revival in 2002. It made stars of the seven leading men including multi-award winning actor Timothy Spall (as gormless Barry), singer and TV star Jimmy Nail (as Oz) and renowned TV actor Kevin Whately (as Neville).

In early 1983, further to his work on Nigel Planer sit-com *Roll Over Beethoven*, eminent producer and writer David MacKay had been asked to provide the theme and incidental music for a new Central television series. MacKay had been shown some rushes of the first series of *Auf Wiedersehen, Pet* as well as having an introduction to the characters and the idea behind the comedy-drama. It needed a main title theme and MacKay was asked to write and produce this.

The same evening, MacKay went to bed with the idea of a lyric 'that's living alright' in his head and a hook for the tune. Writing his ideas in a music manuscript on his bedside table, he awoke the following morning and, with the help of good friend Ken Ashby, had finished putting together a song by mid-morning.

Needing a singer to record the tune, MacKay called on Joe Fagin with whom he had previously recorded an album. Fagin had been a vocalist for over two decades and began his career in the Merseybeat band The Strangers, whose most famous appearance was in a publicized 'Battle of the Groups' contest in 1961 with a new local band by the name of the Beatles.

The series director liked the demo of *That's Livin' Alright* and it was taken to the producer and writer Ian Le Frenais. The production team were reluctant to use MacKay's song, preferring Willie Nelson's *Mama, Don't Let Your Babies Grow Up To be Cowboys* as the main theme. Returning home, MacKay wrote another new song (*Breaking Away*) and invited Ian Le Frenais to contribute by completing its lyrics and melody. This song was chosen for the opening titles on the understanding that *That's Livin' Alright* would be used over the closing credits.

The rest, as they say, is history. The series' first episode, *If I Were A Carpenter* aired on ITV on 8 November 1983 and the show quickly became a huge favourite. By the time several episodes had been aired there was a huge demand for the theme to be released and the double A side single of *Breaking Away* and *That's Living Alright* debuted on the charts the day after the eighth episode of the series.

Despite *That's Livin' Alright* being the official B-side of the record, it was the song that caught the public's attention and gained the lion's share of radio airplay. Buoyed by the popularity of the series, Fagin's single climbed to number Three on the UK Top Forty in January 1984. Unfortunately, it came up against the decade's second biggest single (Frankie Goes To Hollywood's *Relax*) during its chart run, and as DJ Steve Wright told MacKay during a *Top of the Pops* recording, "…if that [*Relax*] hadn't been banned by the BBC, you'd be Number One this week!…"

That's Livin' Alright won an Ivor Novello songwriting award for 'best TV score' and although nominated for a BAFTA for his work on *Auf Wiedersehen, Pet*, MacKay lost out to composer George Fenton's score for popular mid 80s drama *The Jewel In The Crown*.

Fagin went on to appear on The Crowd's 1985 number One charity hit *You'll Never Walk Alone* before recording the theme for the second series of *Auf Wiedersehen, Pet*, the less commercially successful *Back With The Boys Again*. He emerged again in 2006 with a re-recorded version of his biggest hit titled *That's England Alright* – an unofficial record to mark England's 2006 World Cup campaign. Sadly, the lack of association with seven good-hearted (if ill-behaved) labourers meant that this version failed to scale the heights of the original.

18 Nik Kershaw
The Riddle

Released: 17 November 1984 **MCA NIK 6**
Highest UK Chart Position: #3

Nik Kershaw was, for a while, the UK's top solo artist. He spent fifty weeks on the UK singles charts in 1984 - more than any other artist – and had two hit albums within the space of just one year. He also, of course, brought the snood and fingerless gloves to an unsuspecting public...

Nicholas David Kershaw was born in Bristol in 1958. He played with various local bands whilst working full time in his new home of Ipswich but it wasn't until the break-up of his band Fusion in 1982 that the singer-songwriter decided to pursue a full time career in the music industry.

He was signed to MCA Records in 1983 where he released his debut single *I Won't Let The Sun Go Down On Me*. Whilst this song failed to be a hit, his big break came when the follow-up single *Wouldn't It Be Good* reached number Four in the UK in March 1984, spending fifteen weeks on the chart. The song was also a smash across Europe and in Australia.

Kershaw had a further three top Twenty hits from his debut album *Human Racing* including the re-release of *I Won't Let The Sun Go Down On Me* which would ultimately give him his biggest chart hit, reaching number Two in June 1984.

Kershaw spent much of 1984 promoting *Human Racing* across the world and as he did, the deadline for the recording of his second album drew nearer and nearer. In November 1984, Kershaw found himself with just two weeks to complete the recording of his follow-up record. When completed, producer Peter Collins liked the work but complained that there was no 'stand out' single.

Incensed, Kershaw decided to write the single that Collins craved as quickly as possible. He came up with the melody of a song in just ten minutes, but as it was the lyrics that always took the singer longer to write, he decided to put nonsense lyrics over the top of his melody in order that the producer could hear the song.

The result was *The Riddle* and it was always Kershaw's intention to replace the nonsense words with some 'proper' lyrics. After several attempts the replacement lyrics were nowhere near as good as the initial attempt, and so *The Riddle* was eventually recorded with the original, peculiar lyrics.

The song was chosen as the first single from Kershaw's second album, also called *The Riddle*. A clever video accompanied the single which featured a miniature Kershaw looking for clues in a question mark shaped house. A combination of the unusual lyrics and the mysterious video caught the public attention and radio and TV stations became inundated with callers wanting to ask Kershaw what the answer to 'the riddle' was. MCA Records even ran a competition for fans to guess the answer to Kershaw's riddle.

Whilst the whole 'solve the riddle' campaign might have been a clever marketing ploy on behalf of the record label, there was never any hidden meaning in the lyrics. As Kershaw has himself said, the words are "nonsense, rubbish, bollocks; the confused ramblings of an 80s popstar".

The Riddle was a huge hit around the world, peaking at number Three in the UK. Kershaw also unwittingly started a fashion trend for fingerless gloves, having worn them in the video for *The Riddle* and in much of the promotional material. The reality was that the singer wore the gloves in the first month of the album's release – a time when all the promotional pictures were taken!

Kershaw had further top Ten hits with the brilliant singles *Wide Boy* and *Don Quixote* and supported Elton John at Wembley before appearing at the UK *Live Aid* show in July 1985. He only had one more top Forty hit after *Live Aid*, however (1985's *When A Heart Beats*) although he has continued to release albums to much critical acclaim over the last twenty years.

Kershaw has also demonstrated his ability as a songwriter by penning one of the most recognisable number One hits of the 1990s. His song, *The One And Only,* was a massive UK hit for Chesney Hawkes, and Kershaw has also written for the likes of Let Loose and Elton John.

It might have some of the most nonsensical lyrics of the decade but there is no denying that *The Riddle* is a terrific record. We shouldn't forget that for a period, Kershaw was the biggest thing in UK pop and his records are an intrinsic part of the fabric of early 1980s British music.

19 Bananarama
Robert de Niro's Waiting

Released: 3 March 1984 **London NANA6**
Highest UK Chart Position: #3

With a career spanning almost the entire decade, Bananarama remain one of the most well-known and successful artists of the 1980s and, indeed, the past quarter century. Until the advent of the Spice Girls they were the UKs biggest selling girl band of all time. With worldwide album sales of around forty million and a string of successful hit singles throughout the Eighties (although strangely never a number One), they remain one of the best-loved acts of the decade.

Formed in 1979 by childhood friends Siobhan Fahey, Sara Dallin and Keren Woodward, there are varying stories about the choice of the 'banana' in their name but some agreement that the 'rama' came from the Roxy Music hit *Pyjamarama*. Having provided backing vocals and support for many of the eras best-known punk names (including Iggy Pop and the Jam) the three made their first demo in 1981 in a rehearsal room below the apartment they lived, owned by former Sex Pistols Steve Jones and Paul Cook. With their help a version of the Black Blood song *Aie A Mwana* was recorded and a deal was signed, initially with Demon Records and later with Decca (where the girls remained until 1993).

An article about the trio in the Face magazine following the release of *Aie A Mwana* caught the attention of the ex-Specials vocalist Terry Hall and, solely based on their look, he invited Bananarama to collaborate with his new band Fun Boy Three on their song I*t Ain't What You Do It's The Way That You Do It*.

It Ain't What You Do, a jazz number written by Melvin Oliver and James Young and originally recorded in 1939 by both Jimmie Lunceford and Ella Fitzgerald, was a big hit in the UK, reaching number Four in

March 1982. Having achieved mainstream success, Bananarama returned the favour and featured Hall's band on their next single *Really Saying Something* which also reached the top Ten, peaking at number Five in May 1982.

Debut album *Deep Sea Skiving* was primarily written and co-produced by the legendary 80s team of Steve Jolley and Tony Swain. The duo (who had achieved success with Imagination and would later go on to produce such classic albums as Spandau Ballet's *True* and Alison Moyet's *Alf*) wrote the trio's subsequent top Five hit *Shy Boy* and produced their cover of Steam's 1968 American number One hit *Na Na Hey Hey Kiss Him Goodbye*.

The first single from their eponymously titled second album, *Cruel Summer* was a major international hit (partly due to its inclusion in the 1984 movie *The Karate Kid*) and reached the UK top Ten in July 1983.

Whilst their sound was unusual – the girls sang in unison rather than in three part harmony – the band's initial output was not critically well received with them being dismissed as nothing more than a 'covers band' with their output controlled by their writers and producers. Determined to be seen as credible artists the trio wrote a significant part of their second album tackling a number of serious lyrical topics - *Rough Justice* dealt with social apathy and *Hot Line To Heaven* had an anti-drugs message.

Their next single – *Robert de Niro's Waiting* – had possibly the darkest lyrical subject matter of them all. The serious undertones hinted at in the lyrics suggested a rape theme although rumours abounded at the time that Fahey was directed by the other band members not to specify that the song was about rape. It has also been suggested that producer Steve Jolley added the 'talking Italian' line (despite the band hating it) to make the song sound less bloodthirsty.

Robert de Niro's Waiting was one of three Bananarama songs that reached number Three in the UK singles chart (their highest position) – the others being their 1987 Stock, Aitken and Waterman smash *Love In The First Degree* and their 1989's Comic Relief cover of the Beatles' *Help* (alongside comedy duo French and Saunders and actress Kathy Burke).

As well as giving them a top Three hit, *Robert de Niro's Waiting* also gave the girls the opportunity to schmooze with the Oscar winning star after he heard the 'tribute' song. According to Siobhan Fahey, the actor "called our council flat and arranged to meet for drinks and dinner." The story goes that he three girls were so nervous about meeting the *Godfather* actor that they got drunk before he even arrived.

Bananarama's success continued throughout the 1980s with hits such as *Venus*, *I Heard A Rumour* and *Nathan* Jones although Fahey was replaced by Jacquie O'Sullivan in 1988 after she left the group to form a new band, Shakespears Sister. Bananarama also became the only band to feature on both the original and 1989 remake of the Band Aid hit *Do They Know It's Christmas?* although they were overlooked for Band Aid 20's re-recording in 2004.

20 Hazell Dean
Who's Leaving Who?
Released: 2 April 1988   EMI EM45
Highest UK Chart Position: #4

Hazell Dean Poole might have been the Hit Factory's disco diva of the late 1980's, but rather than being plucked from an Australian TV series or elevated from the studio tea maker, a decade of hard work went into her eventual chart success.

Dean began performing as far back as the mid 1970s. Originally a soul singer, she released countless singles (some as the Hazell Dean Orchestra) and whilst these didn't achieve any commercial success, she became extremely popular with the Northern Soul scene and appeared regularly at cabaret venues alongside some of the era's top entertainers. Her first break came when her song *Couldn't Live Without You For A Day* came eighth in the 1976 UK Eurovision heats (behind Brotherhood of Man who won both the Song for Europe and the Eurovision itself that year).

Dean continued to perform in pubs and clubs nationwide, even briefly changing her name to Jessie Miller and recording a rock record called *Jealous Love*, before her next break came in 1983. Although her song *Searchin' (I Gotta Find A Man)* had failed to chart on its original release and had been deleted, her record company agreed to re-release it following Dean's performance in the 1984 UK Song for Europe heat.

Dean's pleading ballad *Stay In My Life* did not fare well, finishing seventh in the competition. Had it been successful, *Searchin'* would never have been released and so Dean's chart success owes a lot to Belle and the Devotions' *Love Games* which was chosen to represent the UK in Luxembourg in 1984, finishing seventh.

After her double A-side single *Evergreen/Jealous Love* had scraped the top Seventy-Five, *Searchin'* was duly re-released as promised. It performed much better this time around, spending sixteen weeks on the chart, peaking at number Six in June 1984. This new dance-orientated sound suited

Dean and following the success of *Searchin'* she teamed up with three little known UK producers, Mike Stock, Matt Aitken and Pete Waterman to record her next single.

Originally a Michael Prince song entitled *Dance Your Love Away*, Stock and Aitken had re-written the song *Whatever I Do (Wherever I Go)* for Dean and, when it entered the top Ten on 11 August 1984, it became Stock, Aitken and Waterman's first ever top Ten hit. It eventually peaked at number Four the following week.

Over the next four years, Dean failed to reach the UK top Forty with any of her releases. She signed to EMI Records in 1985 and whilst the song *They Say It's Gonna Rain* was a number One hit in South Africa, it was in America where she secured most of her success during that time. *Searchin'* had been a US Dance Chart number One record and she was three times voted 'best live performer' by the Federation of American Dance Clubs.

In late 1987, Dean received a call out of the blue from her previous collaborator Pete Waterman. He had heard a fantastic song by the Canadian singer Anne Murray (from her 1986 album *Something To Talk About*) and duly invited Dean into the studio to hear it.

Who's Leaving Who had been a Canadian top Twenty hit the previous year and with the trademark Hit Factory instrumentation, Dean went into the studio and recorded the single straight away. White label copies of the single went to radio stations in early 1988 and London's Capital Radio played the single on regular rotation, even in its white label form.

On its release, and despite Dean's four year absence from the charts, *Who's Leaving Who* rocketed into the top Ten. Its midweek chart position at the end of April 1988 indicated that Dean was going to secure her first number One single, but a dispute that week between EMI Records and Woolworths meant that the chain immediately refused to stock any EMI records. With the song off the shelves of the UK's top singles retailer *Who's Leaving Who* eventually peaked at number Four where it stayed for two weeks. The *Theme From S-Express* topped the charts instead.

Two further Stock, Aitken and Waterman chart hits followed – the hi-NRG *Maybe (We Should Call It A Day)* and the excellent *Turn It Into Love* (originally recorded by Kylie Minogue for her debut album) – before Dean left the Hit Factory after her 1991 single, aptly (but erroneously) titled *Better Off Without You*.

Whilst Dean may have made simple, fun pop-dance records, as she herself said "I certainly think you'd remember a Mel and Kim song or a Hazell Dean song before you'd remember a Morrissey or a Smiths song". And so say all of us.

21 Ray Parker Jr
Ghostbusters

Released: 25 August 1984   Arista ARIST 580
Highest UK Chart Position: #2

One of the longest running pub debates I have been involved in asks the following question: "What is the best ever film soundtrack song to contain the name of the film in the song title?" The key here is that the song title must be the same as the film, which rules out many a great movie tune. The Bond themes are an easy (if lazy) place to begin, but there have been many more over the years. Some are even enclosed herein – the likes of *Footloose* and *Flashdance*.

Whilst there is an oft made case for the great Wings number *Live And Let Die*, we've generally settled on the 'best film soundtrack song ever to feature the movie name' as Ray Parker Jr's 1984 classic *Ghostbusters*.

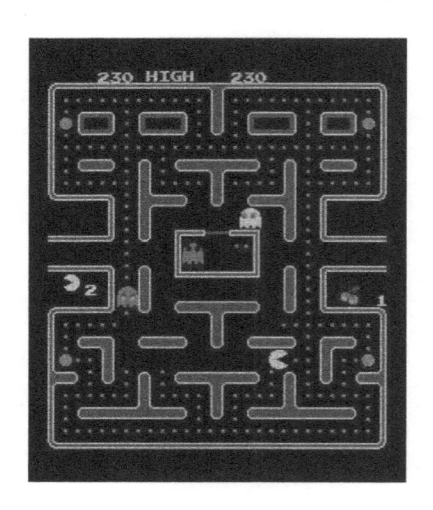

Parker started his music career as a session guitarist in Detroit in the early 1970s. He worked alongside the likes of the Temptations, Gladys Knight and the Pips and Stevie Wonder, and appeared on many of Wonder's early Seventies recordings. In 1977 Parker decided he wanted to be a recording artist in his own right and signed a deal with Arista Records. He formed the band Raydio and the group scored several American hits (including *Jack and Jill* and *You Can't Change That*) before their split in 1981. Parker continued recording as a solo artist and in 1984 was asked to submit a song for the soundtrack of the new Ivan Reitman comedy *Ghostbusters*.

With a score by Elmer Bernstein, the producers had approached Lindsay Buckingham to write a song for the soundtrack (after his work on the *National Lampoon Vacation* movies) but he declined as he did not want to be known as just a soundtrack writer. American rocker Huey Lewis was also approached but he declined as he was working on material for the upcoming *Back To The Future* movie.

Parker had two days to come up with a song that was originally intended to feature in the background of the movie and on the soundtrack. Having come up with a tune he was happy with, Parker was struggling for the words to the song – particularly how to include the awkward movie title. Sitting in a hotel room in the early hours of the morning, Parker switched on his TV and caught a commercial for a local drain company where the number of the company was flashed repeatedly on the screen. He was reminded of the scene in the film where the Ghostbusters team record a similar TV advertisement and immediately came up with the idea of using the 'who you gonna call?' line.

This lyric also solved Parker's other problem of how to incorporate the clumsy word *Ghostbusters* into the lyrics. Not being able to sing the word, he decided that a crowd could shout out the word in response to his 'who you gonna call?' line. Having to record the song at short notice, Parker enlisted his girlfriend's high school friends to be the crowd responsible for yelling the word 'Ghostbusters!' that you hear on the record.

The song was duly submitted for the soundtrack but director Ivan Reitman liked the song so much he asked Parker to record an extended version for use as the film's main theme. Both the movie and the song were a huge success. The Bill Murray and Dan Aykroyd comedy was the second highest grossing film of 1984 and the American Film Institute has ranked it as the 28th best comedy film of all time.

The song *Ghostbusters* was a US number One single, spending three weeks at the top of the Billboard charts in August 1984 and reached number Two in the UK. Interestingly, it was kept off the top spot in the UK by the same song that denied Parker the Academy Award for Best Original Song – his old mentor Stevie Wonder's *I Just Called To Say I Love You*.

The video for *Ghostbusters* was also something of a first and became extremely popular in the early days of MTV. It featured a haunted house built entirely of neon into which sequences of the film were cut. It is also regarded as the first music video to feature cameo celebrity appearances as the likes of Carly Simon, Peter Falk and Chevy Chase participated in the famous 'call and response' chorus. It also ends with the four Ghostbusters dancing behind Parker Jr in Times Square, New York.

The debate will continue to run as to whether there is a finer soundtrack song than this, but, apart from the odd vote for *St Elmo's Fire*, we're yet to find one.

22 Giorgio Moroder and Phil Oakey
Together In Electric Dreams

Released: 22 September 1984   **Virgin VS713**
Highest UK Chart Position: #3

Often erroneously credited as a Human League single, this great song – ostensibly just the theme track to a 1984 film – has become one of singer Phil Oakey's most famous and best-loved singles despite the relative failure of the film from which it was taken.

Oakey had formed the Human League with friends Ian Craig Marsh and Martin Ware in Sheffield in 1977. However, quarrels over the direction of the band led to Ware and Marsh leaving the group in 1980 where they formed Heaven 17 with vocalist Glenn Gregory.

Faced with debts and an impending European tour, Oakey recruited unknown teenagers Susan Ann Sulley and Joanne Catherall to provide backing vocals as well as guitarist Jo Callis and session musician Ian Burden. Success followed almost immediately with singles *The Sound Of The Crowd* and *Love Action (I Believe In Love)* before the 1981 release of their seminal album *Dare*.

Dare was a huge success, reaching number One in the UK album charts as well as being certified triple platinum. It has also become one of the most critically acclaimed albums of the 1980s, being one of the first to be recorded entirely electronically with no 'traditional' instruments. Further top ten single *Open Your Heart* followed before Virgin executive Simon Draper insisted on a fourth single being released and despite opposition from Oakey (who believed it to be the weakest song on the album having relegated it to the end of Side 2 of the vinyl release) *Don't You Want Me* was released in November 1981.

Despite Oakey's reservations *Don't You Want Me* became the band's biggest success becoming the Christmas number One in 1981 on its way to becoming the 25th biggest selling single in UK chart history. The big budget video for the single was directed by well-respected video maker Steve Barron, responsible for several great music videos including Tears for Fears' *Pale Shelter,* and it was this relationship which resulted in Oakey being invited to work on the *Electric Dreams* soundtrack three years later.

Needing a score for his first feature film, Barron had turned to legendary Italian producer Giorgio Moroder to write the score hoping to replicate the success Moroder had achieved with soundtracks such as *America Gigolo* and *Flashdance.* Moroder had written an emotional song called *Together In Electric Dreams* to accompany the end credits of the film, and this required a male vocal. When asked who he would like to record it, Barron immediately recalled Oakey from their previous work.

Renowned as a quick worker Moroder ensured that Oakey's vocals for *Together In Electric Dreams* were recorded in just one take. Believing he was just rehearsing, Oakey insisted on a second take but believes that Moroder used the original recording for the release. The pair also recorded an album together which was also completed in a matter of a few days.

With a promotional video which was to all intents and purposes simply an extended advert for the film *Electric Dreams,* the song became a big hit, reaching number Three in the UK charts in October 1984. Indeed, the success of the single far eclipsed the success of the film – Barron's tale of a love triangle between an architect, a cellist and a home computer called Edgar was not a significant hit at the box-office. Barron returned to music video direction and scored huge success with promotional films including a-Ha's *Take On Me* and Dire Straits' *Money For Nothing* before directing further films including *Teenage Mutant Ninja Turtles* and *Mike Bassett: England Manager.*

The Oakey/Moroder album was only a minor success, and follow up singles *Good-Bye Bad Times* and *Be My Lover Now* failed to reach the UK top Forty. Oakey returned to the Human League to work on their next album *Crash* with US producers Jimmy Jam and Terry Lewis and secured further hits with *Human* in 1986 and then *Tell Me When* and *One Man In My Heart* in 1994.

Although *Together In Electric Dreams* was effectively an Oakey solo release (in conjunction with Moroder) it is generally included on Human League 'greatest hits' compilations and the band often include it in their live performances, with Sulley and Catherall joining Oakey on lead vocals.

For a couple of years in the early part of the decade Moroder was the king of the film soundtrack single – *Flashdance*, the *NeverEnding Story* and this great record which stands the test of time over a quarter of a century later.

23   Jim Diamond
Hi Ho Silver

Released: 22 February 1986   **A&M AM 200**
Highest UK Chart Position: #5

These days, it is pretty rare for the theme tune to a television series to score huge chart success but for a few years back in the 1980s the charts were littered with memorable TV hits. From *Auf Wiedersehen, Pet* to *Howard's Way*, from Su Pollard to Anita Dobson, the top Ten regularly featured songs made familiar from their TV tie-in.

One such hit came from the long-running Central Television series *Boon* which ran for ninety-three episodes from 1986 to 1992. Starring the late Michael Elphick, David Daker and featuring Neil Morrissey in his first starring role, *Boon* was a comedy drama about two retired firemen and their business escapades. Elphick played the eponymous 'hero' Ken Boon who worked his way from an odd-job man to private investigator whilst Daker played Harry Crawford who ran hotels, a country club, a ballroom and a security firm.

Set initially in Birmingham and later in Nottingham *Boon* was hugely popular and scriptwriters included Geoff McQueen (creator of *The Bill*), Anthony Minghella (Oscar winning director of *The English Patient*) and Kieran Prendeville (creator of *Roughnecks* and *Ballykissangel*). Boon's BSA White Lightning motorbike became a trademark of the series, as did Morrissey's studded leather jacket adorned with his 'Rocky' character name.

One of the other main reasons for the show's popularity was its music. Whilst the music for the first series was written by the *Morse* composer Barrington Pheloung, from series two on the show featured some superb incidental music and country and western style songs written by Dean Friedman. American Friedman had scored a top three hit in the UK in

1978 with the song *Lucky Stars* (a duet with Denise Marsa) and had also had a Billboard hit with his song *Ariel*. Songs such as *Handsome Stranger* and *Texas Rangers* often accompanied the credits to the *Boon* series.

The main title theme from the show, however, was written and performed by the Scotsman Jim Diamond. Diamond had first shot to fame in 1982 as part of the trio Ph.D (alongside keyboardist Tony Hymas and drummer Simon Phillips). Their hit *I Won't Let You Down* spent three weeks inside the top Three in May 1982 and despite their video for follow-up single *Little Suzi's On The Up* being the fifth to appear on the first day of MTV broadcasting they failed to achieve another UK chart hit. Diamond contracted hepatitis in 1983 and prevented from touring by the illness, the group disbanded.

Diamond decided to go solo and signed a deal with A&M Records in 1984. His first solo hit was the terrific ballad *I Should Have Known Better* which stormed the charts in the winter of 1984 reaching number One on the first day of December where it stayed for one week. Diamond contributed to his own single spending just one week at the top of the charts by urging the British public to buy another record in place of his: the Band Aid charity single *Do They Know It's Christmas?* which was released the following week. Bob Geldof praised Diamond as "genuinely selfless.... he had just thrown away his first hit for others."

Diamond's two subsequent singles failed to reach the top Forty but in 1985 he was asked by Central Television to write the theme tune for their new drama series *Boon*. He initially declined but when Central persisted he asked to see a copy of the script for the pilot episode which was entitled *Ken Boon - Fireman*. Diamond's father had been a firefighter for many years and had passed away the previous year at which time Diamond had written a tribute song. He was also intrigued by the fact that *Boon* was described as a 'modern day Lone Ranger' – his father was a fan of the TV Series *The Lone Ranger* whose catchphrase, of course, was 'Hi-yo Silver... Away!' which became the title for Diamond's song.

Hi Ho Silver was released in February 1986 after just a handful of *Boon* episodes had gone to air. It climbed steadily up the charts eventually peaking at number Five in March 1986. It also became the last of Diamond's chart hits although the Scottish singer-songwriter remains in the music industry, releasing the studio album *Souled and Heeled* in 2005.

Boon continued until 1992 although a one-off special was aired in 1995. Its charismatic star Michael Elphick had a successful run in the BBC drama *Eastenders* before sadly passing away in 2002. David Daker continued his TV work with appearances in shows as diverse as *Minder* and *Holby City* and Neil Morrissey became one of the country's best-known TV stars after appearing in the comedy *Men Behaving Badly* and in dramas such as *Paradise Heights*. He also scored a number One hit of his own when he voiced the million-selling Bob the Builder novelty hit *Can We Fix It?* in 2000.

24 Baltimora
Tarzan Boy

Released: 10 August 1985 Columbia DB 9102
Highest UK Chart Position: #3

In 1983, Polygram, EMI and Virgin Records released the first album in an unprecedentedly successful series that is still running a quarter of a century later. Devised by Ashley Abram of Box Records (a consultancy specialising in producing compilations), the first *Now That's What I Call Music* album appeared in 1983, opening with the Phil Collins smash *You Can't Hurry Love*.

The *Now!* series (the exclamation mark appeared first on *Now! 18*) took its name from an advertising poster for Danish meat products which showed a pig listening to a whistling cockerel (the pig remained the *Now!* mascot up until *Now! 5*). Whilst compilation albums weren't a new phenomenon, the move to a 'double album' format (thus preventing the abridging of tracks) and the collaboration between several large record companies meant that the first *Now* album boasted a previously unheard-of 'eleven number One hits'.

Seventy or so *Now!* albums later and the series has become something of a cultural icon with many people owning a collection stretching to the entire series. The name has become synonymous with chart compilation records and even now the triannual albums sell in their millions.

Back in the 1980's (in the days before the ability to pick and choose specific records to download) the *Now!* albums were hugely successful, collecting between thirty and forty recent chart hits onto one double vinyl album or cassette. For those of a certain age, our first memory was of *Now That's What I Call Music 4*, released in 1984 and the record that introduced many people to (amongst others), Kim Wilde (*The Second Time*), the Thompson Twins (*Doctor, Doctor*) and Heaven 17 (*Sunset Now*).

The first *Now!* album I owned however arrived from Santa Claus in December 1985. Well, to be entirely accurate, Father Christmas left *Now That's What I Call Music 6* for my sister, although I remember hijacking it for long periods early on. You could do that in those days as they were a 'two cassette' pack, and you could simply borrow the 'other' tape.

Now! 6 opened with Queen's fantastic Bob Geldof tribute record *One Vision* and the first cassette contained more rock classics including Simple Minds' *Alive and Kicking*, Marillion's *Lavender* and the Bryan Adams/Tina Turner duet *It's Only Love*. Side 2 also included the excellent and long forgotten Phil Collins and Marilyn Martin ballad *Separate Lives*.

Sides 3 and 4 were a more eclectic mix, however, and it was a track half way through the final side of the album which became one of the big party tunes of 1985.

Baltimora were an Italian/Irish disco band formed in the mind 1980's. With songs written by band members Naimy Hackett and Maurizio Bassi, the Italian sang the lead vocals but hired a Northern Irish dancer, Jimmy McShane, to front the project. McShane's energetic performances and lip-synching made him the public face of the band.

Their debut single, *Tarzan Boy* was a giant slice of mid 80's eurodisco with a huge jungle rhythm and an amazingly catchy Tarzan-esque 'oh-oh-oh-oh' hook. It was a huge international hit reaching number Thirteen in the USA and number Three in the UK (it was halted by two huge Number One duets – the UB40/Chrissie Hynde *I Got You Babe* and Jagger/Bowie's *Dancing In The Streets*) as well as reaching the top Ten across Europe.

Baltimora's album *Living In the Background* was only moderately successful, and follow-up singles *Woody Boogie* and *Chinese Restaurant* failed to chart, as did their 1987 follow-up album *Survivor In Love*.

McShane, known as 'Ruby' to his friends in the gay community passed away on March 29th 1995 in a specialist care home due to complications from AIDS. *Tarzan Boy* remains his, and Baltimora's, only hit.

It's hard to escape the notion that *Tarzan Boy* was somehow a novelty record, but on reflection it is just a really good (if slightly silly) europop song. Even though Baltimora were a 'one hit wonder', their appearance on countless Eighties compilation albums means the song remains well-known today.

As for the continued success of the *Now!* series, 2008's *Now That's What I Call Music! 69* sold almost 400,000 copies in its first week of release and so there is no evidence to suggest that the twenty-five year old series has lost any of its appeal quite yet. I reckon I had about a dozen of the compilation albums, all in all, although I haven't bought once since about 1995? How about you?

25   Limahl
NeverEnding Story

Released: 13 October 1984   **EMI LML3**
Highest UK Chart Position: #4

In August 1983, a mere seven months after they had scored a number One single with their debut single *Too Shy*, Kajagoogoo decided to fire their popular and well-known vocalist Limahl. Despite having made writing contributions to that single and to their debut album *White Feathers*, the rest of the band (formed before Limahl joined them) decided to continue as a four piece, with Nick Beggs providing the vocals.

The sacking came as a shock to the singer who had become a teen icon and a huge global star. Deciding to pursue a solo career, Limahl had already scored a chart hit with his self-penned debut solo single *Only For Love* when. at the request of EMI, he was invited to perform at the thirteenth Tokyo Music Festival. The Festival was one of the biggest music events on the calendar at the time and had attracted some of the biggest names in music over the preceding years, including Diana Ross, Stevie Wonder and Lionel Richie.

Accompanied by his manager, the larger than life character Billy Gaff, Limahl headed out to Japan to perform. Unbeknownst to him, Gaff had taken legendary Italian producer and composer Giorgio Moroder out for dinner whilst in Japan, and Limahl was therefore surprised to be approached by Moroder at the festival and asked if he would like to perform a then-unknown song for an upcoming film soundtrack.

Moroder was already a huge name in the music industry at the time, having won the 1984 Academy Award for Best Original Song for his composition *Flashdance* as well as an Oscar for his score to the film *Midnight Express*. He had also written and produced other film soundtrack songs including the Phil Oakey classic *Together In Electric Dreams*.

Six weeks later, Limahl flew out to Munich to meet Moroder at the studios and to record the song *NeverEnding Story*, co-written by Moroder and Keith Forsey. Initially Limahl struggled with the song as tiredness had made it difficult for him to hit the many high notes on the record. After going to a restaurant for dinner and a few glasses of red wine, Limahl went back into the studio and re-recorded the song, this time with more success.

Once completed, it became apparent that EMI weren't interested in the soundtrack for the film. Incensed, Billy Gaff called the head of EMI Peter Jameson and (apparently with 'a liberal amount of effing and blinding') convinced the record company head to fly out to Germany to watch the movie and listen to the music. Having been convinced by both the film and Moroder's score, EMI relented and agreed to sign-up the soundtrack.

The film *NeverEnding Story* is based on the 1979 fantasy novel written by Michael Ende. The story tells of a boy named Bastian who encounters a mysterious man in a bookstore and steals a large old book. The large old tome contains the story tells of a terrible plague called the 'nothing' which is spreading across the land of Fantasia. The Empress of the land is critically ill and appoints a warrior named Atreyu to find a cure for the 'nothing' and hands him a magical medallion called the Auryn which acts as Atreyu's guide.

With the help of his horse Artax and a large flying luckdragon named Falkor, Atreyu travels to the Southern Oracle where he is able to save the Empress by giving her a name. With the help of a human child (Bastian) and his dreams and imagination the land of Fantasia is saved and the 'nothing' is defeated. The film is seen as a metaphor for human apathy and despair, and also at a perceived lack of imagination amongst children in an age of video games and television (the 'nothing' destroys a land built from a child's imagination).

The title track from *NeverEnding Story*, unusually for a pop record, fades both in and out. This is designed to make the song appear as if it is just a part of a much longer piece of music – its lack of a definitive beginning or ending references the 'never ending' notion of the film title.

NeverEnding Story sent Limahl back to the top of the charts, reaching number One in several countries including Norway and Sweden. It reached number Four in the UK charts in the winter of 1984 and was the singer's last (and only) solo top Ten hit. Still a radio favourite today, the song has long outlasted the (excellent) film and remains one of the best movie soundtrack themes of the decade.

26 Five Star
Rain or Shine

Released: 13 September 1986 **Tent PB40901**
Highest UK Chart Position: #2

The Americans might have been able to boast the might of the Jackson family, but in the mid 1980s Britain created its own musical dynasty. For a spell, the five Pearson siblings from Romford, Essex became one of the UK's biggest groups selling millions of records and winning countless awards along the way.

Put together by their father and manager, Buster, Five Star were formed in 1983. From oldest to youngest, Stedman, Lorraine, Denise, Doris and Delroy released their debut single *Problematic* in 1983 on their own label, Tent Records. The quintet performed *Problematic* on the BBC show *Pebble Mill At One* in late 1983 and Buster Pearson claims that RCA Records were on the telephone offering the band a deal before the end of their performance.

It would be 1985 before the group would secure their first chart hit when *All Fall Down* made the UK top Twenty. Further singles *Let Me Be The One*, *Love Take Over* and *RSVP* performed progressively less well in the charts and it was only with the release of *System Addict* in 1986 that Five Star really hit the big time. The song reached number Two in the charts and propelled debut album *Luxury of Life* to number Twelve in the UK charts.

System Addict was to start a run of huge singles that kept Five Star in the top Twenty for over two years. They followed it up with the first single from their second album, the catchy *Can't Wait Another Minute* and the further top ten hit *Find The Time*. With their popularity increasing the group began to wear ever more flamboyant matching outfits with most of the dance routines choreographed by Doris Pearson. The band, in much the same way as the Jacksons, held a wholesome, family image which made them as popular with kids as they were with adults.

Five Star's popularity soared and their second album *Silk and Steel* went to number One in the album charts on its release in the summer of 1986. They became the youngest band ever to have a number One album (with an average age of just nineteen and a half) – a record that stood for eighteen years until McFly's *Room On The Third Floor* reached number One in 2004.

It was to be the third single from this album that would give the Romford band their biggest hit. The band weren't writing all their own material at this time and it was the record company and their management that would choose the songs they recorded. Many talented writers contributed songs for *Silk and Steel* including Michael Jay (the man responsible for Martika's solo success) and Billy Livsey, an American writer whose credits include hits for Tina Turner and Kenny Rogers.

Rain or Shine was co-written by Livsey (who had also penned *System Addict*) and Pete Sinfield, the ex-King Crimson lyricist responsible for hits including Bucks Fizz's *Land Of Make Believe*. It became Five Star's seventh Top Forty hit, peaking at number Two in October 1986 where it stayed for two weeks. It took the year's biggest selling single – the Communards' *Don't Leave Me This Way* – to keep it from being what would have been their only UK chart-topper.

Rain or Shine sold over a quarter of a million copies in the UK alone and helped keep *Silk and Steel* in the album Top Ten until January 1987. It was the tenth biggest selling album in the UK in 1986 shifting over 1.2million copies and featuring a mammoth six UK top Ten singles. The group also picked up the BPI (Brit) award in 1987 for Best British Group.

Rain or Shine also holds the peculiar distinction of being the seventh chart hit to mention David Bowie's interstellar hero Major Tom from his number One hits *Space Oddity* and *Ashes to Ashes*. Other songs that namecheck the fictional astronaut have included Peter Schilling's *Major Tom (Coming Home)*, Alphabeat's *Fantastic Six* and Def Leppard's *Rocket*.

Five Star's success continued through 1987 with the Denise Pearson penned *Stay Out Of My Life* reaching the top Ten and further hits *Whenever You're Ready*, *Somewhere Somebody* and *Strong as Steel* all making the UK charts. With falling sales, the band re-invented themselves as leather clad rockers in 1988 although their album *Rock The World* could only reach number Seventeen. The quintet were also infamously abused on the Saturday morning kids show *Going Live* in 1989 when a caller rang in to tell the band they were 'f***ing crap' live on national television.

Although they had no further chart success, Five Star continued until the mid 1990s before they unofficially disbanded. They returned in 2002 as a three piece with Stedman, Denise and Lorraine performing a series of shows including the nostalgia *Here and Now* tour and it is rumoured that the five will reform for further live shows in 2010.

27 Red Box
Lean On Me (Ah-Li-Ayo)

Released: 24 August 1985 Sire W 8926
Highest UK Chart Position: #3

Red Box were one of the less formulaic and more interesting pop bands of the 1980's and are largely credited with bringing so-called 'world music' into the pop arena.

They were formed at the Polytechnic of Central London in the late 1970's and took their name (after some deliberation) from a box left behind by the rock band Slade following a performance at the college. Singer Simon Toulson-Clarke also liked the image of a box (square) being the old North American Indian term for 'white man' ('circle' was the term for man before the Europeans arrived). This imagery was explored further on the band's debut album *The Circle And The Square*, a line taken from the track *Chenko* which would later become a single.

Originally a five-piece, they played live shows in London for four or five years supporting better known bands before paring themselves down to a duo (Toulson-Clarke and Julian Close) and taking a more synth-pop direction. Their cover of the Buffy Sainte-Marie song *Saskatchewan* caught the attention of WEA Records who signed the duo in 1983.

Whilst working on their debut album, Toulson-Clarke was inspired by the work of Sainte-Marie and wanted to create a sound that coupled native ('world') rhythms with a contemporary sound. An interesting feature of the songs that the band were writing at the time was the use of phonetics - indeed 'Ah-Li-Ayo' was the original title given to *Lean On Me* (WEA didn't like the phonetic title and the absence of significant lyrics for *Ah-Li-Ayo* and suggested that the record be re-titled). The use of phonetic language was also apparent in their song *Chenko* (phonetically titled 'tenka-io') and the chorus of follow-up single *For America* with its 'urelei urelei' lyric.

WEA's opposition to the phonetic approach meant Toulson-Clarke also had to write some lyrics for the record (resulting in the 'question/response' verses) and he has described the aptness of the lyrics as a 'bonus'. David Motion was also brought in to add musical ingenuity to the production and assisted with the marimba sound that was so important to the newly-re-titled *Lean On Me*'s sound.

Toulson-Clarke also had some strong ideas for how he wanted the video for the song to look and this became the source of the first of many disagreements with the head of WEA, Rob Dickins. Dickins wanted a simple video with the duo in an open-top car with a couple of good-looking girls but Toulson-Clarke was adamant that his ideas were used. The video that was made (to Dickins' annoyance) featured a roundabout full of people to represent the world and races from all corners of the globe. As the lyrics are all about words and communication, Toulson-Clarke also had the idea of asking a British Sign Language interpreter to provide a translation of the song's lyrics.

Lean On Me was released in August 1985 and by October of that year it had climbed to number Three. At its height it was selling 35,000 copies a day and whilst observers all thought it was going to be a chart-topper, the shoulder padded Jennifer Rush's power ballad *The Power Of Love* and Midge Ure's surprise hit *If I Was* overtook it in the race for number One.

Despite WEA's opposition, the video was very well received and was nominated for 'Best Video' at the 1986 BPI Awards. Rob Dickens' response to the nomination on the night of the awards? "Crap video. Great song."

The argument over the video for *Lean On Me* was the tip of the iceberg as WEA became gradually more and more unhappy about the direction the band were taking. Three and a half months into the making of their debut album, WEA executives visited the studio and were horrified to find a corrugated iron tepee which the band were using to make drum sounds and demanded compromises from the band.

The compromise came in the form of the band's follow-up single, released over a year after *Lean On Me*. This second release was a song written in response to WEA's desire for something more mainstream for the US market entitled, appropriately enough, *For America*. The single reached the top Ten in the UK and was followed by their critically acclaimed debut album *The Circle And The Square* and two further singles *Heart Of The Sun* and *Chenko*.

Red Box's relationship with the record company continued to deteriorate and the band effectively split after just one album. Toulson-Clarke was persuaded back into the studio in 1990 for the follow-up album *Motive* but this was released without publicity and failed to achieve commercial success.

Whilst Paul Simon might have been bringing native sounds to a worldwide audience with his *Graceland* album, Red Box were doing much the same but in the pop music arena. *Lean On Me* (and *For America*) are terrific, beautifully crafted records with a unique sound and interesting videos and it is a crying shame that these singles do not enjoy more regular airplay.

28 Jimmy Nail
Love Don't Live Here Anymore

Released: 27 April 1985   Virgin VS 764
Highest UK Chart Position: #3

In early 1985, if you'd have been asked to pick which one of the *Auf Wiedersehen, Pet* 'Magnificent Seven' would end up having a long and successful pop music career, you'd have got long odds on slovenly Geordie slob Leonard Jeffrey 'Oz' Osborne, played by rookie actor Jimmy Nail. Seven albums and a number One single later, however, Nail has forged a successful TV, film and music career from humble beginnings.

James Michael Aloysius Bradford was born in Benton, Newcastle-upon-Tyne on March 16th 1954. His father was a professional footballer and had played for Huddersfield Town but on leaving school Jimmy took a job as a welder for a local double glazing company. He sang in a 1970s band called King Crabs and appeared as an extra in the classic Michael Caine film *Get Carter* but his first acting break came when he secured a part in the classic Dick Clement and Ian le Frenais comedy drama *Auf Wiedersehen, Pet*.

Auf Wiedersehen, Pet first aired in the UK on 11 November 1983. Nail played one of seven lead characters, British bricklayers working on a construction site in the German city of Dusseldorf. His character – Leonard 'Oz' Osbourne was an argumentative, loud Geordie xenophobe whose passions involved infidelity and his beloved Newcastle United.

In 1985, Nail reinforced his screen reputation as a loveable idiot by starring in the Mel Smith and Griff Rhys-Jones comedy film *Morons From Outer Space* (directed by Mike Hodges, the man responsible for *Get Carter*). Nail plays Desmond Brook, one of the 'morons' who accidentally crash land on Earth after tampering with the controls of their spacecraft during a tedious stop at an intergalactic refuelling station.

Having carved something of a niche as a scruffy, drunken but ultimately harmless fool, the incongruousness of Nail's musical debut was all the more startling. He released his first album *Take It Or Leave It* in 1986, but the previous year had released his debut single which was about as far removed from what the British public expected as was possible.

Love Don't Live Here Anymore was a cover of the classic Rose Royce song. Originally recorded in 1978, Royce's version reached number 32 in the US charts and number Two in the UK and has been covered on numerous occasions by artists from Madonna to Dr Dre.

Love Don't Live Here Anymore is a beautiful soulful ballad and the sight of the giant Geordie builder belting out the song on *Top Of The Pops* (hands in the pockets of his trademark trenchcoat) was quite bizarre. What people had underestimated was the quality of Nail's vocals and they also didn't realize that Nail had been a singer before he became an actor.

The song reached number Three for two weeks in the UK charts in May 1985, kept off the top spot by Paul Hardcastle's *19* and Duran Duran's Bond theme *A View To A Kill*.

Choosing to return to acting, Nail's success continued with a second series of *Auf Wiedersehen, Pet* including an episode where he shocks his fellow labourers by getting up to sing in a country and western pub (his colleagues' response to his dulcet tones mirrored the surprise of the British public when they first heard *Love Don't Live Here Anymore*).

Nail then successfully shrugged off his typecast image by writing and starring in the gritty BBC drama *Spender* which ran between 1990 and 1993. During this time, the Geordie relaunched his music career and released his second single, seven years after the first. The catchy *Ain't No Doubt* reached number One in the UK and paved the way for further singles including the theme to his later TV series *Crocodile Shoes* and the Mark Knopfler collaboration *Big River*. His last hit was the 1996 top Thirty single *Country Boy*.

Nail then turned his talents to the big screen, appearing in several hit movies including a starring role in the 1996 Madonna-led version of the musical *Evita* and a role as aging rocker Les Wickes in the comedy drama *Still Crazy* (where his song *The Flame Still Burns* was nominated for a Golden Globe).

Nail was last seen in the successful BBC revival of *Auf Wiedersehen, Pet* which aired in 2002 and 2004. He reprised his role alongside five of the original Magnificent Seven (Gary Holton had died in 1985 and was replaced by Noel Clarke as his son Waylon in the later two series) as a slightly better-behaved Oz, responsible for reuniting the group.

29 Su Pollard
Starting Together

Released:1 February 1986   Rainbow RBR4
Highest UK Chart Position: #2

If, in a *Family Fortunes* style, you asked a hundred people to name you a long-running and well-loved sitcom of the 1980's you would expect at least an instant prize if you came up with the (quite literally) 'camp' classic *Hi-de-Hi*.

One of the most popular and endearing characters of the BAFTA winning programme's eight year run was motorcycle racing chalet-maid and wannabe Yellowcoat Peggy Ollerenshaw played by Nottingham born actress Su Pollard. Whilst Peggy represents the most enduring memory many have of Pollard, her big break and first taste of success came through her singing career.

Despite being defeated during the 1974 series of *Opportunity Knocks* by a singing Jack Russell terrier, Pollard appeared in numerous West End musicals in the latter part of the 1970s before landing her plum role in David Croft and Jimmy Perry's sitcom.

In 1984, respected British documentary maker Desmond Wilcox embarked on a yearlong project to film a pair of newlyweds through their wedding and through the first months of their married life together. When the twelve part series was completed and ready to be aired in 1986, Wilcox asked for submissions for a theme tune appropriate to the subject matter. One of the songs he received was from Bill Buckley, a colleague of his wife, Esther Rantzen.

Rantzen had presented BBC's hugely popular *That's Life* series since its inception in 1973, a programme whose mixture of hard-hitting consumer affairs and singing animals turned it into a national institution. In 1982

Rantzen was joined on the show by Bill Buckley who, as well as being a accomplished presenter was also a talented songwriter.

Buckley had written a song which he felt would be perfect for Wilcox's series, and having seen Pollard perform in the West End some years before he invited her to record a demo. This was submitted to Wilcox who decided he liked the song (ahead of other submissions by the likes of Barbara Dickson and Cliff Richard) and so the first episode of the series aired in 1986 with a re-recorded version of *Starting Together* as its main theme tune and incidental music.

The Marriage quickly became must-see television. A decade or two before fly-on-the-wall documentaries became the staple of many TV schedules, the story of Karen and Marc Adams-Jones captured the hearts of the British public and the documentary regularly pulled in over 15 million viewers. As well as the show drawing huge interest, there was also a clamour from the public for the theme song and the BBC were asked to release *Starting Together* as a single.

As there had never been an intention to release the song formally, a video had to be quickly filmed. In one of the lowest budget music video efforts of the decade, Su wandered around Hampstead Heath in the snow, wearing what can only (and politely) be described as a luminescent pink tea cosy on her head whilst the newlyweds from the series pelted her (and each other) with snowballs.

Within five weeks of release the song had sold over a quarter of a million copies and had raced to number Two in the singles chart. It was only the might of Billy Ocean's huge *When The Going Gets Tough* that prevented what would have been (in hindsight, certainly) one of the most unlikely artist number One singles of recent years. In one of those lovely incongruous pop moments that happens from time to time, *Starting Together* sat alongside The Damned's *Eloise* in February 1986's top Three.

Starting Together, a simple paean to love, hope and happiness is one of those songs that seems to remain socially unacceptable to admit buying or liking. Whilst is may not be a pop classic, it has a certain charm, appeals to the 'happy endings' in people and, for a few months at least, it was the wedding song of choice for hundreds of brides and grooms. Indeed, Pollard admits to still being invited to weddings to perform the tune (which she pretty much always declines.) Perhaps it is because the abiding memory of Pollard is as *Hi-de-Hi!*'s slightly dippy chalet maid and, twenty years on, people can't get their head around the fact that she actually has a fine voice.

Either way, as TV theme tunes go it remains one of the most commercially successful and as for the newlyweds in the series, they remain happily married twenty-five years later.

30 Adam and the Ants
Antmusic

Released: 6 December 1980   CBS9352
Highest UK Chart Position: #2

At the turn of the decade, when punk was just on the cusp of turning into 'new wave', one vibrant and popular band ruled the charts, led by their stylish and charismatic vocalist. Born Stuart Leslie Goddard in London in 1954, Adam Ant led his band, the Ants, for seven years scoring countless hits worldwide.

Goddard started his musical career as the bass player in a punk outfit called Bazooka Joe in 1975, now most famously remembered as the headline act on the bill where the Sex Pistols played their first live show. The first incarnation of the Ants was formed in 1977 and the line-up altered over the course of the next three years culminating in 1980 when Malcolm McLaren convinced three of the band members to join him to form the band Bow Wow Wow.

Ant then recruited a new band including guitarist Marco Pirroni and the five piece signed a deal with CBS Records in 1980 before setting to work recording their first album with the new line-up, *Kings of the Wild Frontier*.

Although the first single – the title track from the album – failed to make the UK top Forty it wasn't long before the band were flying high in the charts. With one of the most distinctive looks of the decade (who can forget the jackets and the white strip across the nose?) Ant led the band into the top ten for the first time in November 1980 with the song *Dog Eat Dog*.

Their follow-up single was to be the one to catapult the band to international stardom however and start the worldwide Antmania movement. The massive single *Antmusic* was released in December 1980 and, with its accompanying video, urged its young audience to turn away from the current disco music (playing on a giant jukebox in the video) and to listen to their new brand of 'antmusic' instead. The song climbed the UK charts for seven weeks and looked set to become the band's first chart topper until the death of John Lennon in 1980 resulted in his re-released song *Imagine* holding *Antmusic* off the top spot in the UK.

The song also performed well internationally and spent five weeks at the top of the charts in Australia earning the band a platinum certification. It also marked the start of a sustained period of success for the band, as by the time a re-release of the song *Kings Of The Wild Frontier* had hit the top Forty in February 1981, the band had five singles simultaneously on the top 75 chart. The album also won the 'Best British Album' gong at the 1982 BPI awards.

May 1981 saw the eagerly awaited release of the band's new single and this record further cemented Adam and the Ants' position as the most popular chart band of their day. They finally secured their first number One single in the UK with the huge-selling *Stand and Deliver*, which entered the top Forty at number One where it stayed for five weeks. The follow-up single and title track from their second album *Prince Charming* was also a UK number One hit, spending a month at the top of the charts in September and October 1981.

Only one further top five hit followed as Adam and the Ants (1982's *Ant Rap*) as shortly after receiving a Grammy nomination for Best New Artist, Ant decided to disband the group, believing that certain band members 'lacked enthusiasm'. Taking co-writer Perroni with him, Ant immediately launched a solo career and maintained his chart success with the 1982 number One single *Goody Two Shoes*. Further top ten hit *Friend or Foe* followed, and Ant then teamed up with Phil Collins and Richard James Burgess to record his 1983 *Strip* album spawning the top five single *Puss in Boots*.

That was to be the end of Ant's chart domination as despite an appearance at 1985's Live Aid concert, his single *Vive le Rock* failed to make the top Forty and it would be 1990 before Ant enjoyed further top Twenty success with the great single *Room at the Top*. In the meantime Ant had scored moderate acting success appearing on stage in the UK as well as on American TV series including *The Equalizer* and *Northern Exposure*.

Ant returned to the public spotlight in 2002 when he pleaded guilty to affray before returning to court in 2003 after a further incident of affray and criminal damage. Having spent time in psychiatric care, Ant was sectioned under the Mental Health Act in 2003 before later being given a conditional discharge.

Antmusic is the song that really set Adam and the Ants on their way to their huge success in the early decade and whilst it may not have the instant recognition of some of their giant number One singles is still a superb New Romantic record. It was covered by Robbie Williams in 1998 as the B-side to his single *No Regrets* and has also been covered by OK Go, Leeroy Thornhill (formerly of The Prodigy) and by the Charlatans and Dirty Pretty Things (on the Channel Four show *Transmission* in 2008.)

31 Billy Ocean
Caribbean Queen (No More Love On The Run)

Released: 13 October 1984   Jive JIVE77
Highest UK Chart Position: #6

Billy Ocean is, very simply, the biggest selling British black artist of all time. He has sold over thirty million records worldwide, won a plethora of awards and can boast a string of gold and platinum selling international hits including several US and UK number Ones.

Born Leslie Sebastian Charles in Trinidad in 1950, Ocean moved to the UK with his family at the age of seven. His father was a prominent Grenadian musician and Ocean spent much of his teenage years singing in London clubs before he secured his big break by signing to GTO Records in 1975. The singer adopted the name Billy Ocean (from the Ocean Estate where he lived in East London) and had almost instant success with his 1976 UK number Two hit *Love Really Hurts Without You*. The song also reached number Twenty-Two on the US Billboard chart.

Over the next two years, Ocean scored several further UK hits with *L.O.D (Love On Delivery)*, *Stop Me (If You've Heard It All Before)* and the number Two smash *Red Light Spells Danger*. However, after the success of *Red Light...* Ocean failed to make the UK top Forty with his next two releases and so the singer moved to America where his records continued to fly high on the R&B charts. By now Ocean's songwriting talents were being noticed by other artists and he penned several songs for other vocalists, including a track on LaToya Jackson's 1980 debut album.

It was after signing to Jive Records in 1984 that Ocean's major international success began with the release of the single *Caribbean Queen*. The song was co-written by renowned American producer Robert 'Mutt' Lange, responsible for the production on some of the 80s and 90s biggest albums including Def Leppard's *Hysteria*, Bryan Adams' *Waking Up The Neighbours* and Shania Twain's *The Woman In Me*.

Unusually, the song was re-recorded with several different versions for different territories. A story of an exotic and beautiful woman seducing the singer, the track originally made the lower echelons of the UK top Hundred as *European Queen* in the summer of 1984 and Ocean also recorded a version entitled *African Queen*. It was only on its re-release as *Caribbean Queen* in the autumn of 1984 that it successfully climbed the charts on both sides of the Atlantic. The song peaked at number Six in the UK in November 1984, spending fifteen weeks on the charts, but it was the song's success in the USA that propelled Ocean to superstardom. The song dislodged Stevie Wonder's *I Just Called To Say I Love You* from the Billboard number One position in November 1984, spending two weeks atop the charts and selling over a million copies. Ocean also won the 1985 Grammy for Best Male R&B Vocal Performance for *Caribbean Queen*.

Firmly established as a major star, Ocean's album and single *Suddenly* were huge successes worldwide, as was the single *Loverboy*. He performed at the Philadephia leg of 1985's *Live Aid* concert (singing *Caribbean Queen*) before he returned to the studio to record his eagerly awaited follow-up album *Love Zone*.

1986 saw Ocean return with a major UK number One single *When The Going Gets Tough (The Tough Get Going)*. Taken from the Michael Douglas/Kathleen Turner film *The Jewel Of The Nile* the video featured the film leads (plus Danny de Vito) miming to backing vocals. The song would return to the number One spot thirteen years later in the hands of Boyzone who scored the fifth of their six number Ones with their version of the hit.

Ocean's transatlantic success continued with his US number One *There'll Be Sad Songs (To Make You Cry)* before his 1988 album *Tear Down These Walls* spawned the superb hit *Get Outta My Dreams...Get Into My Car*. Featuring a state of the art video mixing animated and live action sequences it gave Ocean his third US Number One hit and reached number Three in the UK.

After a long run of chart success, *Get Outta My Dreams* proved to be Ocean's last major hit. His follow-up *Calypso Crazy* just scraped into the

UK top Forty and his 1989 *Greatest Hits* compilation reached number Four on the album chart. His 1993 album *Time To Move On* (recorded with R Kelly) failed to achieve commercial success and Ocean retreated from the music scene to spend time with his young family.

With his children grown up, Ocean reappeared in 2007 with a major UK tour and his new album *Because I Love You* was released in the spring of 2009.

Whilst not his biggest hit worldwide, *Caribbean Queen* was the song that catapulted Ocean into international superstardom, a full eight years after his first UK hit. It is a slick R&B performance and whilst his popularity fluctuated in the UK during the 1980s he remained a huge star in the US throughout.

32 Sinitta
So Macho

Released: 8 March 1986   Fanfare FAN7
Highest UK Chart Position: #2

Born Sinitta Renat Malone in Seattle in 1968, Sinitta was something of a child star. Her mother Miquel Brown was a well-known actress and soul singer, as was her aunt, Amii Stewart (best known for the disco anthem *Knock On Wood*).

She trained at the Russian Ballet School and spent her school holidays at Pineapple Studios in Covent Garden, where she won the part as the understudy to Dorothy in the famous musical movie *The Wiz*. She was then cast as Francine in the movie sequel to the *Rocky Horror Show* and then spent time working on West End musicals including *Cats* and *Little Shop Of Horrors*.

She signed her first record deal with Magnate Records in 1983 and the first single *Never Too Late* was mixed by legendary American producer Jellybean Benitez. Whilst this solo single was a club hit, it didn't cross over into the pop charts. Several TV appearances followed at this time, including a stint as guest vocalist for the dance group Hot Gossip and as a dancer with the band Imagination.

In 1984, she got her big TV break by appearing in the live elimination final for the UK's *Song For Europe*. Despite beating fellow Hit Factory act Hazell Dean, Sinitta came fourth and Belle and the Devotions ended up representing the UK in Luxembourg where they came 7th (Sweden's *Diggy-Loo, Diggy-Ley* won the contest).

A starring role alongside David Essex in the West End production *Mutiny!* followed before Sinitta went back in the studio to record some more demos. Amongst these was a club hit entitled *So Macho*. This hi-NRG pop single (loved by the singer as it followed the style of her mother and aunt's records) concerned the singer's keenness to find a 'hunk of a guy' and was written and produced by George Hargreaves.

At the time, Sinitta was also undertaking modelling work for an agency in London. The agency offices were below those of a record company called Fanfare run by Ian Burton and a young record executive by the name of Simon Cowell. Whenever the teenage singer was at the agency for a casting, she made a habit of sitting on Cowell's desk and singing *So Macho* (before being chased out by Cowell telling her "she was cute and that she should stick to modelling!") The two later had a relationship and have recently worked together on the ITV talent show *X Factor*.

So Macho began to attract some interest and radio stations started to pick up the fresh, catchy single. A startlingly low budget video, featuring a scantily clad Sinitta and a strange older doctor figure, was filmed in Maida Vale to accompany the single.

So Macho spent literally most of 1986 on the charts. The single embarked on an astonishing thirty week chart run in March reaching its peak position of number Two on 9th August 1986. It was the tenth biggest selling single in the UK in 1986 and was only prevented from reaching the top spot by a bizarre combination of aged Irish crooner Chris de Burgh's timeless *Lady In Red* and Boris Gardiner's surprise reggae hit *I Wanna Wake Up With You*.

Sinitta eventually managed to convince Cowell to sign her and she was also soon noticed by the British songwriting team of Stock, Aitken and Waterman. The legendary producers provided most of the material for her debut album *Sinitta!* including follow-up hits *Toy Boy*, *GTO* and *Cross My Broken Heart*. The team once claimed that Sinitta "was the sexiest voice we ever produced".

Sinitta split with PWL in 1988 due to a perceived lack of credit for her work and the trio's apparent desire to look after their new starlet (one Kylie Minogue) ahead of their existing roster. Working with Pete Hammond and Ian Harding, her success continued with the second album *Wicked* which contained the top ten hit *Right Back Where We Started From*.

So Macho was pretty camp in nature, and thus became something of a gay anthem. This has caused recent controversy as the producer and writer behind the hit (the now Reverend George Hargreaves) admitted that he had used the royalties generated over the years to fund the creation of his political movements, the Scottish and Welsh Christian Parties. These heavily religious groups campaign on a platform of homosexual intolerance and Hargreaves has been accused of hypocrisy considering his claim that *So Macho* was written "...for the gay scene to go mad to on poppers."

So Macho remains Sinitta's most immediately recognisable single and her biggest chart hit. Looking back, it was something of a teenage anthem and had a 'girl power' message which wouldn't rear its head again in music for another decade. As she says herself, the record "was fresh, fierce, full of attitude and camp as hell and at the ripe age of 16 I was fearless and having fun with it." And you can't argue with that, can you?

33 Swing Out Sister
Breakout

Released: 25 October 1986   Mercury SWING2
Highest UK Chart Position: #4

There are many UK places famous for their popular music heritage, and for most major cities you can reel off a list of their musical alumni off the top of your head. Birmingham gave us artists as varied as Black Sabbath, Duran Duran, UB40 and Dexy's Midnight Runners. Liverpool gave us not only the Beatles but Frankie Goes To Hollywood, Gerry and the Pacemakers and the Teardrop Explodes. Manchester is home to Oasis, the Hollies, the Bee Gees and 10cc, Leeds to the Kaiser Chiefs, Soft Cell and the Wedding Present and Glasgow to Altered Images, Wet Wet Wet and Texas.

If you try doing an internet search for 'bands from Nottingham', however, it is a very different story....

Whilst Wikipedia and other websites have lists of household names in pop music for almost everywhere else in the UK, there isn't a page for Nottingham. Considering it is the seventh biggest urban area in the UK, its contribution to popular music in the twentieth century is limited to Alvin Stardust, KWS and Paper Lace. It is a pretty meagre showing when considering that even its smaller East Midlands neighbours can boast the likes of Kasabian, Cornershop and the Enemy.

Nottingham's moment in the pop music sunshine pretty much began and ended in the spring of 1974. Alvin Stardust hit the top of the charts in March of that year with his single *Jealous Mind* and, bizarrely (considering the lack of any significant contribution since) fellow Nottinghamians Paper Lace knocked Stardust off the number One spot with their anti-war hit *Billy, Don't Be A Hero*.

Eighteen years later Nottingham had another number One hit although KWS' chart career was largely limited to their 1992 cover of the KC and the Sunshine Band hit *Please Don't Go* (and that song was only recorded as a plea directed at Nottingham Forest and England footballer Des Walker who was about to sign for the Italian club Sampdoria).

This severe lack of musical legacy for such a vibrant and prominent city is put into acute perspective by the creative talent to have come from the city a mere thirty five miles up the M1 motorway. Sheffield can boast some of the greatest names in popular music over the last forty years and a list of artists to have come from the steel city is like a 'who's who' of pop, particularly in the 1980s. Joe Cocker, Pulp, Heaven 17, Living In A Box, Def Leppard, the Thompson Twins, ABC, the Arctic Monkeys and the Human League all hail from the South Yorkshire city. Indeed, in 1999 the city was chosen as the location for the ambitious but ill-conceived National Centre for Popular Music (the centre was a terrible failure, closing in July 2000).

After considerable research, however, it turns out that there was one more Nottingham based band that did secure success in the 1980s and took their brand of unusual jazz-tinged pop to the top of the UK album charts.

Corinne Drewery was first exposed to the world of live music as a child as her father's band was one of the regular support acts to many of the major stars of the 1960s including Tom Jones, Lulu and Sandie Shaw. Having grown up in the East Midlands, Drewery moved to London in 1976 to study fashion where she became a designer. In 1984 she met Andy Connell and Martin Jackson and formed the band Swing Out Sister, named after the 1945 Arthur Treacher film.

Andy Connell, a classically trained pianist, had paid his way through college by taking a job as a pianist in a Manchester wine-bar. It was during customer requests for songs including *Do You Know The Way To San Jose?* and *You Only Live Twice* that Connell saw the potential in using jazz chord progressions in pop music. These jazz influences would become apparent in the development of Swing Out Sister's sound.

Signed to Mercury Records they released their first single *Blue Mood* in November 1985 although this failed to chart. The follow-up single was not released until October 1986 but after a slow start became a top Five hit.

Breakout is a jazzy pop record which epitomised Swing Out Sister's fusion of synthesisers, strings and real brass. It reached number Four in the UK charts and also appealed to an American audience, where it reached number Six on the Billboard chart as well as being nominated for a Grammy award. The follow-up single *Surrender*, a slower song featuring a well-known trumpet solo also reached the top Ten and their debut album *It's Better To Travel* reached the top of the UK album charts.

Jackson left the band during the recording of their second album *Kaleidoscope World* which also reached the UK top Ten as well as spawning the superb single *You On My Mind*. That was to be the end of the band's commercial success in the UK although the duo did have a couple of minor hits in the 1990's with *Am I The Same Girl?* and *La La La (Means I Love You)*. They have continued to be successful in both American and Japan and their ninth album *Beautiful Mess* was released in 2008.

34 Nick Kamen
Each Time You Break My Heart

Released: 8 November 1986   WEA YZ 90
Highest UK Chart Position: #5

For a time in the mid to late 1980's, there was one sure-fire way to get a hit record. Well, there were two sure-fire ways, really, but the one that didn't include getting Stock, Aitken and Waterman to produce it involved having your song featured in a popular television advert.

For five years or so, commercials from beer to boot cut jeans propelled old songs back into the charts, some of which performed spectacularly successfully. Nina Simone's signature tune *My Baby Just Cares For Me* went top Five in the UK in 1987 after its use in a Chanel Number 5 commercial. A Miller beer advert sent the Hollies' *He Ain't Heavy, He's My Brother* to number One for a fortnight in September 1988 shortly before Robin Beck's ex-Coca Cola jingle *First Time* spent three weeks at the top of the charts.

The most successful series of adverts, however, was for Levi's as their jeans commercials spawned a string of top three smashes in the UK. Twenty nine years after it was first a hit, Jackie Wilson's *Reet Petite* spent a month at number One having been featured in a Levi's ad, three months before Ben E King's *Stand By Me* also hit the top of the charts after featuring in the company's '501s' commercial. Other oldies to re-appear in the top Forty thanks to their exposure in a Levi's advert included Sam Cooke's *Wonderful World* (number Two in 1986) and Percy Sledge's *When A Man Loves A Woman* (number Two in 1987).

Levi's intention with the commercials was to exploit young people's aspirations for the heritage of the 1950's by associating Levi's 501 jeans with a classic period of youth culture. The campaign was staggeringly successful, not only assisting the sale of millions of singles but reviving a flagging jeans market. Sales of 501's went up 800% in the year following the launch of the campaign.

The most famous of these Levi's advertisements was one of their first (for their 'stonewashed' brand), broadcast in 1985. It resulted in Marvin Gaye's classic *I Heard It Through The Grapevine* reaching number Eight on the singles chart (it was marketed with Levi's iconic brand '501' on the record sleeve) and has also become one of the most famous advertisements in television history.

You all remember the one. Set in a 1950's launderette, a young man walks in wearing *Blues Brothers* style sunglasses. Watched by a couple of young children, he empties a bag of rocks into a washer and, to the surprise of the watching women, he then strips down to his boxer shorts, putting his clothes into the machine. The ad finishes with him sitting in between a chubby guy and two giggling women in just his pristine white boxer shorts.

Whilst the advert didn't launch Nick Kamen's career, it certainly put him in the spotlight. Kamen had already been working as a model, appearing on the cover of *Face* magazine in 1984, before he got the part in the laundromat commercial. Spotted by an American rising star, one Madonna Louise Ciccone, Kamen recorded a song written by Madonna and co-writer Stephen Bray (the team behind *Get Into The Groove* and *True Blue*). *Each Time You Break My Heart* was also produced by Madonna and Bray and the American superstar also sang backing vocals on the track.

The song made the top Ten in the UK in December 1986. Reaching number Five, it was a pop oasis in a desert of dubious poodle-rock as its peak chart position was reached in a week where it was outsold by Berlin, Europe and Bon Jovi.

Kamen's follow-up single, a largely ignored but brilliant version of the Four Tops' *Loving You (Is Sweeter Than Ever)* made number Sixteen in March 1987 and despite Madonna's continued involvement (she sang backing vocals on *Tell Me*, the first single from his second album *Us*) further chart success eluded him. He did however provide the song *Turn It Up* for the 1989 Disney hit move *Honey, I Shrunk The Kids*.

If you listen carefully, it's easy to see the Madonna/Bray influence in *Each Time You Break My Heart*. Not only does the singer provide backing vocals on the song, but the backing track is also very reminiscent of early Madonna material. It is not the finest Madonna musical creation of that era, but it's a decent pop song and Kamen does a sound enough job with the vocals. Whilst it is a worthy inclusion here, *Each Time You Break My Heart* is not genius enough to be the one thing Kamen will be remembered for – the sight of him in his boxer shorts on telly saw to that.

35 Curiosity Killed The Cat
Down To Earth

Released: 13 December 1986   Mercury CAT2
Highest UK Chart Position: #3

One of the UK's more stylish and grown-up pop bands of the mid to late 1980s, Curiosity Killed The Cat were formed at a London art school. The band Twilight Children featuring Nick Thorpe, Miguel 'Migi' Drummond and Julian Brookhouse added vocalist Ben Volpelierre-Pierrot in 1984, the singer having appeared regularly in teenage magazines as a young model.

A demo of their song *Curiosity Killed The Cat* was heard by businessman Peter Rosengard who became the band's manager and their name was changed from Twilight Children to that of the song. The foursome were signed to Phonogram in 1985 after a debut gig at the Embassy Club in London in December 1984 and whilst ostensibly a quartet, the band also featured Toby Anderson on keyboards who remained the unofficial 'fifth member' until 1986. As the group had been signed as a four piece it became impossible for them to renegotiate their contract to include Anderson and so he was never officially a member of the band.

Curiosity went into the studio in late 1985 to begin the recording of their debut album *Keep Your Distance* but a change in the production team (after the original team of Sly Dunbar and Robbie Shakespeare was dropped in favour of Stewart Levine) led to a significant delay in the release of their first single.

During 1986 the iconic filmmaker and artist Andy Warhol brought an exhibition to England for the first time in almost two decades. Phonogram Records obtained invitations to the launch of the exhibition and the press featured Curiosity Killed The Cat photographed with Warhol. Warhol drew a wedding ring around the finger of bassist Nick Thorpe for the photographs and the band were then invited to the Cafe Royal for a banquet with the American pop-artist. Warhol asked the band's management to forward a cassette of their work and once received he contacted the group and asked to make the video for their song *Misfit*.

Filmed in New York the video featured Volpelierre-Pierrot dancing in a side-street whilst, in a homage to the famous promotional video for Bob Dylan's *Subterranean Homesick Blues*, Warhol dropped large pieces of white card containing writing in time to the music. Whilst Warhol's involvement secured much exposure for the band, the single was not a success, failing to reach the UK top Forty.

Curiosity Killed The Cat's follow up single was to be a favourite of the band, the funky, soulful *Down to Earth*. Written about the reality of life that people don't want to face – that people have to be 'down to earth' and that this approach isn't altogether a bad one - the record company originally wanted to delay the release until after the Christmas of 1986 as they were worried about the competition associated with the Christmas market. In spite of these concerns *Down to Earth* was released in November 1986.

The song proved to be a slow-burner, actually reaching the top Forty in its ninth week on the chart. It continued to climb slowly eventually peaking at number Three in February 1987 after a full three months in the top Hundred. Several television appearances helped propel the record up the charts, as Volpelierre-Pierrot's trademark image – a fisherman's hat (not a beret) with the peak worn at the back – caught the public attention. *Smash Hits* magazine also nicknamed the singer Ben Vol-au-vent Parrot in mock confusion as to the pronunciation of his surname.

Curiosity Killed The Cat's follow-up single *Ordinary Day* peaked at number Eleven before a re-release of their debut single *Misfit* reached the UK top Ten in July 1987. Their debut album *Keep Your Distance* entered the album charts at number One in May 1987 and spent twenty-four weeks on the album charts.

After a quiet couple of years the band returned to the charts (under a new name, simply Curiosity) in the summer of 1989 with the funky *Name and Number* and after a couple of further years away and a change of record label they made the top Three in 1992 with a cover of the Johnny Bristol hit *Hang On In There Baby*. Follow-up singles *I Need Your Lovin'* and *Gimme The Sunshine* failed to chart however and the group disbanded. They reformed for a National Lottery appearance in the early 2000s and Volpeliere-Pierrot has since performed as Curiosity Killed The Cat on various 80s revival tours.

36 Pepsi and Shirlie
Heartache

Released: 17 January 1987   Polydor POSP 837
Highest UK Chart Position: #2

The Pepsi and Shirlie story begins seven years before the release of their 1987 hit single in the Hertfordshire town of Watford.

Eighteen year old Shirlie Holliman had been pursuing her dream of becoming a horse riding instructor until she developed terrible hay fever which prevented her following her chosen career. Having no other job in mind, Holliman was invited by her then boyfriend, Andrew Ridgeley, to go on stage and dance with him and his friend George Michael's band. Appearing in local nightclubs, Holliman appeared on stage with the two boys whilst their popularity grew and grew.

The band (by then called Wham!) had their big break in November 1982 when they were asked to fill a spot on the BBC's *Top of the Pops* show, despite their record being just outside the top Forty. Performing *Young Guns (Go For It)*, the duo, flanked by Holliman and fellow singer Dee C Lee became an instant sensation and the single eventually reached number Three in the charts.

When Lee left Wham! to work with (and later marry) Paul Weller of the Style Council she was replaced by singer Lawrie 'Pepsi' Demacque and Holliman and Demacque remained Wham!'s backing vocalists and dancers for the rest of the band's lifespan.

Never officially signed to the band, Pepsi and Shirlie were paid for their performances and were ubiquitous in videos and at gigs over the next three years. They starred in the Wham! videos, including wearing the famous Katherine Hammett T-shirts *Choose Life* and *Go-Go* in the *Wake Me Up Before You Go-Go* video. Holliman has said that she particularly enjoyed the making of the films for *Club Tropicana* and *Last Christmas*. The pair appeared for the final time with Wham! at their seventy-three thousand strong *Final* gig at Wembley Stadium on June 28th 1986.

Following the demise of Wham! Pepsi and Shirlie decided to form their own band, and with a more generic pop sound they released their first single in January 1987. Produced by the esteemed Brit Phil Fearon (who had been the brainchild behind the band Galaxy who had scored 80's top Ten hits with the likes of *Dancing Tight*, *What Do I Do?* and *Everybody's Laughing*) and Tambi Fernando, *Heartache* quickly became a hit reaching number Two in the UK charts for a fortnight in February 1987. Ironically, it was their former employer, George Michael, who prevented them reaching number One as his brilliant duet with American soul goddess Aretha Franklin *I Knew You Were Waiting (For Me)* (written by Simon Climie (of Climie Fisher)) was top of the charts.

A further top Ten hit followed for the duo – the similarly uptempo *Goodbye Stranger* - which featured a video with the pair wearing matching dresses looking alarmingly like a set of Laura Ashley curtains. Further singles *Can't Give Me Love*, *All Right Now* (a cover version of Free's classic rock single from the early 1970s) and *Hightime* failed to reach the top Forty and their album (also entitled *All Right Now*) peaked at number Sixty-Nine in November 1987.

At the height of their fame in 1988 Holliman married long-term boyfriend, Spandau Ballet bassist Martin Kemp in a small ceremony in St Lucia. The singer gave birth to their first child, daughter Harley Moon in the summer of 1989 and as she has confessed, "when Harley was born I was so in love with her that nothing else seemed important". Despite commencing the recording of a second Pepsi and Shirlie album in 1989, Holliman plucked up the courage to tell Demacque that her heart wasn't in their music any longer and the pair amicably split.

Holliman spent the 1990's supporting husband Kemp through his recovery from two benign brain tumours and bringing up their two children whilst his acting career flourished (in the acclaimed film *The Krays* and his later appearance in BBC's *Eastenders* as bad-boy Steve Owen). Demacque took part in the 1993 revival of the musical *Hair* alongside

John Barrowman and Sinitta before providing vocals on albums and at live performances for Mike Oldfield, specifically for his *Tubular Bells III* and *Millennium Bell* projects.

Holliman and daughter Harley also appeared in the video for the 1998 Spice Girls number One hit *Mama* and Pepsi and Shirlie reunited in 2000 to record backing vocals for Geri Halliwell's album *Schizophonic* including the number one single *Bag It Up*.

37 Mental As Anything
Live It Up

Released: 7 February 1987   EPIC ANY 1
Highest UK Chart Position: #3

Formed way back in 1976 at East Sydney Technical College (an art school), the first performance as the group Mental as Anything was on the day the news broke in Australia of Elvis' death – 17 August 1977. The band name came from a description that fellow artist Ken Bolton gave to one of their early performances.

The foursome scored some early successes, including the Australian drinking anthem *The Nips Are Getting Bigger* which also reached number One on the UK alternative chart in 1980. They continued to have a string of hit records in their home country at the same time as beginning to achieve some modest successes abroad. They toured with fellow Aussies Men At Work in the USA and Canada, and it was on the tour bus between Edmonton and Winnipeg that keyboardist Andrew 'Greedy' Smith came up with an idea for a song. To this point most of the band's output had been written by bassist Peter O'Doherty and vocalist Martin Plaza, but Smith was beginning to come to the fore as a writer and had written their recent Canadian hit *Too Many Times*.

Although he had never thought of himself as a ladies' man, Greedy Smith had the idea of writing a song about a man trying to chat up a girl and invite her out of a nightclub. The idea of the lyric was that he was trying to save someone from the hell of a loud disco with the line 'hey – yeah you!' Having come up with the idea it took a further two years for *Live It Up* to be completed as it turned from a funky James Brown-esque number into what Smith called a 'shuffle' – taking shape after experimenting with his first ever drum machine.

In 1985, the band was asked to write some music for a forthcoming Australian comedy film. Made on a budget of under $10 million, *Crocodile Dundee* was designed to appeal to a mainstream American audience and was inspired by the real-life story of Rodney Ansell, a bushman who became stranded in the remote Northern Territories in 1977, surviving for over two months on limited resources.

Smith and the band wrote the song *Sloppy Crocodile* which star Paul Hogan liked, although he requested it was re-written with more guitars (before changing his mind and reverting to the original version.) As a thanks to the band, he also asked for their 1985 Australian single *Live It Up* to be included in the film, and it was duly incorporated in the background of the finished movie. The song had already been a huge hit in Australia (in fact, it was the biggest selling single of the year) and had won two Australian Countdown awards for 'best single' and 'best songwriter'.

Crocodile Dundee became a worldwide phenomenon and was the second highest grossing film in the USA in 1986. Richard Evans from Epic Records in London liked the inclusion of the song *Live It Up* and wanted it released as a single in the UK and Europe. Paramount agreed that Epic could use the film poster as the single sleeve for the record and with a giant picture of Paul Hogan on the cover, the song became a big international hit. On the back of the film's success (and due to the fact that it is a great record) the song climbed to number Three in the UK charts in March 1987, as well as topping the charts in Scandinavia and reaching number Two in Germany.

Despite permission to do so, the American record company refused to associate *Live It Up* with the movie. They didn't want to give free promotion to *Crocodile Dundee* by having the film poster on the single cover and this resulted in the song failing to be a big hit in the States.

Mental as Anything continued to have musical success in their homeland throughout the 80s and 90s and, moreover, they are also extremely well-respected and critically acclaimed artists. Several exhibitions of their work have been held in Sydney and across Australia with pieces being bought by the likes of Patrick White and Sir Elton John.

The band is still very much active, performing over a hundred live shows every year in their homeland and overseas. Whilst they may be considered a one-hit wonder in the UK and Europe they remain one of Australia's longest-running, successful and well-loved rock bands.

38 Mel and Kim
F.L.M

Released: 11 July 1987   Supreme SUPE113
Highest UK Chart Position: #7

Of all the huge superstars who came out of the PWL studios, two unassuming girls from East London could have been, according to Pete Waterman, amongst the biggest stars of them all. It was only tragedy that prevented Mel and Kim from becoming one of the great Stock, Aitken and Waterman acts, although we do have four great singles to remember the girls by.

Sisters Melanie and Kim Appleby (Kim is the elder) were born in Hackney to British Jamaican parents and were first spotted as nightclub dancers in London in 1986. They were signed to Supreme Records and, under the guidance of production team Stock, Aitken and Waterman, in 1986 they began recording records under the name of Mel and Kim.

A track called *System* was intended as their first single, but both the duo and the production team weren't entirely happy with it, and it became the B-side of their first single *Showing Out (Get Fresh at the Weekend)* which was released in September 1986. The track caused some confusion at first as it shared a title with the ITV Saturday morning kids programme *Get Fresh* and many thought it had a link to Gaz Top's zany morning show.

The sound of the single and the girls' visual style, which combined high fashion and urban streetwear, was immediately popular and *Showing Out* reached number Three on the British charts and number one on the US Dance charts. Stock, Aitken and Waterman decided to follow-up *Showing Out* with the fantastic *Respectable* which reached number One in the UK in March 1987 and became one of the year's biggest hits. Indeed, Pete Waterman maintains that *Respectable* would have become one of the biggest selling singles of the decade had it not been knocked off the top of the charts after just one week by the Ferry Aid single *Let It Be*, recorded to raise money for the victims of the Zeebrugge ferry disaster.

The girls were so famous that their band name was even stolen in the winter of 1987 when comedian Mel Smith and singer Kim Wilde teamed up as an alternative Mel and Kim to record a festive charity single *Rockin' Around The Christmas Tree*.

During a promotional visit to Japan in June 1987, Mel became ill with a suspected spinal disc herniation, after complaining of a back problem for several months. Upon returning to the UK, Mel was diagnosed with secondary cancer of the spine, after previously being treated for liver cancer when she was 18, prior to the duo's rise to fame. The cancer was malignant paraganglioma. While the media speculated that Mel was terminally ill, both sisters categorically denied this, stating that Mel had suffered a debilitating back injury.

During this time the girls' third single was released. *FLM* is a less well remembered, but no less brilliant catchy pop record, the '*FLM*' standing for 'fun, love and money'. The sisters withdrew from publicity while Mel underwent treatment for her illness, and footage from their Montreux Festival performance was used to compile the *FLM* music video, along with some clever dancing marionettes in the style of the two girls.

FLM reached number Seven for two weeks in July 1987 and its success would arguably have been greater had the sisters been able to promote the record with media and TV appearances. The song was also the title track of their debut album which peaked at number Three on the UK charts, selling three million copies worldwide.

Despite their huge success, work on a second Mel and Kim album was never started. Mel's health deteriorated very quickly and the singer had to check herself out of the cancer hospital in order lay vocals down for their next single *That's The Way It Is* which reached number Ten in the spring of 1988.

The doctors believed that it would be at least twelve months before Mel would be able to record further material and so the producers put the second album on hold, praying that the singer would recover. Tragically that never happened. Mel Appleby died of pneumonia on 18 January 1990 after contracting a cold; her immune system weakened by chemotherapy.

With the aid of her boyfriend, ex-Bros bassist Craig Logan, Kim launched a solo career with much of her debut solo album composed of songs co-written with Mel. She scored a number Two hit in 1990 with the fantastic *Don't Worry* before following it up with the further top Ten hit *G.L.A.D* the following year.

We can leave the final word to their producer Pete Waterman. "To me they really were the original Spice Girls; they had such confidence, such bravado - and they epitomised the whole concept of Girl Power completely. It's quite painful to think about what happened and how things turned out. I really enjoyed working with them."

39 Living In A Box
Room In Your Heart

Released: 23 September 1989   Chrysalis LIB7
Highest UK Chart Position: #5

A trivia question for you – name the late 80s band whose name, debut single and debut album were all the same?

1985 saw Sheffield based vocalist Richard Darbyshire join forces with keyboard player Marcus Vere and drummer Anthony Critchlow. Taking their name from the time they spent writing and recording in a small disused Sheffield steelworks, Living In A Box were signed to Chrysalis in 1986 and recorded their first album in Los Angeles with producer Richard James Burgess. Burgess had a string of successful production credits including Kim Wilde and Five Star as well as Spandau Ballet's first two gold albums.

Their debut album, also entitled *Living In a Box* contained their successful debut single, handily also called *Living In A Box*. The single made the top Five in the UK as well as reaching number Seventeen in the American Billboard charts. Their pop-funk sound proved popular and follow-up singles *So The Story Goes* and *Scales Of Justice* also made the UK top Forty in 1987.

For their follow-up album, the band teamed up with legendary songwriter Albert Hammond. Hammond had written a string of fantastically successful records over the previous fifteen years or so, including standards such as *The Air That I Breathe* (for the Hollies) and *When I Need You* (later taken to number One by Leo Sayer). The father of the Strokes guitarist, Albert Jr, had also written or co-written a string of massive 80s hits including Starship's mammoth number One record *Nothing's Gonna Stop Us Now* (from the film *Mannequin*) and Whitney Houston's 1988 Olympic theme *One Moment In Time*.

In a basement flat in Westbourne Grove, London ('in a state of mild inebriation', as Darbyshire put it) Hammond and the band came up with a stripped-back, soulful ballad, somewhat of a departure from the high-energy pop-funk sound that Living In A Box were associated with. A demo of the song *Room In Your Heart* was recorded and later re-recorded and produced by Chris Porter who had previously worked with George Michael on his solo albums.

In early 1989, Living In A Box returned to the UK top Ten with the first single from this new second album. *Blow The House Down* featured Queen's Brian May on guitar and made its way to number Ten in March 1989. Building on this - their second top Ten hit - Chrysalis were all set to release the bands next single, *Gatecrashing*, a similar up-tempo slice of pop-funk.

What they hadn't (and couldn't have) accounted for were the terrible events at the Hillsborough football ground on April 15th, 1989. During an FA Cup semi final between Liverpool and Nottingham Forest, a crush at the Leppings Lane end of the stadium lead to the death of 96 Liverpool football fans, and injuries to 766 others. In the aftermath of such a tragedy, the record company could clearly not sanction the release of a single (or an album) entitled *Gatecrashing* and the single was removed from the release schedule.

This delay in release damaged the band's momentum and a low-key release of the record meant it only just scraped the lower echelons of the Top Forty. The album was also released later than planned, in July 1989.

Having already decided that *Room In Your Heart* would be the third single taken from the album, it was eventually released much later than planned, in September 1989. Hammond had wanted the song to be more of an out and out rock number, but Darbyshire wanted a slightly softer sound despite his own electric guitar solo featuring. To appeal to British radio playlisters the song had been made 'fuller' with the addition of a mock choir at the beginning and enhanced backing vocals (the last ninety seconds of the song feature strong backing vocals with Darbyshire's soulful voice freestyling over these). A stylish video featuring the band in Tuscany accompanied the release (some of it being filmed in the bar where the crew and band sat for three days waiting for the rain to stop).

Room In Your Heart climbed slowly up the UK top Forty in the autumn of 1989 eventually reaching number Five and spending fifteen weeks on the chart – longer than any of their other singles. It is a departure from the more synthesised sound most associated with Living In A Box although it showcases Richard Darbyshire's terrific vocals much more than anything else they recorded. It's a really simple song – as the singer admits, "it could have been written in any era" and Darbyshire continues to include it in his sets today, albeit a more stripped down, acoustic version - perhaps as originally intended.

40 Wet Wet Wet
Sweet Little Mystery

Released: 25 July 1987   Precious JEWEL 4
Highest UK Chart Position: #5

The Eighties gave us many great male vocalists. There were lead singers of the iconic bands (the likes of Boy George, Tony Hadley, Simon le Bon and Phil Oakey), superstars (George Michael, Michael Jackson) and talented solo artists (from Paul Young to Rick Astley). You could argue all day about who the best singer of the decade was but, if you had to pick a vocalist from that era, there would be many who would nail their colours firmly to the mast of Marti Pellow.

Born Mark McLachlan in Clydebank in 1965, the singer joined the band Vortex Motion in 1982 with schoolmates Tommy Cunningham, Neil Mitchell and Graeme Clark. Pellow was the last to join the group, invited by Clark who said, "At break we all went behind the kitchen for a fly smoke, and there in the corner was this quiet kid who said very little, but when he sang, everyone listened..."

They later changed their name to Wet Wet Wet (a name taken from a line from the Scritti Politti song *Getting', Havin' and Holdin'*) and McLachlan changed his name to stage moniker Marti Pellow. In 1983, guitarist Graeme Duffin joined the band and remained their unofficial 'fifth member' throughout their successful years.

Signed to Polygram Records in 1985, the Wets (as they became known) scored their first chart success with debut single *Wishing I Was Lucky* in 1987. Drummer Tommy Cunningham recently revealed that the highlight of his two decade career with Wet Wet Wet wasn't achieving a number One single or playing for Nelson Mandela but hearing this song for the first time whilst standing in a queue in a Glasgow chip shop.

The mixture of influences the band members brought helped to give them a deeper and richer sound than many of their pop contemporaries. Influences as diverse as the Clash, Stevie Wonder and Otis Redding gave the band an output which was more than just throwaway pop records. The title of their debut album *Popped In, Souled Out* explicitly defined their identity.

Having established themselves with the success of *Wishing I Was Lucky*, Wet Wet Wet followed this up with another upbeat soul-pop single, *Sweet Little Mystery*. Accompanied by a jaunty video filmed in Gambia, the song's sing-along and catchy lyrics propelled the song into the UK top Five in September 1987 spending three months on the chart.

Debut album *Popped In, Souled Out* followed and eventually reached number One (fourteen weeks after release) spending nearly a year and a half on the album charts and achieving five times platinum status.

Further top Five single *Angel Eyes* followed before the great *Temptation* and *Sweet Surrender* also made the top Twenty. The Wets also scored their first number One single in 1988 with their cover of the Beatles' *With A Little Help From My Friends* which, with help from a double A-side contribution from Billy Bragg, raised £600,000 for the charity Childline.

The first two singles from their 1991 album had not performed particularly successfully in chart terms, but the release of third single *Goodnight Girl* sent the band back to the top of the charts and became their only self-penned number One. It re-invigorated the Scottish band's career and their album *High On The Happy Side* also topped the charts.

Fuelled by its appearance in the blockbuster movie *Four Weddings And A Funeral*, Wet Wet Wet's cover of the Troggs 1968 hit *Love Is All Around* also shot to the top of the charts in 1994 where it stayed for an astonishing fifteen weeks (its deletion at the bands request effectively stopped it equalling Bryan Adams record of weeks at number One) and spent thirty seven weeks on the chart. It remains the 12th biggest selling single in the UK of all time.

The band eventually split in 1999 after Cunningham and Pellow's departures and a mildly successful solo career for Pellow followed until the reformation of the band in 2004 and their twenty-sixth top Forty single in 2008.

Wet Wet Wet managed to sustain a longer chart career than many of their contemporaries, thanks in part to Pellow being one of the best vocalists of his generation. His cheeky boyish looks also helped his appeal, but he has a terrific voice and the quality of the band's songs set them apart from many of their more 'poppy' peers.

41

Johnny Logan
Hold Me Now

Released: 23 May 1987   Epic LOG1
Highest UK Chart Position: #2

Since 1956, the *Concours Eurovision de la Chanson* has captivated and irritated Europe in equal measure. One of the longest running television programmes of all time with viewing figures estimated at between 100 and 600 million every year, the Eurovision Song Contest has been a staple part of the spring entertainment calendar for over fifty years.

The Eighties were something of a golden era for the Contest, launching the careers of acts including Nicole, Bucks Fizz and Celine Dion. The hugely successful chanteuse won the 1988 Contest for Switzerland, beating the UK entry (Scott Fitzgerald's *Go*) by a measly one point after the Yugoslavians awarded Royaume-Uni the subsequently customary 'nul points' in the final round of voting.

The biggest success story of 1980s Eurovision however was a little known Irish singer who has managed to win the competition an astounding three times, once as a songwriter (in 1992) and twice as a singer (in 1980 and 1987).

Born in Australia, Sean Patrick Michael Sherrard moved to Ireland with his family when he was three years old. Adopting the stage name Johnny Logan, he released his first single in 1978 and unsuccessfully entered the Ireland National Song contest in 1979. The following year he entered again, and his performance of the Shay Healy song *What's Another Year?* won both the national contest and, on April 19th 1980, the Eurovision. The song sold three million copies worldwide and reached number One in the UK charts.

Logan's solo career failed to take-off after his Eurovision success, although he wrote two further Irish National Song Contest entries in

1984 (for Linda Martin) and 1986 (for Mike Sherrard). Martin's song *Terminal 3* was chosen to represent Ireland in the 1984 Eurovision Song Contest, finishing second to the Swedish entry *Diggy-Loo, Diggy-Ley*. In 1987 Logan entered the contest himself with his own composition, the ballad *Hold Me Now* and the song comfortably won the Irish National Song contest and then the 32nd Eurovision in Brussels.

Hold Me Now remains many people's most vivid early memory of the Eurovision Song Contest. Performing twentieth of the twenty-two entries the song was so instantly recognisable that audiences were able to sing the chorus of the record even before they had heard it all the way through. Logan was overcome with emotion after the win, failing to hit the high notes when he reprised the song at the end of the show.

Hold Me Now is one of the few self-penned songs that has won the Eurovision and remains one of the high points in the history of the contest. In 2005, it was voted the 'third best Eurovision song of all time' (behind ABBA's *Waterloo* and Domenico Mudogno's *Nel blu dipinto di blu*, more commonly known as *Volare*) and it sold six million copies worldwide. It reached number Two in the UK singles chart (only failing to hit the top of the charts thanks to Whitney Houston's mammoth hit *I Wanna Dance With Somebody (Who Loves Me)*) and spent eleven weeks on the chart.

Again, the success of the Eurovision winning record failed to sustain a chart career and Logan's follow-up single, a cover of 10cc's *I'm Not In Love* failed to make the top Forty. Still, Logan's love affair with Eurovision continued in 1992 when he wrote *Why Me?* which, sung by Linda Martin, won the 37th Eurovision in Malmo, starting an unprecedented run of success for the Irish who also won the 1993 and 1994 Contests.

Johnny Logan remains the most successful individual in the history of the Eurovision and in many people's opinion *Hold Me Now* (despite what the voting public think) remains the finest song ever to grace the Eurovision. It is fundamentally a break-up song - the story of a man whose lover is leaving him for someone else – but the singer pleading for one last night to celebrate their relationship and his assertion that he will always love her adds an optimism and uplifting tone to the record. It may be somewhat formulaic in construction but as simple, straightforward break-up ballads go it remains one of the decade's best examples.

There are countless people whose love of the Eurovision Song Contest began in 1987 with this terrific record. Thousands of long-suffering husbands and wives, girlfriends and boyfriends of Eurovision addicts, therefore, have Johnny Logan to blame.

42 Spagna
Call Me

Released: 25 July 1987 CBS 650270 7
Highest UK Chart Position: #2

The invention of the package holiday is generally credited to an ex-Soviet national, Vladimir Raitz, the founder of the Horizon holiday company in 1949. His first 'package tours' were to Corsica in 1950 and within the next five years he organised the first such holidays to Sardinia, the Costa Brava and Palma.

The popularity of cheap package holidays grew in the 1960s and 1970s and by the turn of the 1980s, there were hundreds of thousands of Brits every year holidaying in Mediterranean destinations as varied as Greece, Yugoslavia and Spain. With flights from all four corners of the UK, families and couples and 18-30 singles could afford to spend two weeks in the sun drinking strange coloured beverages whilst enjoying the local nightlife.

One of the side-effects of this mass exodus to the sun is that, on occasion, some of Europe's finest/most appalling pop is heard in a local discotheque by thousands of British holidaymakers who then demand to find that tune on their return. History is littered with summer smash hits that have been released in the UK in response to mass public demand after hearing them in the continent's nightclubs.

Glenn Medeiros' number One hit *Nothing's Gonna Change My Love For You* was released in the UK after a DJ on holiday in America heard it on a local station. Eiffel 65's multi-million selling Europop smash *Blue (Ba Da Bee)* was a number One hit in the UK in 1999 after achieving huge success right across Europe whilst Sabrina's *Boys* was released in the UK after filling dancefloors across Europe in the summer of 1988.

Possibly the most famous of all 'summer hits' though was this particular slice of hi-NRG Italian disco which swept the continent in the summer of 1987.

Ivana Spagna was born in Verona, Italy in 1956 and released her first single *Mamy Blue* as early as 1971. For a decade she worked as a backing singer for other artists before forming the pop duo Fun Fun which released several singles in her native Italy between 1983 and 1986.

Her solo career took off in 1986 when the single *Easy Lady* became a hit across Europe although, strangely, not in the UK. It was to be her follow-up single, however, that catapulted her to international stardom in the summer of 1987. *Call Me*, co-written by Spagna, Alfredo Larry Pignagnoli and Giorgio Spagna is an upbeat, catchy Europop song which concerns a long-time single girl who meets a boy, has a good time and is urging him to now get in touch.

With one of the catchiest and most annoying hooks of the entire decade (and despite Spagna's pidgin English vocals) *Call Me* swept across Europe reaching the top Ten in countries including France, Norway and Ireland as well as topping the European Chart. Imported from the Mediterranean discos, it was also released in the UK and after a slow start it accelerated up the charts in August 1987, peaking at number Two behind Michael Jackson's 'comeback' single *I Just Can't Stop Loving You*. Her debut album *Dedicated To The Moon* sold in excess of half a million copies worldwide.

The video was actually filmed in England's East Midlands with most of the scenes recorded at Ritzy's nightclub in Nottingham and at the Belvoir Castle, the home of the local Duke of Rutland.

Much was made at the time of the Italian popstress' enormous hair and her liberal use of hairspray, which led *Smash Hits* magazine to christen it a 'frightwig' (and anyone subsequently to have 'larger' hair was said to be sporting a 'Spagna frightwig"'. It also led to the singer protesting "Is not, 'ow you say, a frighten wig. Is real hair."

After a re-release of her earlier hit *Easy Lady* failed to make the UK top Forty, it looked like Spagna was going to be a one-hit wonder, but her single *Every Girl and Boy* spent two weeks at number Twenty-Three in September 1988.

Spagna continued to be successful across the continent until in 1995 she returned to her native Italy where she has recorded nine albums in her native language. She has also competed several times in the Sanremo Festival, Italy's premier songwriting contest.

Call Me remains one of the catchiest summer hits in pop music history although it is questionable whether it is the song, or that majestic hair that will live longest in the memory.

43 Wax
Bridge To Your Heart

Released: 1 August 1987   **RCA PB41405**
Highest UK Chart Position: #12

Bridge To Your Heart is a proper little pop-gem that, when mentioned, tends to make people either salivate in fulsome praise or scratch their head in bewilderment.

Graham Gouldman's musical career is just about as sparkling as they come. Born in Broughton, Salford in 1946, he played in a succession of bands throughout the Sixties combining his day job in a man's outfitters with writing and performing music. Whilst his own bands at the time didn't achieve massive success, Gouldman made a name for himself as a songwriter, penning a string of million-selling songs including *Bus Stop* for the Hollies, *Heart Full Of Soul* for the Yardbirds and *Listen People* for Herman's Hermits.

In 1972 alongside friends Kevin Godley, Lol Crème and Eric Stewart, Gouldman was signed by music mogul Jonathan King. The renamed band 10cc became one of the most successful bands of the 1970's scoring five top Ten albums and three number One singles, including the modern classics *I'm Not In Love* and *Dreadlock Holiday*.

By the end of the 1970's, 10cc were down to a two-piece with just Gouldman and Stewart and their popularity had begun to wane. For the recording of their 1981 album *Ten Out of 10*, head of A&R at Warner Brothers Lenny Waronker suggested that 10cc enlist the help of American singer/songwriter Andrew Gold to give the record a sound more tailored for the US market. Gold had been a successful solo artist since the mid 1970s and had scored hits in the UK with the fantastic *Lonely Boy* and *Never Let Her Slip Away*.

The collaboration with Gold was a successful one (he co-wrote three tracks and co-produced a further three for the album) – so successful in fact that Gold was invited to join 10cc, an invitation he declined due to other work commitments.

Even though *Ten Out Of 10* wasn't a huge commercial success, Gouldman and Gold kept in touch and, before long, Gouldman invited the American back to the UK to work on some further songs. What was originally intended as a short stay ended up being anything but, as Gold stayed in England for seven months. Taking time out from 10cc, the pair eventually wrote a complete album of material and despite several band name changes (their first single *Don't Break My Heart* was released under the name World In Action and the second single *Victoria* under the name of Common Knowledge) the duo ended up with the first Wax album in 1986.

The name 'Wax' was eventually chosen, according to Gouldman, for several reasons – including that it fitted well with 'ear', the fact that a record was 'waxed' and that the literal meaning of 'wax' was 'to become bigger'.

It was during the recording of the band's second album that the pair came up with the song that would be their biggest (and only) UK top Forty hit. In the studio at Gold's Los Angeles home, with Gold on keyboards and Gouldman on guitar, *Bridge To Your Heart* took shape. The title was Gold's idea, and influenced by the Jam and Lewis music popular in the US at the time, the pair used a horn section to come up with what Gouldman called a 'Janet Jackson pastiche'. Gold had written the original chord sequences for the song but, inspired by the chord sequence for the Andy Williams classic *Can't Get Used To Losing You*, Gouldman based the middle eight of the song on this sequence.

Although the duo thought *Bridge To Your Heart* was 'OK' there were other songs recorded for their second album *American English* that they liked better. It was only when the tracks were played to producer Chris Neal that he picked out *Bridge To Your Heart* as a potential hit single. The finished version of the song ended up being very similar to the initial demo, even to the point where Gold's mistake in counting in the introduction was left in the final version.

Released in July 1987 with a great animated video directed by Storm Thorgerson, the song made a slow and steady climb up the charts eventually reaching number Twelve where it stayed for three weeks in September.

One further studio album followed for the band before Gouldman was reunited with 10cc in 1992 to record the album ...*Meanwhile*. Whilst Wax may have waned since the late 80s, Gouldman and Gold continue to work together on various projects to this day.

44 Rick Astley
She Wants To Dance With Me

Released: 24 September 1988   RCA PB 42189
Highest UK Chart Position: #6

If there is one name that is synonymous with the musical landscape in Britain in the late 1980s it is Richard Paul Astley, the fresh-faced 'tea-boy' turned pop-star who scored seven smash hit singles in an astonishing eighteen month period towards the end of the decade.

Leaving school at the age of sixteen with no qualifications, Astley only ever wanted to become a musician. On leaving his first group Give Way, Rick joined some school friends to form FBI, ostensibly a rock band named after the old Shadows hit. Balancing his job as a delivery driver for his parent's Newton-Le-Willows garden centre with his band commitments, FBI became well known locally for both their covers of chart material and their self-penned songs. Securing management, FBI arranged for pop svengali Pete Waterman to see them perform at a Warrington club in May 1985. Whilst Waterman was impressed with Astley's vocals and made him an offer, he wasn't interested in signing the band. Remaining loyal to FBI, Astley didn't immediately accept Waterman's invitation but on the advice of bandmate Will Hooper, Astley later contacted Waterman and made the move to London.

Rather uncharitably labelled the 'tea-boy', Rick actually worked as a tape operator at PWL Studios, learning how to write, record and produce music with the hugely successful Hit Factory team. Several early recordings followed (including uncredited backing vocals on Ferry Aid's 1987 number One single *Let It Be*) before he recorded his first single, the Stock, Aitken and Waterman penned *Never Gonna Give You Up* in October 1986. Mixed on New Year's Day 1987, Waterman felt the time wasn't right for release and it was delayed until July of that year.

The song became a huge worldwide smash hit reaching number One in countries as diverse as Chile and Australia and it became the biggest selling UK single of 1987. It won the 'best song' award at the 1988 BPI (Brit) awards and remains one of the biggest selling and most instantly recognisable records of the 1980s.

Much of the conjecture at the time regarded Astley's soulful singing voice as some quarters believed that he was merely a front, miming for a black American singer. His deep baritone vocals led many to assume that he was black, despite the presence of a white guy in a beige raincoat in the music video!

The astronomical success continued for Astley throughout 1987 as debut album *Whenever You Need Somebody* sold half a million copies in its first month of release and ended up selling over fifteen million copies worldwide. Unlike many of his fellow Hit Factory artists, Astley did have some creative influence with Stock, Aitken and Waterman and four of his own compositions appeared on his debut album. However, none were considered strong enough for release as a single as instead the title track from the album, the insanely catchy *Together Forever* and the faithful cover of the Nat King Cole classic *When I Fall In Love* all followed *Never Gonna Give You Up* into the UK top Three.

Astley's second album was written and recorded during 1989 and this time he took on both songwriting and co-production credits. The first single to be released from the album was also Astley's first self-penned release, the soul-pop *She Wants To Dance With Me*. Accompanied by a record sleeve featuring Rick wearing a peculiar gold jacket, *She Wants To Dance With Me* reached number Six in both the UK and US charts.

A fire at the PWL studios destroyed the master tapes for Rick's second album and so with re-recorded vocals, *Hold Me In Your Arms* was eventually released in January 1989, some time behind schedule. Two more top Ten hits followed before the singer split with PWL in search of greater artistic control and to try to prove to the media that he was more than just a simple 'pop' singer. The superb 1991 single *Cry For Help* (co-written with

Climie Fisher's Rob Fisher) was Astley's last top Ten hit and he effectively retired from the industry in 1993.

The singer returned to the public eye in 2008 when an internet phenomenon featuring the vocalist spread across the web. 'Rickrolling' involves a person providing a web link that they claim is relevant to the topic at hand, but the link actually takes the user to the video for Astley's single *Never Gonna Give You Up*. When a person clicks on the link and is led to the web page, he or she is said to have been 'Rickrolled'. A survey in April 2008 found that over eighteen million Americans had been 'Rickrolled'.

She Wants To Dance With Me is by no means Rick's most recognisable single but the less synthesised production (it was clearly distinguishable from the Stock, Aitken and Waterman sound of other records of that era) and the quality of the vocals stand it apart from his catchy, but more formulaic work.

45 Glenn Medeiros
Nothing's Gonna Change My Love For You

Released: 18 June 1988   London LON184
Highest UK Chart Position: #1

The third of four children born to parents of Portuguese ancestry, Glenn Alan Medeiros was born on the Hawaiian island of Kaua'i on 24th June 1970. His mother, Dorothy, was the musician of the family and the one who encouraged a young Medeiros to sing in his spare time. His father, Robert worked as a tour guide based in the island capital of Lihue and a young Glenn would often entertain tourists by singing on his father's minibus tour.

At the age of twelve, Medeiros made the transition to the Kauai High and Intermediate School where his music teacher Arnold Meister spotted talent in the young student. Inspired by Meister to join theatre classes and talent contests, this encouragement was repaid when Medeiros won a regional Kaua'i talent contest. In 1986, he also became the Regional State champion after triumphing in a state talent contest entitled *Brown Bags to Stardom* run by a local radio station.

Medeiros' winning performance in the Regional contest was a cover of the George Benson song *Nothing's Gonna Change My Love For You* and his prize was $500 and the opportunity to record the song as a single in the May of 1986.

The song *Nothing's Gonna Change My Love For You* was written by the esteemed songwriting team of Gerry Goffin and Michael Masser. Goffin had been a successful songwriter since the early 1960's with his then wife Carole King, penning hits as varied as *The Loco-Motion, Will You Love Me Tomorrow?* and *I'm Into Something Good*. Ex-stockbroker Masser wrote a string of soul classics in the 1970s and 1980s including Whitney Houston's *Didn't We Almost Have It All* and *The Greatest Love Of All*, Diana Ross'

Touch Me In The Morning and Roberta Flack and Peabo Bryson's *Tonight I Celebrate My Love*.

Masser and Goffin teamed up on several occasions (including for Houston's number One *Saving All My Love For You*) and their gentle ballad *Nothing's Gonna Change My Love For You* was originally recorded by soul legend George Benson on his 1984 album *20/20*. Medeiros' smooth cover was immediately a smash hit in Hawaii and his success was translated to mainland USA when a visiting record executive from KZZP in Phoenix, Arizona heard the song and took a copy of the single back to the station.

The popularity of the song quickly spread and Medeiros appeared on the *Johnny Carson Show* as well as being signed up to a recording contract by Leonard Silver, president of Amherst Records. Medeiros recorded his first album in 1987 as the single climbed to number Twelve in the Billboard chart in the spring of that year.

A year after the record had swept across the America, and in a manner reminiscent to how the singer had achieved his success in mainland USA (a DJ brought the single back from a US vacation where it started to gain airplay on European radio stations), *Nothing's Gonna Change My Love For You* became a smash hit across Europe. Released in the UK in the summer of 1988 (when it was already over two years old) and featuring a low budget video of the hirsute young singer serenading his love on a deserted beach the song took just over a month to reach the summit of the charts where it stayed for four weeks. Its success was replicated across the continent as it reached number One in Belgium, Ireland and Holland and in France, where it achieved gold status.

Although further singles were released from Medeiros' debut album and were successful in the US and Europe, none reached the top Forty in the UK. Exhausted after worldwide promotion for both the *Glenn Medeiros* and *Not Me* albums Medeiros disappeared from the music scene in early 1989. During this time off, he decided on a change of musical direction towards a more R&B style and this transformation was complete when the debut single from his third album (also confusingly titled *Glenn Medeiros*) shocked the world by featuring one of the world's biggest R&B

stars, Bobby Brown. The slick, funky *She Ain't Worth It* was a Billboard number One single as well as reaching number Twelve in the UK in July 1990.

Medeiros success diminished after this third album and further releases were only moderately successful. In 1995, Medeiros decided to fulfil a life's ambition and enrolled at college (and later the University of Hawaii) where, in February 1999 he graduated as a history teacher. The singer now lives in Hawaii with his wife and two children - Chord and Lyric - and teaches history at the Maryknoll High School whilst spending his spare time as the performing host at Waikiki's Hale Koa Hotel.

46 Bros
Drop The Boy

Released: 19 March 1988   CBS ATOM3
Highest UK Chart Position: #2

There is no real question that Bros were the most famous pop act in the late 1980's. They weren't the most successful in terms of chart positions or record sales, but for a couple of years the Goss brothers experienced hysteria on a Beatles-esque scale.

Twin brothers Matt and Luke Goss (Matt is the elder) became friends with Craig Logan whilst at Collingwood School in Camberley, Surrey in 1984. Despite their music teacher awarding them a grade 'F' and telling the boys they would 'never amount to anything', they began to secure gigs in local working men's clubs and came to the attention of several record companies. In 1987 they signed with Massive Management and under the control of former Pet Shop Boys manager Tom Watkins they signed a deal with CBS Records.

Also working for CBS at the time and credited with 'discovering' Bros, Nicky Graham was the driving force behind the band's success. Using the pseudonym 'The Brothers' (to imply that it was the Goss' who had written the songs), he wrote the material for the band's debut album. Chapman had previously worked with artists as varied as David Essex, Andy Williams and Bonnie Tyler (and would later work with Let Loose and Ant and Dec's pop-star incarnation PJ & Duncan, amongst others).

Bros' first single, the catchy *I Owe You Nothing* failed to reach the top Seventy-Five in the UK on its release in 1987. It looked like their follow up-single, the aptly titled *When Will I Be Famous*? was also going to miss out on the top Forty when it failed to reach the charts in late 1987. On its re-release in 1988 though it did chart, and eventually reached number Two in February 1988.

As *When Will I Be Famous?* hit the charts, the trio became massive stars. Their pop-star looks and image created a mass hysteria the likes of which hadn't been seen since the Beatles and the Bay City Rollers in the 1960s and 1970s. Hundreds of weeping Brosettes camped outside their homes in an attempt to catch a glimpse of their heroes and thousands turned up to personal appearances and record signings. It was also rumoured that they had the biggest fan club in the UK with over thirty thousand members. Their trademark fashion was also the copycat image of choice in 1988, comprising of a leather jacket, white t-shirt, blue denim and black shoes. Sales of a premium Dutch lager also increased sharply in early 1988 as thousands took to aping the Goss brothers by wearing Grolsch bottle tops on their shoes.

Building on their newfound stardom, the *Smash Hits* favourites (Matt, Luke and 'Ken', as the magazine had christened Logan) immediately released their follow-up single. A slower paced record, *Drop The Boy* was written from the perspective of a young adult desperate to be treated as a grown-up rather than as a child. The video featured twin blonde haired toddlers and Goss with his trademark 1950's style microphone.

Charting the week after *When Will I Be Famous?* dropped out of the top Forty, it jumped from number Seventeen to number Two where it frustratingly stayed for a month, being outsold first by Aswad's *Don't Turn Around* and then by the Pet Shop Boys third number One single *Heart*. Their album *Push* followed and despite spending over a year in the album charts it never reached number One, peaking at number Two in both April and July 1988, selling five million copies worldwide.

The band finally secured a number One hit with their next single when the re-release of *I Owe You Nothing* topped the UK charts for a fortnight in June 1988. It was to be their only chart-topper as subsequent singles *I Quit* and *Cat Among The Pigeons* reached number Four and number Two respectively.

At the height of success in 1989, bassist Craig Logan left the band and successfully sued the brothers for £1million in unpaid royalties which left the duo near bankrupt. As a two piece their success continued with their second album *The Time* (featuring the top Ten hits *Too Much* and *Chocolate Box*) and the duo became the youngest artists ever to sell out Wembley Stadium. However, their popularity continued to diminish and the brothers called it quits after their third album *Changing Faces* in 1991.

Whilst *Drop The Boy* might be the least well known of their major hits, it's an interesting single as it's very different in style to the more straightforward formulaic pop of the band's other big hits. Its funky bassline and unusual tempo (rather than the overt verse/chorus pop of *When Will I Be Famous?* and *I Owe You Nothing*) might make it difficult to dance to in a club, but at least it showed the band had a musical identity of their own.

47 Tiffany
Could've Been

Released: 19 March 1988 **MCA TIFF2**
Highest UK Chart Position: #4

There was no bigger teen pop idol in 1988 than the flame haired Tiffany. Whilst her giant number One *I Think We're Alone Now* has become part of the pop furniture, the Californian's hits extended way beyond the now ubiquitous Tommy James and the Shondells cover.

Tiffany Renee Darwish was born in Norwalk, California on 2 October 1971. She began singing at an early age and made her first professional appearance in California in 1981, spending several years performing across the US, mainly in country and western venues. She was signed as a soloist in 1984 and made an appearance on American talent show *Star Search* in 1985, eventually finishing second.

In 1986, Tiffany signed a contract with producer George Tobin and started the recording of her debut album. As a young teenager, the singer had mainly performed country songs but for her album she wanted to do more pop and rock music (inspired by the likes of Stevie Nicks). Over the course of that year, a total of forty-eight songs were recorded for Tiffany's debut album at Tobin's North Hollywood studio. One of these came from a simple piano vocal demo from the writer Lois Blaisch about the break-up of a relationship entitled *Could've Been*. Tiffany immediately fell in love with the powerful ballad and recorded the song in one take, aged just fourteen.

The record company were reluctant to include *Could've Been* on the singer's debut album. They were of the opinion that it sounded too mature and thought that a teenage audience wouldn't be able to relate to the lyrics. Tiffany thought otherwise, believing that as dating was everything to a young teenager, they would be able to understand and empathise with the sentiment. Assisted by her ability to showcase the song with a powerful live performance, Tiffany fought the record company and managed to have *Could've Been* included on her eponymously titled debut album.

MCA Records had paid $150,000 for the advance for the album *Tiffany*, but once it was completed it remained in the warehouse as the label was unsure of how to market the singer to a wide audience. Tobin had the novel idea of promoting the singer and her record on a tour of major shopping malls across the country. Starting at the Bergen Mall, Paramus, New Jersey and entitled *The Beautiful You; Celebrating The Good Life Shopping Mall Tour 1987*, Tiffany headed on her cross-US promotional tour. Performing to small crowds at first, the substantial coverage of her novel promotional campaign resulted in significant crowds by the end of the ten mall tour.

People magazine also featured an article on the singer's appearance at the Woodfield Mall in Schaumburg, Illinois, by which time MCA Records had agreed to release the much-requested *I Think We're Alone Now* as a single. The song was a huge hit on both sides of the Atlantic, reaching number One on the Billboard chart in November 1987 and in the UK in January 1988.

Despite their initial reluctance to include the ballad *Could've Been* on the album, MCA decided it would be the singer's follow-up single. Proving to many that she wasn't a 'manufactured' artist with her powerful live renditions of the song, Tiffany secured another major hit when the heartfelt break-up song knocked Michael Jackson's huge *Bad* from the Billboard number One spot to secure her second chart-topping single. The song also performed well in the UK, reaching number Four in the charts for three weeks in April 1988.

Further hits followed (including a gender-changed cover of the Beatles classic *I Saw Him Standing There*) and her debut album *Tiffany* made her the youngest ever female artist to have an American number One debut album, eventually selling over four million copies. Tiffany also watched a young boy band by the name of New Kids On the Block audition for her in her tour dressing room at the Westbury Music Fair. Impressed with the band, she gave them their first live performance as her support act on 30 April 1988.

At the height of her fame in 1988, the singer became embroiled in a bitter legal dispute with her mother and manager George Tobin over control of her career and earnings and Tiffany's request to be declared an 'emancipated minor' was thrown out by the court. The case took a toll on the singer and her late 1988 second album *Hold An Old Friend's Hand* failed to chart in the UK, despite the single *Radio Romance* making the top Twenty. Further albums and a famous nude *Playboy* appearance followed and the singer continues to tour on both sides of the Atlantic as she shares her time between the US and the West Midlands where she lives with her British husband.

48 Eighth Wonder
I'm Not Scared

Released: 20 February 1988 **CBS SCARE1**
Highest UK Chart Position: #7

The route to international success for most British bands normally involves them hitting it big in the UK before they head off to conquer Europe and the rest of the world. Eighth Wonder, however, bucked that trend as their homeland was almost the last place they achieved any success.

Formed in 1983 as Spice, Jamie Kensit had put together a band but lacked a lead singer. His sister - fourteen year old Patsy - was successful at the audition and they played their first gig in West London in the autumn of 1983. Their music was mainly influenced by the white-funk popular in London clubs at the time – the likes of Haircut 100 and Stimulin.

Towards the end of 1984, the band line-up changed with the addition of keyboard player Alex Godson and the band name was changed to Eighth Wonder (after a song by the Sugar Hill Gang). The younger Kensit also started having more of an input on the band's songwriting.

At a pre-Christmas gig in 1984, Kensit was spotted by Steve Wooley, the co-owner of Palace Films and, alongside director Julian Temple, offered her the role of Crepe Suzette in the upcoming film *Absolute Beginners*. She had acted since childhood, famously starring in a frozen peas advert at the age of four as well as appearing on stage with the Royal Shakespeare Company and in television dramas such as the 1981 adaptation of Dickens' *Great Expectations*.

Eighth Wonder were signed to CBS Records in April 1985 and, in October of that year (after the filming of *Absolute Beginners* had ended) their debut single *Stay With Me* was released. Whilst it barely scraped the top Seventy-Five in the UK it reached number One in Italy and, after a successful promotional tour, in Japan. Their appearance at the Montreux

Festival in May 1986 was their final as a six-piece (Lawrence Lewis and Jake Walters left at this time) and in August the four band members headed to Los Angeles to record their debut album.

In LA, the band worked mainly with the writer and producer Mike Chapman. Chapman was one half of the 1970's songwriting team of Chinn and Chapman who had written a string of huge hits for the likes of Sweet, Mud, Smokie and Racey – as well as the Toni Basil smash hit *Mickey*. Many well-known songwriters were interested in working with the band, including the Eurythmics' Dave Stewart (although his song was not eventually used) and Billy Steinberg and Tom Kelly – the writers of *Like A Virgin* and *True Colours*.

In January 1987, the Chapman produced song *Will You Remember* was released, and whilst it only reached number Eighty-Three in the UK, it climbed to the top Ten in Italy and gave the band another Japanese number One. *When The Phone Stops Ringing* (co-written by Bernie Taupin – Elton John's lyricist) had also reached the top spot in Japan and prompted CBS to release a mini-album of singles and B-sides in Japan entitled *Brilliant Dreams*.

The band returned to London to resume work on the album in April 1987 and completed the tracks with producer Richard James Burgess and PWL engineer Pete Hammond. The album *Fearless* was almost ready, except for one final track.

Written by Neil Tennant and Chris Lowe – the hugely successful Pet Shop Boys – *I'm Not Scared* was recorded in London and co-produced by Tennant, Lowe and Ian Harding. Complete with trademark PSB electronica and the clever use of both English and French lyrics, *I'm Not Scared* was chosen as the next single.

With the Pet Shop Boys' influence apparent and accompanied by a video focusing heavily on the stunningly beautiful lead singer, the single was a major international hit reaching number Seven in the UK in April 1988 as well as the top Five in Italy, Germany, Switzerland, Portugal and

France. Tennant and Lowe also recorded their own version of the song which appeared on their 1988 album *Introspective*.

Eighth Wonder had one further UK hit – the bouncy *Cross My Heart* (originally recorded by American star Martika for her debut album) - before the failure of the follow-up single *Baby, Baby* meant the band parted ways and Kensit began to focus more heavily on her acting career. Whilst this stalled in the mid-90's (amongst high profile marriages to both Jim Kerr and Liam Gallagher) Kensit returned to our screens in the ITV soap opera *Emmerdale* in 2004 and subsequently BBC's hospital drama *Holby City* in 2007.

49 Danny Wilson
Mary's Prayer

Released: 22 August 1987   Virgin VS934
Highest UK Chart Position: #3

Scotland has always been a hotbed for musical talent and there have been some eras when it seemed as though every other act in the charts was from north of the border. In the late 1980's there appeared a number of talented, melodic guitar bands from various corners of Scotland – the likes of Deacon Blue, Aztec Camera, the Blue Nile and Del Amitri, but it was a threesome from the country's only south-facing city who lit up the charts with one of the late 80's finest piece of pop music.

Gary Clark and his younger brother Kit formed a band with their friend Ged Grimes in their home city of Dundee in 1984. With the elder Clark on vocals, the younger on guitar and Grimes on bass, the trio started their musical life as the band Spencer Tracy, although this had to be changed after an objection from the late actor's estate.

The Clark's father was a huge fan of the music and film of the 1950's and so when the band were forced to change their name they picked another Fifties reference, calling themselves Danny Wilson after the 1952 Frank Sinatra, Shelley Winters and Raymond Burr movie *Meet Danny Wilson* (which would also would become the name of the band's 1987 debut album.)

Originally spotted whilst busking around Dundee in the mid 1980's – a mixture of self-penned songs and Bacharach and David covers - the trio signed to Virgin Records in 1986 and set about recording their debut album. Clark had been writing songs for a number of years by that time, having been lent a keyboard by his friend Ally Thompson at the age of twenty. He had never played keyboard before and began to come up with lyrics and music for songs using only the white notes on the keyboard!

The verse for what ended up being their signature tune, *Mary's Prayer* came easily, but it took Clark several months in 1983 to come up with a chorus that he was happy with. Three years later the band eventually recorded the song for their debut album and, as the stand-out tune, it was released as their debut single in the UK. Although it spent eleven weeks on the chart in March and April 1987, it spent a month inside the top Forty-Five singles whilst falling tantalisingly short of the all-important top Forty position.

Despite its failure to penetrate their home market, the record became a surprise hit in America. On its release in 1987, it climbed to number Twenty-Three in the Billboard charts and became one of the rare instances where a British band achieved success elsewhere in the world before charting at home.

Virgin believed strongly in the record and buoyed by the success of the song in America (and despite the chart failure of their follow-up song *A Girl I Used To Know), Mary's Prayer* was released for a third time in April 1988. With an interesting part-animated video, the song was finally a hit this time around, reaching the top Ten in only its third week on the top Forty. It eventually climbed to number Three in April 1988 where it stayed for two weeks, outsold only by *Theme from S-Express* and Fairground Attraction's *Perfect*.

Whilst many people believe it to be a song about religion – the inclusion of a line about 'ten Hail Mary's' (and the title itself), it is in fact a simple song about a lost love. The lyrics included references to religious imagery, but they were simply memories of Clark's own Catholic upbringing, not hiding any more significant religious undertones.

Despite the success of *Mary's Prayer*, Danny Wilson never really hit the big time as their lush, sophisticated arrangements didn't quite fit with the 'pop' music of the time. They did appear on the top Forty once more, however, with the brilliantly catchy *The Second Summer Of Love* which reached number Twenty-Three in the summer of 1989.

The trio split after their third album *Sweet Danny Wilson* in 1992 and Gary Clark embarked on a short solo career before he began using his songwriting talents for the benefit of other artists. After working with the likes of Julia Fordham and Eddi Reader, Clark co-wrote and produced much of Natalie Imbruglia's 2001 album *White Lilies Island*.

50 Aztec Camera
Somewhere In My Heart

Released: 23 April 1988 **WEA YZ181**
Highest UK Chart Position: #3

There are fewer more instantly recognisable opening lines in 80s music than that of this superb 1988 summer anthem. *Somewhere In My Heart* remains one of the most loved late 80s pop songs, particularly on a beautiful, sunny British day.

Aztec Camera are, essentially, Scottish songwriter Roddy Frame. Born in East Kilbride in 1964, Frame released several low budget records before forming his band with a name that originated from one of a 15 year old Frame's 'deep thinking, psychedelic periods'.

In 1983, Aztec Camera released label their debut album *High Land, Hard Rain* which became label Rough Trade's first ever album release. *High Land, Hard Rain* gave a nineteen year old Frame his first hit single (the catchy *Oblivious*) which reached number Eighteen on its re-release in December 1983. With a primarily acoustic sound the band became popular in the 'indie' scene whilst maintaining moderate mainstream chart success.

Second album *Knife*, (produced by Dire Straits frontman Mark Knopfler) followed in 1984, spawning the minor hit *All I Need Is Everything*. After an extensive tour and concerns over the direction that the current incarnation of Aztec Camera was taking, Frame took some time out and headed to America to write and record his next album.

Making a conscious effort to make his lyrics more direct, and drawing inspiration from the soul artists popular in America at that time (great vocalists such as Anita Baker and Luther Vandross), Frame spent a lot of time in the US searching for producers and musicians to work with him on his new project.

The album *Love* was recorded in a four month period in New York with a range of producers and musicians, mainly as those Frame wanted to work with were busy on other projects and could only spare the time to work on one or two songs. Capturing the soul/R&B sound he was looking for, producers Russ Titelman, Tommy LiPuma, David Frank and Rob Mounsey helped Frame assemble the album that would become his most commercially successful.

The one remaining track to be recorded for *Love* was the up-tempo, horn-led *Somewhere In My Heart*. Recorded in Boston and produced by the respected Mike Jonzun (who later went on to have huge production success with New Kids On the Block), *Somewhere In My Heart* also featured the talents of Steve Gadd – a drummer whose career has spanned forty years and who has worked with the likes of Paul Simon, Eric Clapton and George Benson.

Over three years after second album *Knife*, *Love* was released in the UK in November 1987 and although the lead single *Deep and Wide and Tall* failed to reach the top Forty, the follow-up single (the stunningly beautiful feminist ballad *How Men Are)* spent eleven weeks on the chart reaching number Twenty-Five and re-introducing Frame to the record buying public.

Considered by many commentators as a commercial sell-out, the album *Love* (and particularly the next single *Somewhere In My Heart*) met with mixed critical reaction. Many preferred the acoustic, indie sound of yore, but Frame's American influences led to a slicker, more soulful sound that many critics dismissed as average commercial rock.

What it did mean is that *Somewhere In My Heart*, with its bouncy pop melody and catchy singalong lyrics, took the charts by storm. The leather-jacketed Frame's boyish good looks in the retro-looking black and white video, coupled with the song being a perfect radio friendly summer anthem, led to it spending fourteen weeks on the chart in the summer of 1988. It eventually climbed to number Three in June, kept off the top of the charts only by Kylie's *Got to Be Certain* and Wet Wet Wet's *With A Little Help From My Friends*.

The success of *Somewhere In My Heart* also led to the album *Love* reaching the top Ten in June, a full eight months after release. *Love* was also nominated for the Best British Album award at the 1988 BPI Awards, losing out to Sting's *Nothing Like the Sun*.

Aztec Camera continued their success with the 1990 album *Stray* that included the hit singles *The Crying Scene* and *Good Morning Britain*. Frame continued to make albums under the Aztec Camera banner until 1995 after which all his releases have been under his own name.

Somewhere In My Heart remains a radio favourite, as perfect a soundtrack to a hot British summer's day now as it was two decades ago. It may have been seen as a commercial sell-out at the time but both it, and the album *Love*, are intelligent, clever pop music of the highest calibre.

51 Belinda Carlisle
Circle In the Sand

Released: 7 May 1988 **Virgin VS1074**
Highest UK Chart Position: #4

As a boy of a certain age in the mid to late 1980's, there was certainly no shortage of female celebrities on whom to develop a teenage crush. Pictures of goddesses from Eighth Wonder's Patsy Kensit to Rachel Friend (the lovely Bronwyn from *Neighbours*) were carefully torn from *Smash Hits* magazine and pinned lovingly on bedroom walls up and down the land.

Whilst the stunningly beautiful Martika might have run her close, there was only really ever one 'world's sexiest woman' in those late 80s years – the diminutive but perfect Belinda Carlisle.

After leaving the successful all-girl rock band the Go-Gos in 1985, Carlisle embarked on a solo career and became successful in her own right in the US with her debut album *Belinda* and chart singles *Mad About You* and *I Feel the Magic*. In December 1986, having interviewed several producers, songwriter Rick Nowels was asked to write and produce Carlisle's second album having previously worked with another pop-rock vocalist, Stevie Nicks.

Accompanied by friend and fellow songwriter Ellen Shipley, Nowels set to work in writing the *Heaven and Earth* album in time for the recording to start in March 1987. After coming up with the song that would be Carlisle's biggest transatlantic hit – *Heaven Is A Place On Earth* – the duo's next project was to set about writing a mid-tempo song. Using a Linn drum and a sixteen track recorder, the aim was to come up with a simple, folky melody that could be sung around a campfire. Inspired by songs such as Fleetwood Mac's *Dreams* and by the famous photo of Marilyn Monroe on a Malibu beach (from the film *The Misfits*), the pair came up with the basic structure for *Circle In The Sand*.

The ideas were taken into the Ocean Way studios in Hollywood and the song was created by a live group featuring not only guitarist John McCurry (from Cyndi Lauper's backing band) but also 80s star Thomas Dolby who contributed the distinctive keyboard sound and the seagull cries heard in the song. The record was mixed at A&M Studios in Hollywood by Shelly Yakus (previously responsible for mixing work by artists including Tom Petty and Patti Smith) and Carlisle's vocals were also recorded at Ocean Way in an studio adjacent to that being used by one of the great Canadian songwriters, Joni Mitchell.

Picked as the third single from the *Heaven and Earth* album (the Diane Warren penned *I Get Weak* had reached number Ten in the UK after the number One success of *Heaven Is A Place On Earth*), *Circle In the Sand* was released in the UK in May 1988. With a popular video featuring Carlisle in various beach scenes it reached number Four in the UK in June 1988 as well as reaching the US top Ten.

Carlisle's career continued to flourish with an impressive string of hit singles including *Leave A Light On*, *(We Want) The Same Thing*, *Runaway Horses*, *Do You Feel Like I Feel?* and *In Too Deep*. Further successful albums followed including 1989's *Runaway Horses*, 1991's *Live Your Life Be Free*, 1995's *Real* and 2007's *Voila* – an album of French pop tunes and covers of songs by the likes of Edith Piaf and Francoise Hardy inspired when Carlisle moved to France in the early 1990s. Carlisle also rejoined her bandmates the Go-Gos to record and tour a new album *God Bless The Go-Gos* in 2001.

Since the turn of the century Carlisle has also forged a television career with appearances on shows including *Celebrity Duets*, where Carlisle teamed up with actress Lea Thompson (famous for playing Lorraine Baines-McFly in the *Back to the* Future movie series) to sing both *Heaven Is A Place On Earth* and *I Get Weak*.

Carlisle's name is synonymous with great guitar power pop of the late 1980s and her energetic, catchy, hits have become standards worldwide. In some ways *Circle In the Sand* is a perfect summer song – the ideal soundtrack to driving an open top car down a beach highway. Its early-Sixties inspired sound and summery subject matter combined with its easy to remember, catchy chorus evoke memories of classic Sixties Americana and it was also an interesting departure compared with Carlisle's other singles of the time, which were predominantly great up-tempo power pop.

52

Yazoo
Only You

Released: 17 April 1982 Mute MUTE 020
Highest UK Chart Position: #2

Flying Pickets
Only You

Released: 26 November 1983 10 TEN 14
Highest UK Chart Position: #1

As well as being one half of the late 1980's most popular bands – Erasure - Vince Clarke contributed strongly to the success of two other of the decade's most popular groups. His first success came in the initial line-up of Depeche Mode and he penned two of their earliest hit singles *New Life* and *Just Can't Get Enough*.

Clarke surprisingly quit Depeche Mode after just one album before teaming up with Basildon based vocalist Alison Moyet to form the electropop duo Yazoo. Moyet claimed that this name came from the label of old blues albums Yazoo Records, although Clarke later claimed that it had come from a mis-hearing of the word 'kazoo' – the small mouth instrument popular at the time. The name had to be changed to Yaz in the USA after a threatened lawsuit by a relatively unknown American rockband of the same name.

Signed to Mute Records in the UK their debut single was released in April 1982. *Only You* was a ballad written by Clarke and was a song that he had offered to Depeche Mode as he was leaving the band. They declined (preferring to release the Martin Gore penned *See You*) and so Clarke recorded the song with his new bandmate.

Only You was an instant success, climbing to number Two in the UK (improbably kept from number One by Germany's one and only Eurovision winner, Nicole's *A Little Peace*) and it spent fourteen weeks on the chart.

It also became one of only two Yaz songs to chart in the US (ironically, it was the original B-side of Only You – *Situation* – that was the other).

Yazoo followed up the success of *Only You* with the top three hit *Don't Go* and their debut album *Upstairs At Eric's* became both a platinum seller and, latterly, one of the most influential records of the early 1980s. Second album *You And Me Both* was a UK number One and the single *Nobody's Diary* also made the UK top Three. Shortly before the release of *You And Me Both*, Clarke and Moyet announced that they were going their separate ways after just four UK singles releases. Moyet went on to have a successful solo career with hits such as *All Cried Out, Is This Love?* and *That Ole Devil Called Love* whereas Clarke formed the Assembly with Feargal Sharkey before teaming up with Andy Bell as Erasure.

A year earlier, in 1982, Welshman Brian Hibbard had formed a vocal group with a group of colleagues from John McGrath's 7:84 Theatre Group. Named the Flying Pickets (after the name given to mobile strikers who travel at short notice in order to form a picket) they came up with the novel idea of bringing 'a cappella' music to the pop scene. Originally an eight piece, the band became well-known for their flamboyant looks (Hibbard's huge sideburns became famous, as did the band's gaudy suits and large headwear) although the band were reduced to a six piece by the time of their debut release.

Choosing *Only You* (the original of which had been a hit only eighteen months previously) the Flying Pickets first single was released with no fanfare on 26 November 1983. As a complete surprise, and out of practically nowhere, it was the UK's number One single two weeks later. It stayed at the summit of the charts for five weeks (including the coveted Christmas number One in the UK in 1983) becoming the first a-cappella song to reach the top of the UK charts. It went on to be a number One single in Germany and also a hit in Canada but didn't repeat Yaz's success in the USA where it failed to chart.

The Flying Pickets followed this up with another top Ten hit – *When You're Young And In Love* – but their subsequent releases all failed to make the top Forty. The membership of the band changed regularly throughout the 1980s and 1990s (there have now been nineteen members in total) but none of these incarnations has had further success. The original band members have had varied careers since the Pickets days, from lead singer Hibbard's appearance in *Doctor Who*, Gareth Williams touring with the English Shakespeare Company, Rick Lloyd winning a BAFTAs for his TV work to David Brett appearing as Dedalus Diggle in the film *Harry Potter and the Philosopher's Stone*.

Further versions of the song have been recorded by the likes of Rita Coolidge and Jocelyn Enriquez and Enrique Iglesias' Spanish version of the song *Sólo En Ti* spent ten weeks at the top of the US Billboard Hot Latin Tracks chart in 1997.

The song has become a modern classic and, whilst not a Christmas song, *Only You* is now often played at Yuletide thanks to the Flying Pickets' version being a Christmas number One hit. It was also famously used in the special Christmas edition of the hit TV show *The Office* in 2003.

53 Jona Lewie
Stop The Cavalry

Released: 29 November 1980   Stiff BUY104
Highest UK Chart Position: #3

One of the keenest annual musical battles in British popular music is the fight for the coveted Christmas number One position. Every December a myriad of diverse artists jostle for airplay and exposure to try and propel their record to the top of the festive hit parade. Whilst Christmas is a good time to chart in sales terms (big-selling Christmas records often feature near the top of annual singles sales charts), the number One single also tends to receive additional press coverage and exposure on programmes like the *Top of the Pops'* Christmas special.

It is thought that the additional press interest in the annual battle for the Christmas number One started in 1973, when two of the UK's biggest acts at that time simultaneously released Christmas based singles. Slade's enduring classic *Merry Xmas Everybody* eventually won that battle from Wizzard's *I Wish It Could Be Christmas Everyday*, although both have since become festive standards.

The Christmas number One battle raged hard in the 1980s and the ten festive chart toppers in the decade were as odd a mixture as you could imagine, as were the records they narrowly beat to the top spot.

Four traditional Christmas themed songs made it all the way to number One – these by Shakin' Stevens, Band Aid, Band Aid II and Cliff Richard – whilst three more just missed out (Shaky again, The Pogues and Kirsty MacColl and Wham). Wham's *Last Christmas* of course remains the biggest selling single in the UK never to top the charts, having been denied by *Do They Know It's Christmas?* on which singer George Michael heavily featured.

The 1980s also saw three of its classic pop tunes top the festive top Forty. 1981 saw the Human League's *Don't You Want Me* at number One,

1983's Christmas chart-topper was the brilliant *Only You* (albeit the Flying Pickets cover rather than the Yazoo original) and 1987 saw the Pet Shop Boys secure the Christmas number One with their hi-NRG cover of the Elvis classic *Always On My Mind*. A nod should also go to Stock, Aitken and Waterman's biggest selling single *Especially For You* which narrowly failed to dislodge Cliff's *Mistletoe and Wine* in December 1988 (although Kylie and Jason did subsequently spend three weeks atop the UK charts).

The remaining 1980s Christmas chart toppers were records that you could politely put at the 'novelty' end of the musical spectrum. A brilliant animated video in 1986 and exposure on a Levi's jeans commercial sent Jackie Wilson's 1957 hit *Reet Petite* to the top of the Christmas charts in 1986, leading to successful re-releases of his other hits *I Get The Sweetest Feeling* and *(Your Love Keeps Lifting Me) Higher and Higher*. 1982 saw the passionate ballad *Save Your Love* by Renee and Renato deny Shaky a Christmas number One and landed Renato the role in the 'Just One Cornetto' TV commercial.

1980, however, saw the ultimate in novelty Christmas number One records and this, coupled with the premature death of ex-Beatle John Lennon, denied a British singer a number One record with a song that has become one of the season's most popular.

Jona Lewie (born John Lewis) had started earning a living in the music industry as early as 1968 and scored a number Two hit in the UK in 1972 under the pseudonym of Terry Dactyl and the Dinosaurs with the song *Seaside Shuffle*. It wasn't until 1980 however when he finally had his first solo hit, the imaginatively titled *You'll Always Find Me In The Kitchen At Parties*.

Lewie's next single, *Stop the Cavalry*, was never intended to be a Christmas record. The song is set at the British front during World War One, although it is intended to represent soldiers at wars throughout the centuries rather than a specific conflict. Stiff Records however spotted the 'wish I was at home for Christmas' line and, with the brass band sound, decided it would be a perfect record for a Christmas release. The song eventually peaked at number Three in December 1980, kept off the top of the charts by John Lennon's *(Just Like) Starting Over* and *Imagine* and, in between, by the combined efforts of the St Winifred's School Choir with their implausible chart-topper *There's No-One Quite Like Grandma*.

Stop the Cavalry was Lewie's final hit in the UK, although he did secure further hits overseas including 1981's Australian number Two hit *Louise (We Get It Right)*. This song has, however, become one of the staple Christmas records on radio stations and compilation albums in the UK - and all this despite its non-Christmas theme.

54 Kylie Minogue
Got To Be Certain

Released: 14 May 1988   PWL PWL12
Highest UK Chart Position: #2

The songwriting and production team of Stock, Aitken and Waterman helped launch (and in some cases resurrect) the careers of many a pop star in the UK, but by far the most successful of their alumni is a petite Melburnian whose sixty million record sales have made her one of the most popular and enduring pop stars of the modern era.

Kylie (famously meaning 'boomerang' in some Aboriginal languages) was born in Melbourne on 28th May 1968. She began her showbiz career at the age of twelve with small parts in TV dramas such as *Skyways*, *The Sullivans* and the *Henderson Kids* and whilst she had also sung on the weekly show *Young Talent Time*, sister Dannii was seen as the more talented of the two sisters and the younger Minogue's success overshadowed that of her sibling.

That changed in 1986 when Kylie secured the part of Charlene Mitchell in the soap opera *Neighbours*. The popularity of the show (particularly in the UK) catapulted a young Kylie to superstardom as her on/off screen relationship with blond heartthrob Jason Donovan kept Minogue in the public spotlight as well as helping *Neighbours* draw audiences of up to twenty million viewers.

A year into her successful TV career, Kylie joined fellow *Neighbours* cast members at a benefit concert for the Fitzroy Football Club, a local Melbourne AFL team. Performing the 1962 Gerry Goffin and Carole King song *Locomotion*, she was subsequently signed to Australia's Mushroom Records who decided to release her cover of the Little Eva hit as her debut single.

Re-titled *The Loco-Motion*, the song was a huge hit in Australia, spending seven weeks at number One and becoming the biggest selling single of the 1980s in that country. The success brought her to the UK where she was invited to work with the British production team of Stock, Aitken and Waterman. Waterman had never seen *Neighbours* and the trio knew little of Minogue – so much so that they actually forgot she was arriving to work with them. The team quickly wrote a song for her whilst she waited outside the studio and in less than an hour *I Should Be So Lucky* was written and recorded.

Kylie returned to Australia to work on *Neighbours*, and in the meantime *I Should Be So Lucky* became a huge hit worldwide, spending five weeks at number One in the UK. Mike Stock flew to Australia to persuade Kylie to return to the UK to record songs for her debut album which was completed in early 1988.

Whilst it was anticipated that the 'new' Hit Factory version of *The Loco-Motion* would be the follow-up single (the trio had re-recorded the hit as they didn't like the chords and thought the male voices on it were 'obnoxious'), PWL instead decided to release a new record. They chose the less-bubblegum *Got To Be Certain* as the next single and recorded a video featuring the singer (dressed alternately in a strange black and white crop-top and a classy black cocktail dress) wandering around her home city of Melbourne.

The song was released in May 1988 and quickly reached number Two in the charts. It failed to replicate the number One success of *I Should Be So Lucky* however, spending three weeks at number Two behind Wet Wet Wet and Billy Bragg's double-A side Childline charity single.

Kylie continued her association with Stock, Aitken and Waterman until 1992, scoring three further number Ones with the Hit Factory (*Hand On My Heart, Tears On My Pillow* and her duet with co-star Jason

Donovan *Especially For You*). Despite a waning of her popularity in the 1990s as she sought to create a new image for herself, 'sexy' Kylie returned in 2000 when she reaffirmed her position as pop's number One female starlet. Further number One singles *Spinning Around*, *Slow* and the mammoth *Can't Get You Out Of My Head* followed, as well as a series of spectacular world tours and starring roles in blockbuster films including 2001's *Moulin Rouge*.

Got to Be Certain is an interesting song as it often gets forgotten amongst Kylie's better-remembered early work, like fellow number Two hit *Je Ne Sais Pas Pourquoi* (another really good pop single). Whilst the likes of *Better The Devil You Know* and *I Should Be So Lucky* are the radio-friendly memories of early Kylie, *Got To Be Certain* is at least as good a record and certainly deserves more recognition than it gets.

55 Sabrina
Boys (Summertime Love)

Released: 6 Feb 1988   IBIZA IBIZ1
Highest UK Chart Position: #3

56 Sam Fox
Touch Me (I Want Your Body)

Released: 22 March 1986   Jive FOXY1
Highest UK Chart Position: #3

Two curvaceous models with 'S' names, two sex-inspired songs, two number Three hits and four of the most viewed knockers of the 1980s....

Sabrina Salerno and Samantha Fox were two of the leading glamour models of the mid to late 1980s and both made their name after contest successes. Salerno's 1985 Italian TV debut on the prime time show *Premiatissima* followed her triumph in a beauty pageant in her home region of Ligurnia, whilst a 16 year old Fox secured her first topless shoot after taking the runners-up spot in the *Sunday People* newspaper's *Face and Shape of 1983* contest.

Sabrina launched her singing career immediately, scoring her first hit in her native Italy with the formulaic eurodisco song *Sexy Girl,* complete with a video which was little more than a magazine cover shoot set to music. Second single, a cover of Labelle's 1974 classic *Lady Marmalade* was released with limited success in France and Holland.

Fox also shot to immediate fame. After the *Sunday People* contest, and with her parents' consent she appeared topless on Page 3 of the *Sun* newspaper on 22 February 1983 under the headline 'Sam, 16, quits A-Levels for Ooh-Levels'.

Over the next three years, Fox became Britain's premier sex symbol mainly thanks to her outgoing personality, working class background and, of course, 36d breasts (insured at one stage for a quarter of a million pounds) winning the *Sun*'s Page Three Girl Of The Year in 1984, 1985 and 1986.

After retiring from topless modelling aged 20, Fox turned to her music career with a debut live performance at Peter Stringfellow's club *Hippodrome* and a debut single *Touch Me (I Want Your Body)*. Beating Sabrina to the UK charts by two years or so, *Touch Me* was a hit on both sides of the Atlantic, reaching number Three in the UK in April 1986 and number Four in the American Billboard charts later that summer.

Whilst Fox had opted for a denim-clad, Bonnie Tyler-esque soft-rock approach, Sabrina's career was built on high energy Eurodisco. After the success of *Sexy Girl*, Salerno released the single *Boys (Summertime Love)* which became a huge hit across Europe, reaching number One in Italy (for two months), France (becoming the country's 292nd biggest selling single of all time) and Switzerland. It made the top Five in nine other countries, including a number Three position in the UK in June 1988.

Whilst Fox's video had made a conscious effort to eschew the singer's modelling background (she appeared on stage with a band), Sabrina decided to that the opposite view and to make the most of her assets. The video for *Boys* became the first to be censored in the UK, as the Italian temptress spent the majority of it bouncing up and down in the swimming pool of the Florida Hotel in the Italian resort of Jesolo in a see-through white bikini. The song became christened 'Boing, Boing, Boing' thanks to the nature of her 'performance' in the video which later became one of the internet's most downloaded.

It is difficult then to determine which of the two artists had the most enduring music career. Both artists progressed to working with British producers Stock, Aitken and Waterman with Fox's *Nothing Gonna Stop Me Now* making number Eight in June 1987 and Salerno's *All Of Me* reaching the top Thirty in the summer of 1988. Fox's final album for Jive Records was 1991's *Just One Night* and despite an attempt at a comeback in 1995 when she fronted the band Sox's Song for Europe entrant *Go For*

The Heart (it finished fourth) her following releases achieved only moderate chart success.

Sabrina Salerno (as she then became known) released two further albums, the 1996 all-Italian language *Maschio Dove Sei* and 1999's *Flower's Broken* but both were largely unsuccessful.

Both singers then turned their hand to television – Salerno in an Italian 'where are they now?' celebrity show and Fox in appearances on reality shows including *The Club* and *Celebrity Wife Swap*. Fox, of course, will also be ever remembered for her contribution to the rebranded Brit Awards show in 1989 when she and co-presenter Mick Fleetwood presided over one of the most shambolic nights of television in living memory.

It is difficult to work out which is the better of these two model-turned-singer records. Fox's was probably the more serious effort but Sabrina's is the catchier and will be forever associated with its colourful video. Still, both were top Three hits and both represented the high point of their respective music careers. Make of that what you will.

57 Hue and Cry
Labour Of Love

Released: 13 June 1987   **Circa YR4**
Highest UK Chart Position: #6

Brothers Pat and Greg Kane formed Hue and Cry in Coatbridge, Scotland in 1983 and whilst their first single was released on a local independent label, out of their first batch of demos *Labour of Love* really stood out to their publishers and was, according to Pat Kane, 'the song that got us our record deal with Circa Records.'

The song was originally penned in the songwriting room at Chappells Music in London in the spring of 1986. The duo were 'plonked in a room with a piano and a very ancient beatbox' and it was the cyclical Latin groove coupled with the bass part of Greg's piano riff that came together first. Lyrically, rap was becoming an important force in music and whilst Pat hardly wanted to rap, the pair looked for a percussive lyric to bounce along with the riff they had created.

The lyrics of *Labour of Love* describe the disillusionment of working class Conservative voters in the mid 1980s who had worked hard to believe in Thatcher's story of a proud, individualist Britain but were now realising that there was more 'pain' than 'gain' in doing so. Pat Kane was a self-confessed 'compulsive political philosopher' and had been reading works by left-wing writers, puzzled as to why the working class would vote for Thatcher when her agenda was to destroy their jobs and livelihood.

The books Kane read propounded that the working classes in a confusing world liked the idea of a strong leader coupled with the notion of the 'rights of the individual' in a growing lifestyle culture. However, the song was built around the idea that these people were now seeing Thatcherism for what it really was, and that the veneer was wearing thin.

An entirely Scottish backing band laid down the basic track in the sessions for the *Seduced and Abandoned* album in late 1986 but it was when the song was taken to New York by the band's American producers Harvey Goldberg and James Biondolillo that it really sprang into life. At Jimmy's flat in Carnegie Mews, the band worked out the string/horn lines for *Labour of Love*, with Biondolillo recording these on a cassette player in order that the sheet music writers could notate the music. Over two days at Sigma Studios (above the Ed Sullivan Theatre on Broadway), the horn and string sections (including contributions from some of Sinatra's old players) were recorded.

Once mixed, the whole album was taken to the band's record company and manager to pick the singles. *I Refuse* was chosen as the debut release (peaking outside the top Seventy-Five) and it was agreed to then release *Labour of Love* as the second single. Pat Kane admits with complete embarrassment that he had severe doubts about the song being released as a single as he felt it too rhythmically and lyrically radical. However (thankfully) he was overruled by A&R man Ashley Newton and the single was scheduled for a June release.

This was unfortunate timing as *Labour of Love* was nearly derailed by Thatcher calling a summer General Election. A song that had strong political meaning with 'Labour' in the title was being sent out to radio stations, although thankfully the track was playlisted. The band's big break came when American band Los Lobos failed to obtain work permits for a *Top Of The Pops* performance and the brothers (who after six weeks on the chart had crept to number Thirty-Four) were asked to step in at the eleventh hour. The song then leapt up the charts, eventually peaking at number Six in August 1987.

Ultimately, the song made no difference to the outcome of the Election as Thatcher's Conservative government comfortably won a third term in office. Hue and Cry continued to make clever, beautiful pop singles until 1999 including further hits *Violently* and *Looking For Linda* before making a return to performing, starring on the ITV series *Hit Me Baby One More Time!* in 2005. The Kanes beat Sinitta, Hazel O'Connor, China Black and The Real Thing on their way to the final having performed *Labour of Love* and a cover of Beyonce's *Crazy In Love*. They lost to Shakin' Stevens in the Grand Final on 21 May, 2005.

Pat Kane sums up their attitude to *Labour of Love* nicely: "Am I happy that such an energetic, innovative, funky record is the one that defines our career, even to this day? Very happy indeed. *Labour of Love* is entirely continuous with who we are and who we'll continue to be."

58 S-Express
Hey Music Lover

Released: 18 February 1989   Rhythm King LEFT30
Highest UK Chart Position: #6

Credited with kick-starting the UK acid house music scene, S-Express are, in some ways, an unlikely act to feature in a book about pop music. A bizarre selection of club DJ's, producers and vocalists, the troupe set the charts alight at the end of the decade becoming one of the first acts in the UK to capitalize on the new 'sampling' culture.

Formed in 1988, the band's membership was loose and inclusive. The primary force behind S-Express was DJ, remixer and producer Mark Moore who, accompanied by vocalists Michelle and Jocasta, Mark D (trumpets) and fellow producer Pascal Gabriel, formed the initial incarnation of the band.

Debut single *Theme From S-Express* (based on the Rose Royce hit *Is It Love You're After*, and with its hi-hat sampled from an aerosol spray) was a smash hit single, reaching number One in the UK in only its third week on the singles chart. Follow-up single *Superfly Guy* also reached the top Five in the UK in 1988.

Whilst the sounds for their record were engineered primarily by the quartet, Moore had stated in a *New Musical Express* magazine interview that "anyone could be a member of S-Express." The DJ was subsequently approached in a London club by Billie Ray Martin, a German singer keen to audition for the band and Moore was so impressed by her vocals she ended up contributing to several of the songs on the band's debut album.

Although the majority of the material for the *Original Soundtrack* album was written by Moore and the band, Capitol Records (the band's American label) suggested a cover be included. Having already decided to incorporate their interpretation of an old song, they agreed on the Sly and the Family Stone song *Music Lover*.

Sly Stone (born Sylvester Stewart) was one of the biggest names in American music in the late 1960s and early 1970s and helped popularize soul and funk music worldwide. Most famous as the frontman of Sly and the Family Stone – the first major American band to have an integrated line up in both race and gender – the singer's hits included such soul classics as *Everyday People, Dance To The Music* and *Family Affair*. The song *Music Lover* was written in 1967 and originally included on their seminal 1968 album *Dance To The Music*.

The backing track for S-Express' *Hey! Music Lover* was recorded in 1988 (updated, but fundamentally faithful to the original) and the vocals were provided by Eric Robinson (who had worked with disco stars Sylvester and Diana Ross as a child prodigy) and by Billie Ray Martin (much to the disgust of vocalist Michelle who had provided the female vocals on the band's previous two hits).

The S-Express image by this time was based heavily on the Seventies-inspired artists such as the Jackson Five and Sly and the Family Stone themselves. Inspired by films by the likes of Fellini and Russ Meyer the video for *Hey! Music Lover* featured a Ken Russell-esque revolving record player stage on which an ensemble cast danced and performed in brightly coloured, extravagant costumes. Legendary Australian performance artist Lee Bowery was also slated to appear in the video but had to withdraw at the eleventh hour with his part as 'black and white alien' taken by fellow performer David Cabaret.

The song followed in the footsteps of S-Express' previous singles reaching the UK top Ten, peaking at number Six in March 1989. Its chart run also coincided with the release of the *Original Soundtrack* album, which peaked at number Five.

Whilst Pascal Gabriel went on to produce and write for the likes of New Order, Billie Ray Martin achieved success as part of Electribe 101 and as a solo artist (*Your Loving Arms* reached number Six in the UK in

1995). This meant that S-Express were a duo by the time their second album *Intercourse* was released in 1990 (the band comprised of Moore and DJ/vocalist Sonique who would later achieve a solo number One with the monster hit *It Feels So Good*.)

Moore has spent the period since S-Express as a successful club DJ and record producer.

Moore once described S-Express "as being to dance what Talking Heads were to punk". Although they were part of the dance scene they released songs which weren't archetypal dance records, mixing influences from the house, disco and funk scenes to excellent effect. That's the reason *Hey! Music Lover* is included here – although there are house music elements in evidence, its reliance on the brilliant Sly and the Family Stone melody coupled with its fun vocals make it a great dance/pop crossover hit.

59 Jane Wiedlin
Rush Hour

Released: 6 August 1988   Manhattan MT36
Highest UK Chart Position: #12

The second of the American punk-band the Go-Gos to secure top Twenty solo chart success (after 80s megastar Belinda Carlisle) Jane Wiedlin's great single *Rush Hour* became a big hit in the summer of 1988 and the theme tune to 'eye in the sky' traffic news bulletins the world over….

Born in 1958 in Wisconsin, Wiedlin formed the Go-Gos with Carlisle in 1978 and they had their first single and album success in 1981 with the number One album *Beauty and the Beat* and single *We've Got The Beat*. Weidlin also co-wrote the band's first top Ten hit *Our Lips Are Sealed* with British vocalist Terry Hall after the pair had a short-lived affair.

Weidlin left the Go-Gos in October 1984 to pursue both an acting and solo career. One of her first acting roles was a small part in the fourth Star Trek film *The Voyage Home*. She also appeared as Joan of Arc in the hit comedy *Bill and Ted's Excellent Adventure* and in the 1985 film *Clue* (based loosely on the board game Cluedo).

The guitarist's first solo release was her self-titled album *Jane Wiedlin* in 1985. Despite promising reviews (Rolling Stone said "Wiedlin's taste for the offbeat and her punchy pop know-how as well as the record's pinball-arcade bustle of guitars, synths and sound effects keep things fizzing") it was not a huge commercial success. Single *Blue Kiss* reached number Seventy-Seven on the Billboard chart although the album failed to break into the Billboard top 100 album chart.

After the lukewarm success of the first album Wiedlin continued to act whilst deciding in which direction she wished to take her second album. Featuring collaborations with ex-Naked Eyes keyboardist Rob Fisher (who would subsequently team up with Simon Climie to record as Climie Fisher), the album was produced by legendary synth producer Stephen Hague fresh from his work with the Pet Shop Boys in the UK.

Fur was released in both the UK and US in the summer of 1988. Its title relates to Weidlin's longstanding involvement as an animal rights activist and she has been involved with People for the Ethical Treatment of Animals (PETA) since the 1980s. The first single to be released from *Fur* was the jaunty pop single *Rush Hour* co-written by Wiedlin and Peter Rafelson. Rafelson (the son of Hollywood legend Bob Rafelson) studied film composing at music school before establishing himself as a songwriter with the likes of Elton John and Jackson Browne. As well as co-writing *Rush Hour*, he also wrote Madonna's worldwide hit *Open Your Heart* and co-produced the Corrs 1998 single *Dreams*.

Rush Hour, with its insanely catchy hook, was Weidlin's biggest hit. The song reached number Nine in the US Billboard chart and number Twelve in the UK, spending eleven weeks on the chart. The video passed up the opportunity to mirror the 'traffic' concept, instead being a straightforward film of Weidlin performing the song interspersed with clips of her swimming with dolphins.

Weidlin had one further chart hit *Inside a Dream* (although this failed to reach the top Fifty in either the UK or US) and her 1990 album *Tangled* was her final solo release. As well as continuing to act, Weidlin has reunited with the Go-Gos on several occasions since the early 1990s including for the 2001 album *God Bless the Go-Gos*.

Rush Hour made a return to the UK singles chart in 1996 when a cover by the Northern Irish band *Joyrider* spent one week at number Twenty-Two.

60 Erasure
A Little Respect
Released: 1 October 1988   Mute MUTE85
Highest UK Chart Position: #4

In the 1980's, if you were an aspiring band and needed a lead singer there were two place where you would always place your advertisement. The *NME* and *Melody Maker* are responsible for several bands finding their vocalist – Limahl answered a small ad to audition for Kajagoogoo and Alison Moyet answered Vince Clarke's request for a singer for his new band Yazoo.

After the relative failure of his band the Assembly, ex Depeche Mode and Yazoo songwriter Clarke placed an ad in the *Melody Maker* looking for a 'versatile singer' to work with an 'established songwriter'. Two days of auditions and forty hopefuls later, he had still not found his new vocalist but on a wet Tuesday morning, the penultimate 'interviewee' arrived, 21 year old Andy Bell.

Extremely nervous, Bell sang *Who Needs Love Like That* and *My Heart...So Blue* and despite there being one further singer to audition, Clarke was sure that he had found the vocalist he was looking for. After a lengthy list of band name suggestions was accumulated, the pair picked Erasure and one of the most successful acts of the late 80s and early 90s was born.

After their initial singles failed to chart, Erasure hit the big time in 1986 with their number Two single *Sometimes* from their second album *The Circus*. The song marked the start of an astounding run of twenty-three consecutive top Twenty hits for the band over the course of the following decade.

Their third album, *The Innocents* was released in April 1988. Produced by the American Stephen Hague (also responsible for great synthpop records by the likes of the Communards, New Order, OMD and the Pet Shop Boys) the album reached number One in the UK selling over 600,000 copies. The two lead singles *Ship Of Fools* and *Chains Of Love* were big hits across Europe, but it was the album's opening track and third single which endures as one of the bands most popular songs.

The impassioned plea of a lover to show compassion, *A Little Respect* has become one of Erasure's signature tunes. Their tenth single, it reached number Four in the UK singles chart in October 1988 when many commentators believed it was a certain number One hit. There was speculation that had it been released as the opening single from *The Innocents* that it might have secured the band's first number One single, but as it was its progress was halted by Whitney Houston, Bobby McFerrin and D-Mob.

Clarke was also heavily involved in the video for the single, which remains one of the decade's most memorable. It features both Bell and Clarke acting out the very literal meanings of the lines of the song, including a tiny model of the word 'respect' being given by one to the other. Highlights also included a lump of sugar being dropped into a cup of tea ('something to make you sweeter'), a telephone ringing ('I hear you calling….') and Bell with two large fish hanging from his ears (…'that you give me no sole'). Ridiculous it might have been, but brilliant also.

Erasure's success continued into the 1990's with further huge hits including *Blue Savannah, Drama!* and *Chorus* although they had to wait until 1992 for their first (and to date only) UK number One single – their *Abba-Esque EP* reaching the summit for a month. Having covered four of the Swedish legend's records in an Erasure style, the well-known Abba tribute band Bjorn Again decided to record four Erasure hits in an Abba style on their own 1992 EP *Erasure-Ish*. This release reached number Twenty-Five in the UK and included their Abba-esque version of *A Little Respect*.

There has also been a Spanish version of the song (*Un Poco De Respeto*) recorded by Argentinean band Attaque 77 which featured on their 1997 album *Otras Canciones*.

Most famously, however, Wheatus followed up their massive international hit *Teenage Dirtbag* in 2001 with a cover of *A Little Respect*. Their guitar based version is one of Clarke's favourite Erasure covers and it outperformed the original version in the UK charts, reaching number Three in July 2001.

A Little Respect is one of the finest pop records of the late 1980s with its heavily synthesised backing accentuated by Clarke's gentle acoustic guitar. Like a number of great records, it successfully combines a melancholy sentiment with an uplifting pop melody. Quite how it only reached number Four, I'll never know.

61 Milli Vanilli
Girl You Know It's True

Released: 1 October 1988   Cooltempo COOL170
Highest UK Chart Position: #3

The story of Milli Vanilli remains one of rock and roll's most ignominious – a tale of huge success built on deception and lies.

Fabrice Morvan and Rob Pilatus met whilst working as breakdancers in a Munich club in the mid 80s. German producer Frank Farian (previously responsible for Boney M) had developed a new dance-pop act named Milli Vanilli using vocals by Charles Shaw, John Davis and Brad Howell. The three singers lacked a marketable image, however, and having spotted the young, photogenic Morvan and Pilatus in a Berlin dance club they were recruited to front the act.

Milli Vanilli's debut single *Girl You Know It's True* was not an original composition but a cover of an obscure 1987 song by the band Numarx. Written by Bill Pettaway, a gas station attendant from Annapolis, Maryland along with Sean Spencer, Kevin Lyles, Rodney Holloman, and Ky Adeyemo, it was distributed in Germany and became a hit in the dance clubs. It was there that it was picked up by Farian.

Debut album *All Or Nothing* was released in Europe in mid-1988 before being noticed by Arista Records who signed the duo, renamed the album *Girl You Know It's True* and released it in the US in early 1989.

The album and singles were a huge success. *Girl You Know It's True* climbed to number Two on the Billboard chart and their following three singles (*Baby Don't Forget My Number*, *Blame It On The Rain* and *Girl, I'm Gonna Miss You*) all hit number One. *Girl You Know It's True* climbed to number Three in the UK in November 1988 and made the top Three all over Europe, including reaching number One in Austria and Germany.

Hugely successful, selling thirty million singles and fourteen million albums worldwide, the duo rode the wave of success culminating in beating Tone Loc, Neneh Cherry, the Indigo Girls and Soul II Soul to the Grammy Award for Best New Artist in 1990.

All, however, was not well. In December 1989, vocalist Charles Shaw told New York's *Newsday* that he was one of the vocalists on the record and that Morvan and Pilatus were imposters. The comments were quickly retracted (allegedly due to a sizeable payoff by producer Farian). The duo were then caught out in a live MTV performance when their backing track stuck, repeating the chorus line over and over.

Eventually, in November 1990, frustrated by the two frontmen's insistence that they sing on their impending second album and in the midst of rumour surrounding the source of the real talent in the band, Farian confessed to reporters that Morvan and Pilatus did not actually sing on the records.

There was a huge public outcry and it took a mere four days for their Grammy award to be withdrawn. Arista Records dropped the act and deleted the album giving Milli Vanilli the dubious honour of holding the record for the biggest selling album ever to be deleted. Countless lawsuits also followed under fraud protection laws approving refunds for consumers who had attended Milli Vanilli concerts or bought their recordings.

The follow-up album had already been recorded, and Farian attempted to continue with its release by crediting the actual vocalists, hiring a Morvan/Pilatus lookalike named Ray Horton and altering the name to 'The Real Milli Vanilli'. The album spawned three moderately successful singles. Rob and Fab (as they became known) released an eponymous album in 1993, but the scandal surrounding Milli Vanilli still shrouded them and the record was a commercial failure.

Whilst Morvan continued working as a DJ, session musician and solo performer, Pilatus was on a downward spiral. In 1995 he was arrested several times for a spate of assaults and vandalism and, in 1996, he was found guilty of several charges and jailed for several months as well as being admitted to a rehab centre for his cocaine addiction. He then returned to Germany, but was found dead in a Frankfurt hotel room on 2 April 1998 after mixing a fatal combination of prescription pills and alcohol.

Milli Vanilli remain one of music's greatest ever scandals and the infamy of their deceit and their legacy of being the first act ever to be stripped of a Grammy will long outlive their music. Huge record sales showed their popularity, but their singles were generally unashamedly similar and formulaic and, whilst no-one can doubt the catchiness of singles like *Girl You Know It's True*, they were never critically acclaimed.

However, as Fabrice Morvan says on his website: "Through scandal, through ruin, and ultimately through tragedy, the duo has demonstrated a deep connection with their audience that speaks directly to the profound relationship between performers and fans." That'll be the same fans that filed a class action lawsuit demanding refunds for their album purchases, will it?

62 Angry Anderson
Suddenly

Released: 19 November 1988   Food for Thought YUM113
Highest UK Chart Position: #3

It is easy to see why the popularity of long-running television drama *Neighbours* led to many of its stars finding the transition from TV star to pop icon relatively straightforward. Regular exposure to an enthusiastic, hungry teenage audience provided the perfect platform for the likes of Kylie and Jason to launch their stratospheric pop careers, although the show also had strange spin-off successes in addition to the creation of some of the decade's biggest stars.

In 1988, Australian rock singer Gary "Angry" Anderson was a relative unknown outside his home country. Apart from an appearance as Ironbar Bassey in the 1985 film *Mad Max: Beyond Thunderdome*, his fame was largely restricted to his homeland. Anderson first came to prominence as the vocalist for rock band Buster Brown in the early 1970s alongside Phil Rudd who would later join the hugely successful rock outfit AC/DC. Anderson joined the band Rose Tattoo in 1975 and remained as the vocalist for the popular four piece until the group was disbanded in 1987.

Whilst not major international stars, Rose Tattoo had a number of big Australian hits including *We Can't Be Beaten*, *Scarred For Life* and *Bad Boy For Love* and their songs have been covered by the likes of the LA Guns and Guns'n'Roses. They also performed at the UK's Reading festival in 1981.

After Rose Tattoo's demise in 1987, Anderson set to work recording his debut solo album *Beats From A Single Drum*. At the same time the cast of the Network Ten soap opera *Neighbours* were recording their 523rd episode and were looking for a song to soundtrack the wedding of popular characters Charlene Mitchell (played by Kylie Minogue) and Scott Robinson (Jason Donovan). Anderson's album included a gentle rock ballad entitled *Suddenly* which was apparently suggested to the producers as an appropriate track by the show's diminutive female star.

Neighbours had already quickly attracted a significant audience in both Australia and the UK by the time the wedding of Scott and Charlene was broadcast on Network Ten on 1 July 1987 (the same day as the show's two main stars appeared in Parramatta, Sydney cutting an exact replica of the *Neighbours* wedding cake). The UK audience had to wait until 8 November 1988 to see the episode, the ceremony soundtracked at the altar by Anderson's hit.

The wedding proved to be a historic and defining moment for the Australian series. Seventeen million BBC1 viewers watched Scott and Charlene tie the knot in what has become one of the drama's best known episodes. The late 1980s was certainly the heyday for the soap and this particular episode epitomised the humour and drama associated with the show and, unusually, featured all the lead characters. The off-screen romance between the two leads also only served to whet the appetite of viewers yet further.

Due to the spectacular success of both episode 523 and the show in general, Anderson's song was released in the UK in the week of the wedding with the single cover branded heavily as the 'wedding theme from *Neighbours*' and featuring 'Scott and Charlene' in large red letters on the cover. Due in no small part to the success of the show, the song charted almost immediately, becoming an unlikely contender for the 1988 Christmas number One slot. It eventually peaked at number Three in December 1988, outsold by Cliff Richard's festive chart-topper *Mistletoe and Wine* and, coincidentally, by Kylie and Jason's own *Especially For You*. Unsurprisingly, the song reached number One in Australia.

Anderson's solo career continued to flourish in Australia, although *Suddenly* remains his only hit in the UK. He is now recognised in his home country as much now for television presenting and for charitable work, both as a youth advocate and as a campaigner for men's health (having lost four former Rose Tattoo band members over recent years).

Whilst some might view *Suddenly* as a rather naff, overblown ballad, those members of the *Neighbours* generation celebrate the song as representing everything that made the show so unmissable during the late 1980s. It had the good fortune to provide the soundtrack to one of the most watched TV moments of the entire decade and many a tear was shed as Reverend Sampson pronounced Scott and Charlene man and wife on that November day in 1988. It is probably true to say that whatever song was chosen to accompany that iconic TV kiss would have been a major smash, but that is not to diminish the appeal and quality of Anderson's charming hit.

63 Boy Meets Girl
Waiting For A Star To Fall

Released: 3 December 1988   RCA PB 49519
Highest UK Chart Position: #9

Following their meeting at a Seattle society wedding at which the two of them were asked to perform, George Merrill and Shannon Rubicam teamed up and formed the band Boy Meets Girl. Signed to Thom Bell's publishing company, Mighty Three Music, the couple had an office in Pioneer Square, Seattle from where they wrote songs for the likes of American jazz and soul stars Phyllis Hyman and Deniece Williams.

Bell also produced Williams and the duo's first taste of hit music came when they were asked to sing backing vocals on Williams' huge worldwide smash *Let's Hear It For The Boy* as well as touring the world with the star.

Their eponymous debut album was released in 1985 and spawned the top 40 hit *Oh Girl*. Still continuing to write for other artists, however, their big breakthrough came after they submitted an up-tempo pop track to Janet Jackson as a commitment to their publishing company. The song *How Will I Know* was "dashed off" in order that George and Shannon could get back to the business of writing their own material, and although Jackson passed on the song (she was recording the *Control* album with Jam and Lewis at the time), the publishers also forwarded it to the producers of a niece of Dionne Warwick who liked the song and invited George to work with them on it.

After a couple of false starts, Narada Michael Walden and Randy Jackson recorded *How Will I Know* with the then up-and-coming star Whitney Houston. Featuring on her eponymous debut album the song was a huge hit worldwide and an American number one single (Houston actually knocked her aunt, Dionne Warwick, off the Billboard number One spot with the song.)

Merrill and Rubicam then submitted a further song to Houston, which was recorded in 1987 and became one of the most well-known songs of the decade. The Boy Meets Girl penned *I Wanna Dance With Somebody (Who Loves Me)* catapulted Whitney to international stardom selling over four million copies worldwide and reaching number One in the USA, the UK, Germany and Switzerland.

It was whilst watching Houston perform their two songs at an open-air gig at the Greek Theatre in Los Angeles that the inspiration for the duo's own biggest hit came. As invited guests of the star, Whitney had just performed their song *How Will I Know* to a rapturous reception when Rubicam looked to the sky and saw a shooting star. Immediately getting the idea for the lyric 'waiting for a star to fall', the singer wrote the line on a scrap of paper and kept it in her purse.

Writing lyrics around this one line, the duo came up with a song about 'the longing for what appears to be unobtainable' entitled *Waiting For A Star To Fall*. The demo for the song was recorded in the couple's garage in Venice, California during quiet moments – the garage wasn't very well insulated and so any extraneous noises (car alarms, animals) would tend to appear on the recording! *Waiting For A Star To Fall* was, once again, a song submitted first to Whitney Houston, but this time the star elected to pass. Moving towards a more R&B sound, it was felt that this song was too 'poppy' for her new direction.

Deciding to record the song themselves, Boy Meets Girl met with the legendary producer Arif Mardin who, after hearing *Waiting For A Star To Fall* amongst other demos was unequivocal that the band should record and release it as a single. The mix by David Leonard was superb, a video was filmed featuring the couple's daughter and some pre-school friends and the song was released in late 1988 with both the duo and record company convinced that it was going to be a hit.

A hit it was, reaching number Five in the US and number Nine in the UK charts and it was also used in the film *Three Men And A Little Lady*. The signature six note sequence before the chorus has become instantly recognisable, and to a new generation thanks to the songs usage in two samples in 2005. Merrill re-recorded some vocals for the Cabin Crew hit *Star To Fall* whilst English group the Sunset Strippers used a sample from the original record for their top three hit *Falling Stars*.

Whilst the duo's two most famous songs might well be those that they wrote for Whitney Houston, *Waiting For A Star To Fall* remains a great upbeat slice of late 80s pop in its own right. As Merrill happily confessed, "our best work ended up being heard by millions of people" and you can't much argue with that.

64 Howard Jones
What Is Love?

Released: 26 November 1983 **WEA HOW2**
Highest UK Chart Position: #2

There are a few names that will forever be synonymous with early 1980s pop music. Those that took synthesizers and turned them from avant-garde new wave music into chart-based pop live long in the memory and there was no-one that is more fondly remembered for his brand of catchy 80s synth-pop than Howard Jones.

Born John Howard Jones in Southampton in 1955, Jones spent his formative years in High Wycombe and in Canada before returning to the UK to spend a year at the Royal Northern College of Music in Manchester. In 1983 he hired the Marquee Club in London and invited record companies to come and watch him perform and his well received set secured a session on John Peel's radio show and support slots with OMD and China Crisis. He signed with WEA Records in the UK and Elektra Records in the USA shortly after.

Jones' live shows at the time were famous for featuring the mime artist Jed Hoile. Hoile performed improvised choreography on stage whilst doused in white paint as Jones performed behind him. The mime artist remained an integral part of Jones' live shows until 1985 and appeared in one of Jones' most famous *Top Of The Pops* performances.

Jones' debut single *New Song* was released in September 1983 and was an unexpected immediate success, reaching number Three and spending five months on the charts.

The follow-up single proved to be his biggest hit in the UK as the superb *What Is Love?* climbed to number Two in January 1984. Whilst it had a terrifically catchy melody, *What Is Love?* had a downbeat lyrical message, questioning 'does anybody love anybody anyway'?

With a popular video filmed in Paris, *What Is Love?* was held off the top of the charts by Paul McCartney's *Pipes of Peace* but helped to propel Jones' debut album *Human's Lib* to the top of the UK album charts where it spent two weeks as part of a yearlong chart run.

Human's Lib was well received by both critics and the public alike on both sides of the Atlantic and around the world. It went gold in the UK, USA, Australia, Germany, Italy and Japan and, whilst Jones did not score the run of top Ten hits in the USA as he had in the UK, singles including *What Is Love?* and *New Song* both reached the Billboard top Forty.

After further hits *Hide and Seek* and *Pearl In The Shell*, Jones set to work on his second album *Dream Into Action*. The album featured his own backing group Afrodiziak who included both renowned session singer Claudia Fontaine and also Caron Wheeler who would sing on Soul II Soul's classic 1989 number One *Back To Life*. Lead single *Like To Get To Know You Well* reached number Four in the UK and the follow-up *Things Can Only Get Better* also reached the top Ten.

The album also featured the brilliant *No One Is To Blame* which reached number Four in the American singles chart and has since had over three million radio plays in USA. *Dream Into Action* went platinum in USA and remained in the US top Twenty album chart for the best part of a year making Jones one of the very few British artists to have comprehensively 'broken' America in the past twenty-five years.

In 1986 the singer was voted 'Keyboard Player of the Year' in Rolling Stone magazine, and in 1987 he toured the world extensively headlining Madison Square Garden in New York, the Forum in LA and The Budokan in Tokyo. Jones also performed at the UK leg of Live Aid performing his hit single Hide and Seek on a piano that belonged to Queen frontman Freddie Mercury.

Chart action eluded Jones after his minor 1986 hit *All I Want* although he continued performing, recording and touring throughout the 1990s and 2000s. On 20 September 2003, he played a sold out twentieth anniversary concert at the Shepherds Bush Empire, London, commemorating the release of his first single. He was joined on stage by fellow 80s artists Midge Ure and Nena, as well as his mime artist, Jed Hoile.

Howard Jones hits, particularly *What Is Love?* are perfect examples of the high quality hits that peppered the UK charts in the early to mid 1980s. With both catchy hooks and deeper lyrical meaning, Jones led the way in synth-pop for two superb albums and his music is some of the most popular and recognizable of the era.

65 Donna Summer
This Time I Know It's For Real

Released: 25 Feb 1989   **Warner Bros U7780**
Highest UK Chart Position: #3

You may ask how it is possible to include an artist who has sold an estimated 130 million records worldwide in a book about 'forgotten pop hits', but with a career as long and as illustrious as Donna Summer's, there is bound to be the odd song that falls under the pop radar.

Born LaDonna Adrian Gaines in Boston on New Year's Eve 1948, Summer left home at the age of eighteen to pursue a career on Broadway. An audition for the musical *Hair* led to a prime job with the show's road company where she joined the German (and later the Austrian) cast of the show, settling in Munich where she married Austrian actor Helmut Sommer and took the 'Summer' name.

Whilst working in Germany, Summer met Pete Bellotte and Giorgio Moroder who produced her first album *Lady of the Night*, from which came a couple of sizeable European hits. In 1975 Summer approached Moroder with an idea for a song written around the lyric 'love to love you, baby'. Moroder was interested in the new musical style of 'disco' and utilised Summer's lyric and her orgasmic moaning on what ended up being a seventeen minute version of the song. It was Summer's first big US hit (reaching number Two) and the emergence of disco as a musical genre was complete.

Summer continued to have a string of huge disco smashes throughout the remainder of the 1970s including classic hits such as *Hot Stuff*, *MacArthur Park* and *On the Radio*. Her most famous recording, however remains *I Feel Love*, which has been enormously influential in the development of dance music over three decades thanks to Moroder's innovative production. It is widely regarded as being the first disco-style song recorded entirely with a synthesised backing track and was Summer's only UK number One single.

The early 1980s remained good to Summer as her new deal with the fledgling Geffen Records and relationship with producer Quincy Jones produced such hits as *State of Independence* and *She Works Hard For The Money*. As the decade progressed, her albums became less and less successful and her relationship with David Geffen deteriorated, leading to her signing with Atlantic Records in 1988.

In 1989, seeking a return to the Euro-dance/Europop approach that had served her well in the early years, Summer turned to British producers Stock, Aitken and Waterman to work on her next project. In the late 80s, the Hit Factory trio were as important to European dance-pop as Giorgio Moroder and Pete Bellotte had been to the Euro-disco of the late 1970s. The album *Another Place and Time* was written and produced by Stock, Aitken and Waterman with three tracks co-written with Summer. As Waterman said, "For a producer to get goosebumps, that's saying something. Donna could do that. Get Donna to sing the times-table and you'd go 'f*cking hell!' Unbelievable."

The hi-NRG pop sound of the album coupled with the Midas touch of the production team propelled Summer back into the top Ten. The first single, the terrific *This Time I Know It's For Real* climbed to number Three in the UK charts – Summer's first top ten single in a decade. The song also made number Seven in the Billboard chart.

Co-written by Summer, *This Time I Know It's For Real* remains one of Stock, Aitken and Waterman's finest and most recognisable singles. It raced to number Three in only its fifth week on the chart where it stayed for two weeks, being denied the top spot by Madonna's smash *Like A Prayer* and another Hit Factory song (Jason Donovan's *Too Many Broken Hearts*). It spent longer on the UK singles chart than any other of Summer's hits and achieved gold status on both sides of the Atlantic.

The follow-up singles, S/A/W produced *I Don't Wanna Get Hurt* and *Love's About To Change My Heart* also made the UK top 20, before Summer fell out with the production team and the songs they had written for her were instead recorded by Lonnie Gordon. Indeed, echoes of *This Time I Know It's For Real* can be heard in Gordon's 1990 single *Happenin' All Over Again*.

Being such a great tune, it was inevitable that it would return to the charts at some point and Aussie girl band the Young Divas took their version of the hit to number Two in the Australian charts in 2006. Their interpretation achieved platinum status and became the sixth biggest selling song in the country that year.

Whilst it may not be one of the classic records with which the Queen of Disco is associated, *This Time I Know It's For Real* remains one of her best known singles and biggest hits. From the second the instantly recognisable Hit Factory drums begin (four seconds in), it bounces along breathlessly with one of the catchiest choruses you'll ever hear. Whether it represents a critical low point in her career is debatable but it remains a great pop record and didn't prevent Summer retaining her position as one of the all-time icons of dance music.

66 Abba
Super Trouper

Released: 15 November 1980   Epic EPC 9089
Highest UK Chart Position: #1

Arguably the greatest pop band in the history of music, whilst the majority of their smash hits came in the previous decade, Abba were still a force to be reckoned with in the early part of the 1980s.

The Abba story is well-told. Formed in the early 1970s by Benny Andersson, Blorn Ulvaeus, Agnetha Faltskog and Anni-Frid Lyngstad and named as an acronym of the quartet's first names the band hit the big time in 1974 when their song *Waterloo* became the first Swedish winner of the Eurovision Song Contest. When their follow-up singles failed to replicate *Waterloo*'s success it was thought that they would become Eurovision 'one hit wonders' but the success of 1975 singles *SOS* and *Mamma Mia* established Abba as a major chart act.

The group scored eight number One singles in the UK in the 1970s on their way to selling an estimated three hundred and seventy million records worldwide. Singles such as *Dancing Queen, Take A Chance On Me, The Name Of The Game* and *Knowing Me, Knowing You* have become modern classics and their greatest hits compilation *Abba Gold* is the third biggest selling album in UK chart history, behind Queen's *Greatest Hits* and the Beatles' *Sergeant Pepper's Lonely Hearts Club Band*.

As the 1980s began, it looked like Abba's star was beginning to wane. Their six singles since *The Name Of The Game* had all failed to reach the top of the charts and Ulvaeus and Faltskog had announced that they were to divorce. However their superb single *The Winner Takes It All* sent Abba back to the top of the UK and international charts, resulting in pre-orders for their seventh album *Super Trouper* exceeding a million in the UK alone.

The last song to be written and recorded for this album was the title track itself. Originally called *Blinka lilla stjärna* (the Swedish title of the nursery rhyme *Twinkle, Twinkle Little Star*) the song refers to the giant spotlights used in stadium and arena concerts. *Super Trouper* is a registered trademark of Strong Entertainment Lighting of Omaha and the corporation has been manufacturing the spotlights since 1956. The lights became a favourite with many artists because of their excellent light field and are used as a 'follow' spotlight by many stage artists.

It was well-known that Abba were not always the most comfortable of live acts. Despite a number of extremely successful tours across the world the band generally preferred the confines of the studio atmosphere rather than a giant tour stage. The lyrics of *Super Trouper* are typical Abba – a great upbeat pop tune hiding a melancholy lyrical content, this time about being on tour.

The single and album cover for *Super Trouper* also utilised the spotlight theme with the band on a stage in the Europa Film studios in Stockholm surrounded by two local circus troupes. The video of the song also featured the band on stage, cut with scenes from this photoshoot.

Super Trouper was another major international hit, reaching number One in the UK for three weeks in November and December 1980. The song also reached the top of the charts in Belgium, Holland, Germany and Ireland and the album *Super Trouper* was the UK's biggest selling of 1980. Although Abba were firmly re-established as the leading pop band of the age, *Super Trouper* was their final number one single as the further breakdown of the band's relationships led to just one further album (1981's *The Visitors*) and two further UK Top Ten hits, *Lay All Your Love On Me* and *One Of Us*.

Although the band never officially split, their last performance as Abba was on Noel Edmonds' *The Late, Late Breakfast Show* on December 11th 1982. The foursome have only been reunited twice in public since 1986 – at the 2005 Stockholm premiere of the stage production of *Mamma Mia!* and in 2008 at the film premiere in Sweden.

The motion picture release of *Mamma Mia* starring Meryl Streep and Pierce Brosnan introduced the music of Abba to a whole new audience on its release in 2008. The film has become the highest grossing in UK cinema history and its unprecedented success propelled *Abba Gold* back to the top of the UK album charts in August 2008.

Whilst there is no indication that the quartet will ever perform together again, the vast success of Abba will ensure their place in musical history is guaranteed. It is estimated that the value of their back catalogue is exceeded only by the Beatles and their string of superb catchy, weighty pop records – typified brilliantly by this 1980 number One – will live forever.

67 London Boys
London Nights

Released: 1 July 1989 **WEA YZ393**
Highest UK Chart Position: #2

Ah, the London Boys. Their energetic gymnastic dance routines, hi-NRG Europop and fantastic matching outfits lit up the charts across Europe for an all too brief period in the late 1980s....

Dennis Fuller and Edem Ephraim were born within a fortnight of one another in the summer of 1959 – Fuller in Jamaica and Ephraim in London. The pair met when at school in Greenwich, London although both moved to the German city of Hamburg in the early 1980's where they spent the early part of the decade working as dancers and as rollerblade artists. Fuller was part of a rollerskating disco act called the Roxy Rollers who actually released a single of their own, *I Need A Holiday* in May 1979.

The pair formed their pop duo the London Boys (based on the fact that, despite their long term residence in Germany, they were both from the English capital) in 1986 as a vehicle for the German songwriter and producer Ralf-Rene Maue. Indeed, Maue became known as the 'third London Boy' for his input to the band's success in the late 1980's.

Whilst their sound may have been considered traditional Eurodisco, the music actually blended a number of styles. Based on a high-energy disco sound, the band's songs also incorporated distorted rock guitar, rap, elements of glam-rock, contemporary dance rhythms, anthemic choruses and, for the first time in pop music, Gregorian chants. Producer Maue also added a huge 'wall of sound'-like drama to the production which gave the songs a powerful, disco feel.

The duo's first single in the UK was the up-tempo disco stomper *London Nights*, but this failed to chart. In December 1988 the follow-up single *Requiem* was released and this hovered around the lower reaches of the top 100 for a couple of months before eventually making the top Forty in April 1989. Whilst not PWL artists, Pete Waterman was friends with Maue and had remixed *Requiem*, blending the unique Hit Factory sound with Maue's disco production. The song climbed to an eventual high of number Four where it stayed for three weeks in May 1989.

Following the success of *Requiem*, the duo decided to re-release their first single. In the same mould as *Reqiuem*, *London Nights* was a hi-NRG slice of Eurodisco with Ephraim taking the main lead vocals. To capitalize on their newfound success, *London Nights* was released immediately – indeed it charted the very same week that *Reqiuem* dropped out of the Top Forty.

It was an instant hit, jumping from number Nineteen to number Three in its second week on the chart before peaking at number Two in July 1989 (Sonia's Stock, Aitken and Waterman penned *You'll Never Stop Me Loving You* stopped it topping the charts.)

A big part of the London Boys appeal was their stage presence. From their training and work as rollerblade artists in Germany in the early Eighties, the two had a good knowledge of dance and choreography and their performances formed a huge part of their overall image. Two extremely fit young guys with a professional dance background gave them a strong visual aspect and their athleticism was their trademark. Whether it was spinning on their heads or performing somersaults and back flips (as they did when opening *Top of the Pops* with *London Nights* in 1989) their stage routine was always energetic and captivating.

The duo's success continued with their number Two album (*The Twelve Commandments Of Dance*) from which was taken the top Twenty single *Harlem Desire*. Their subsequent releases all failed to make the top Forty and whilst they continued to make albums (1991's *Sweet Soul Music* and 1993's *Love 4 Unity*) they were ultimately dropped from their record label and effectively the band split. It is estimated that the pair sold over four and a half million records worldwide.

Unfortunately, this particular story has a terribly tragic ending. Not long after the duo had reformed to record the crossover album *Hallelujah Hits* (mixing Eurodance with traditional religious arrangements) they were both killed in a car accident. On January 21st 1996 whilst on a skiing holiday in the Austrian Alps, a car being driven by a Swiss motorist collided with them head-on in bad weather whilst attempting an overtaking manoeuvre. Both Edem Ephraim and Dennis Fuller were killed in the accident alongside Edem's German wife Bettina, a mutual friend (a Hamburg DJ) and the driver of the other vehicle.

Whilst the boys may no longer be with us, their Eurodance legacy of two of the most upbeat, anthemic disco records of the late 1980's remains. *London Nights* in particular is a great floor-filler – the video showing the duo and a nightclub audience all punching to air to the chorus will be remembered by many, I am sure.

68 Martika
Toy Soldiers

Released: 29 July 1989 **CBS 655049 7**
Highest UK Chart Position: #5

America in the late 1980's produced a seemingly endless conveyor belt of beautiful, teen-friendly female pop talent. From Tiffany through Debbie Gibson to Belinda Carlisle, the covers of teenage magazines and the pop charts were monopolized by these video-friendly artists.

One of the least well remembered (unless you were a fan, in which case I would contend that she would categorically have been your favourite) was the stunning and talented Marta Merrero, born in Whittier, California to Cuban parents in May 1969.

Martika, as she became known, was a child star, first coming to public attention with her performance as an orphan girl in the 1982 motion picture version of the *Annie* story. This film role led to her being signed to appear in the popular Disney Channel show *Kids Incorporated*, a series about a group of young neighbourhood children who rose to fame through their singing.

Producer and writer Michael Jay had achieved success in the mid 1980s with artists such as Five Star and Gloria Estefan. Looking for a solo vocalist for his next project, Jay discovered Martika entirely by chance – spotting her during a lunch meeting with his sister who worked on the *Kids Incorporated* show. The pair wrote several songs together and the demos were taken to several record companies where interest was high. A bidding war ensued before the young vocalist was eventually signed to CBS Records.

Recording her debut album, Jay's original intention was to record and produce a dance/pop album but the sheer quantity of other artists at the time producing that sort of material led to a rethink. The aim then was to come up with an album and some singles which would stand out from the teen-pop records domination the charts and this led to the inclusion of the song *Toy Soldiers*.

Toy Soldiers had been recorded as part of the original demo package produced to secure a recording contract. The chorus of the song had been written first although Jay admitted that this didn't have any particular meaning. The rest of the song was different, however, as its extremely serious message was missed by most. Whilst on the face of it *Toy Soldiers* sounds like a standard break-up ballad it is in fact the story of one of the singer's friends who was battling a serious drug addiction at the time. Written about how drugs can take over control of a person (in the same simple way a child 'controls' their toys), the video for the record also reinforced this anti-drug message. The short film featured Martika's relationship with a drug-dealer culminating in the death of the addict and the singer placing a flower on his grave.

The recognizable chorus of the song also featured backing vocals from some of Martika's fellow cast members from *Kids Incorporated*, including future stars Stacy Ferguson (Fergie from the Black Eyed Peas), Shanice and Jennifer Love Hewitt.

After the release of debut single *More Than You Know* (the first release was originally to be the catchy *Cross My Heart* but British band Eighth Wonder had already released their version of this song) radio stations picked up the unusual downbeat song. Not intended as a single, it was only released after radio stations became inundated with requests for the song leading to the record becoming an almost instant hit.

It climbed to number One on the American charts, becoming the 29th biggest selling single in the USA in 1989. It also performed well on the British charts, reaching number Five.

After further chart successes with her up-tempo cover of Carole King's *I Feel The Earth Move* and a re-release of *More Than You Know* the singer made the decision to sever her relationship with Jay (even though it was he who had helped her achieve her success) and decided to record her second album with the help of diminutive musical legend Prince.

Although her second album was a flop in her home country further success followed in the UK and overseas with the songs *Love....Thy Will Be Done* and the single and album *Martika's Kitchen*. The singer faded from the public eye in 1993 and despite forming the band Oppera with husband Michael Mozart in 2003 further success has not been forthcoming.

The song *Toy Soldiers* did achieve further success however when international rap star Eminem sampled the record on his 2004 hit *Like Toy Soldiers*. Although the chorus of the Martika song is frequently used in the record, the subject matter is different as Eminem's hit concerns violence and murder linked to rap music and not to drug addiction.

69 Big Fun
Blame It On The Boogie

Released: 12 August 1989 **Jive JIVE 217**
Highest UK Chart Position: #4

Big Fun were Philip Creswick, Jason John and Mark Gillespie and met whilst working as the dance group Seventh Avenue in 1986. The trio were employed as dancers in discos across Scotland and the North of England mainly miming to disco hits with their own choreographed dance routines. Although the work was fun, the money was poor and so the three boys decided to form their own pop band ('the male Bananarama').

Working with house producer Marshall Jefferson, the trio decided not to record house music tracks but to become a 'traditional' pop group. Seventh Avenue had some success on the club scene and on a trip to Japan they met legendary producer Pete Waterman who confessed to be looking for an all-male dancing group. Waterman didn't sign the trio immediately, however after hearing their recording of Carole King's classic *I Feel The Earth Move* he took an interest. He asked the boys to join his Hitman Roadshow – a nationwide series of shows featuring the best of the Stock, Aitken and Waterman stable including Hazell Dean, Sinitta, Sonia, Kylie Minogue and Jason Donovan.

The crowds at the Roadshow were extremely enthusiastic for the now renamed Big Fun (after the Inner City smash hit of the time) and having secured a recording contract the three boys moved in to a shared house in London whilst they set about recording their material. The fact that all three were gay had to be carefully managed also so as not to alienate the huge gaggle of adoring female fans.

Waterman wasn't a fan of *I Feel the Earth Move* and hadn't produced this record. It had also become a chart hit for the American singer Martika by this time and so an alternative record was sought, and it was a cover of an old 1970's disco classic that was to be their debut single.

Blame It On The Boogie is a classic 1978 disco record written by Michael Jackson. Whilst the Jacksons recording of the song has become the most well known the song was actually not written by *the* Michael Jackson - by complete coincidence it was penned by a British based singer-songwriter by the same name. Yorkshireman Mick Jackson originally intended the song for Stevie Wonder but it was at the Modern Music Festival in Cannes in 1978 that the Jacksons' record executives heard the song and adopted it for their clients.

Also coincidentally, the Jacksons cover of *Blame It On The Boogie* was released at the same time as Mick Jackson's original and the 'Battle of the Boogie' (as the press labelled it) was fought in the charts in October 1978. The Jackson's cover eventually triumphed reaching number Eight in the singles chart whilst Jackson's original peaked at number Fifteen.

Waterman suggested the band record a further cover of this hit and it was released in August 1989 as Big Fun's first single. It became the most successful version of the song (in chart terms), reaching number Four in the UK in September 1989 as well as reaching number One in Belgium and number Two in Spain. The band actually became hugely popular in Spain, at one point having three songs in the top Twenty simultaneously.

The band tell the story of being in a London taxi when the familiar opening beats of their Stock, Aitken and Waterman tune came on the radio. Excitedly asking the cabbie to turn up the volume, it became immediately apparent that the song wasn't *Blame It On The Boogie* but another PWL number – the introductions of many of them were so similar that even the artists couldn't tell them apart!

Blame It On The Boogie has, by virtue of both the Jacksons and Big Fun versions, become something of a party staple over the years. The famous dance routine to the record (right hand extended at eye level, left hand extended at waist level, simulated sex, dancing) was actually 'invented' by Creswick in their shared house in Hampstead. One of the highlights for the band was seeing 120,000 people at a festival in Zaragoza all simultaneously join in the camp, catchy routine which has become a wedding disco favourite.

Big Fun had two further chart hits from their top Ten album *A Pocketful Of Dreams* – the astonishingly catchy Can't Shake *The Feeling* and *A Handful Of Promises* – in addition to *You've Got A Friend*, a top Twenty duet featuring fellow PWL artist Sonia. Despite selling over a million records the band were dropped by Jive records in 1991 after just one album.

70 Damian
The Time Warp

Released: 19 August 1989,   **Jive JIVE 182**
Highest UK Chart Position: #7

One of the best loved stage musicals, *The Rocky Horror Show* was the brainchild of British writer Richard O'Brien and opened in the West End on 19 June 1973. It has been regularly revived and performed over the last thirty odd years, but only one song, the Act One dance number *Time Warp*, has ever been a success on the UK singles charts.

Featuring the likes of Julie Covington, Tim Curry and O'Brien himself, the musical exceeded all expectations on its opening and ran for an initial seven years and almost three thousand appearances. It premiered in Los Angeles in 1974 before transferring to Broadway in 1975 with O'Brien, Curry and a young Meat Loaf amongst the stars of the New York show.

After its Broadway success, the musical was turned into the much-loved movie *The Rocky Horror Picture Show* in 1975. Directed by the stage director Jim Sharman the film also featured many of the actors from the London and Broadway casts as well as Oscar winner Susan Sarandon as the sweet and naive Janet Weiss.

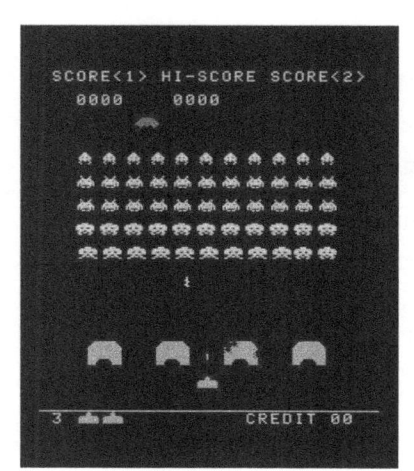

The Rocky Horror Picture Show was never actually pulled from cinematic release and so it continued to be shown in cinemas across the world throughout the 1970s and 1980s. The 1980s also saw several revivals of the popular show and there have been over two dozen cast recordings to date of the music from the show.

Mixing sex, science fiction and strange goings on, the story of Brad and Janet has become one of the stage's most popular, coming eighth in a BBC Radio 2 listener poll of the 'Nation's Number One Essential Musicals'.

The song *Time Warp* appears as the fourth song in the film (after *Science Fiction/Double Feature*, *Dammit, Janet!*, and *Over at the Frankenstein Place*), but fifth in the original stage show (after *Sweet Transvestite*) and consists of verses sung by alternating characters (Riff-Raff, Magenta and Columbia) and choruses sung by the chorus of 'Transylvanians' (in the film) or 'phantoms' (in the musical).

The song has also become popular beyond the reaches of the musical and is now a party favourite as well as being one of that small but select bunch of 1980s pop records that came with its very own accompanying dance.

In the same way that *Agadoo* encouraged you to push your pineapples and shake your tree, the *Time Warp* is difficult to perform on a dance floor without following the clear instructions. Jumps to the left, steps to the right, hands on your hips and, of course, those pelvic thrusts are an intrinsic part of the song's appeal, and one of the reasons that it has become such a popular party favourite.

Damian Davey, a twenty-two year old musician and actor first released his high-energy version of this classic *Rocky Horror* song in March 1986, although it failed to reach the UK Top Seventy-Five. Confusingly, a second version of the song, *Time Warp II* was released twice, in December 1987 and August 1988 although both these versions also failed to chart. It was only when a remixed version of the original *Time Warp* was released in 1989 that it finally became a chart smash.

The remixed single was also accompanied by an odd video, which mixes images of Damian in some extremely avant-garde outfits (a cross between the Joker from *Batman* and something from an old Pet Shop Boys promo) and some hilarious footage of old age pensioners attempting to perform the *Time Warp* dance outside a branch of Dixons in Manchester.

Time Warp spent fourteen weeks on the chart, peaking at number Seven in the UK in September 1989. Damian would have no further chart success, however, as his follow up single *Wig Wam Bam* peaked at number Forty-Nine in December 1989.

Although it will be always intrinsically linked with *The Rocky Horror Show*, the *Time Warp* has carved a solid niche for itself as a must-hear Eighties party tune. The annoying but critical accompanying dance is certainly a factor, as is the extreme catchiness of the song itself. Cover versions have also been released by artists as diverse as Jive Bunny, Alvin and the Chipmunks and Sebastian Bach from the rock band Skid Row.

Writer Richard O'Brien, of course, later went on to star as the host of the popular Channel Four game show *The Crystal Maze*.

71 Debbie Gibson
Foolish Beat

Released: 9 July 1988   Atlantic A 9059
Highest UK Chart Position: #9

Since the dawn of time music history has been littered with rivalries between artists. The Beatles versus the Stones, Spandau versus Duran, Blur versus Oasis – the list goes on and on. If you were an American teenager in the late 1980's, however, it is probable that your playground arguments would have been on the subject of whether you preferred Tiffany or Debbie Gibson.

Deborah Ann Gibson was born on 31 August 1970 and grew up in the Long Island suburb of Merrick. From a very young age she showed musical talent and started performing in community theatres with her sisters at the age of five. She also began piano lessons with the noted American pianist Morton Estrin (who had previously taught Billy Joel to play the instrument).

Her first song - *Make Sure You Know Your Classroom* - was written at the age of six and at the age of eight she sang in a children's chorus at the Metropolitan Opera House in New York. It was a song called *I Come From America*, written at age twelve, that gained Gibson widespread recognition for her talents after she won $1,000 for the song in a songwriting contest. This prompted her parents to sign a management contract with Doug Breithart who helped Gibson learn several further instruments and also taught her how to arrange, engineer and produce records. By 1985 at the age of fourteen Gibson had recorded over one hundred of her own songs.

Whilst still at Calhoun High School, Long Island, Gibson signed her first contract with Atlantic Records and set to work recording her debut album *Out Of The Blue* with producer Fred Zarr. The album was recorded in just a month (in between performances around the country in nightclub venues) and Gibson's debut single *Only In My Dreams* was released in the US in the summer of 1987 reaching number Four in the Billboard charts. The follow-up single *Shake Your Love* also reached number Four as well as being Gibson's first success in the UK, reaching number Seven in February 1988.

The album was released in the autumn of 1987 and eventually climbed to the top Ten in the US in the spring of 1988 achieving triple platinum status. The upbeat poppy title track was then released as a single and reached number Three in the US (and number Nineteen in the UK).

For her fourth single, Gibson took a slight change of direction by releasing a slow break-up song. The song *Foolish Beat* was written in the winter of 1987 for her *Dream* tour, several months before its inclusion on her debut album. It is a lush piano-led ballad that captures the fantastical feelings of a teenage girl who has had her heart broken and wonders if she 'will ever love again'. Showing a remarkable maturity in her lyrics and arrangement, the song was a huge success on both sides of the Atlantic, giving Gibson her first American number One single.

When *Foolish Beat* made number One in the USA, Gibson became the youngest ever artist to write, perform and produce a number One single, a record that (as a female artist) she still holds today. The song performed well in the UK also, reaching number Nine in the singles chart for two weeks in July 1988. Shortly after the success of *Foolish Beat*, Gibson graduated from high school with honours.

Gibson's career continued to flourish in the US, and her next single – the *Foolish Beat*-esque *Lost In Your Eyes* stayed at number One for three weeks. Her second album *Electric Youth* was a smash hit in the USA and elsewhere selling ten million copies worldwide and spawning further singles including the tremendous *We Could Be Together*.

A less successful third album followed, before Gibson left the pop industry to take a part in the Broadway version of *Les Miserables* in 1992. She also had a successful stint in the West End version of the musical *Grease* (playing Sandy opposite Craig McLachlan's Danny) and their duet version of *You're The One That I Want* was Gibson's last appearance in the British charts.

In the 2000s, Gibson had a varied career, starring in the TV movie *Mega Shark vs Giant Octopus*, appearing naked in *Playboy* and appearing on the Fox TV show *Skating With Celebrities*.

Whilst she might not have ever translated her American success to the UK, Gibson still managed to score seven UK top Forty singles. For a magic eighteen months or so, Gibson was the biggest American teen idol and it was only the fact that we had our own pop icons at the time that prevented her being one of the biggest names around. *Foolish Beat* might sound slightly sentimental today but considering it was written and produced by a seventeen year old, it's a very polished and likeable pop ballad.

72 a-Ha
The Living Daylights

Released: 4 July 1987 **Warner Bros W8305**
Highest UK Chart Position: #5

When coming up with my original list of 101 records for this book, it seemed an obvious oversight not to include a James Bond theme from the decade, and the 80s threw up no shortage of possibilities. From the gentle Sheena Easton ballad *For Your Eyes Only* to the grand Gladys Knight ballad *Licence To Kill* Bonds 12 to 16 were all released in the 80s.

The unusual choice would have been the superb and oft-overlooked Rita Coolidge ballad *All Time High* (from *Octopussy*) but it barely scraped the top Seventy-Five and so it possibly a little too 'forgotten'. The obvious selection would therefore have been to go for the grand Duran Duran theme from Roger Moore's last outing *A View To A Kill* but, on reflection, I went for what I consider the best Bond song of that, or any, era.

a-Ha were formed in Norway in 1982 and the threesome moved to London in 1984 to pursue their music career and where they signed with Warner Brothers. Keyboardist Magne Furuholmen, guitarist Pal Waaktaar and singer Morten Harket scored their first major success with their single *Take On Me* in 1985. The song (originally called *Lesson One*) sold an estimated eight million copies worldwide and was accompanied by a groundbreaking pencil sketch animation/live action video that has become one of the most iconic and well-remembered music videos of all time.

The Scandinavian trio were finishing off their second album *Scoundrel Days* and preparing for their first world tour when they got the call about the possibility of recording a song for the upcoming James Bond film. After Timothy Dalton's casting as 007, several artists (apparently including

Queen and the Pet Shop Boys) were invited to submit a song for the new post-Moore era Bond.

Armed with the title, guitarist Waaktaar put together a song and played it to his band mates just before an appearance on UK music show *Top Of The Pops*. Movie producer Cubby Broccoli heard and loved a-Ha's demo for *The Living Daylights* and the Norwegians were given the honour of providing the theme for Bond 15.

Co-writing credits for the song were taken by the legendary film composer John Barry. Barry had worked on the Bond series since the first film *Dr No* and *The Living Daylights* turned out to be Barry's last Bond score. Not a fan of busy, frilly string arrangements, Barry added very simple strings to the trio's song which gave the record its Bond-esque sound.

Various sources intimate that the relationship between Barry and the band was not a cordial one. Barry claimed the band were difficult to work with due to their insistence that their original version of the song was the one used in the film. However, Waaktaar claims that the band enjoyed working with Barry and being regaled with tales of Bond movies past whilst recording the song. It was the Barry arranged version that was released as a single and appears on both the film soundtrack and the band's *Headlines and Deadlines* greatest hits album.

With a video featuring the band in the famous Bond 'gunbarrel' sequence and recorded at the giant Bond soundstage at Pinewood Studios (in which many of the Bond movies were filmed), the single was one of the bands biggest hits, reaching number Five in the UK in July 1987. Whilst the Barry version might have been the version of choice by the record company, the band used their original (and less dramatic) version on their excellent third album *Stay On These Roads*.

Part of the reason that *The Living Daylights* continues to be performed as a centrepiece of the band's live gigs is that, whilst it might have gained an iconic status as a Bond theme, it's also, very simply, a great pop record. The title is pretty much the only thing that the song shares with the blockbuster movie and the band's original version of the song (even stripping out any 007 connotations) is terrific.

In a departure from one of the longstanding Bond conventions, *The Living Daylights* used different songs over the opening and closing credits of the film. Whilst a-Ha's song accompanied the opening sequence, the Chrissie Hynde song *If There Was A Man* closed the film. The movie itself grossed $191.2 million although Dalton only reprised his role as 007 in one further film – 1989's *Licence To Kill*. a-Ha went on to have further hits in the UK and although they took a four year hiatus in the mid 1990s, they reappeared in 2000 with their album *Minor Earth, Major Sky*. Their subsequent albums *Lifelines*, *Analogue* and *Foot of the Mountain* are much underrated and even approaching their fiftieth birthdays the Norwegians returned to the UK top Ten with their single *Analogue* in January 2006.

Sadly, the trio have announced that they will split after a final 'farewell' tour in 2010.

73 Jason Donovan
When You Come Back To Me

Released: 9 December 1989   PWL PWL46
Highest UK Chart Position: #2

If you were looking for a ready-made teen pop idol in the late Eighties – someone who already had mass appeal with the youth market and was already famous in their own right – there was no better place to start than with Australia's Network Ten series *Neighbours*.

Neighbours most famous male alumnus is, of course, the Melbourne born actor and singer Jason Donovan. In the show's original run (from 1985) the part of young journalist Scott Robinson was taken by Darius Perkins but on the shows move to Network Ten, Perkins was fired due to problems with his behaviour on set. Donovan (who had previously appeared as a young actor in Australian dramas *Skyways* and *I Can Jump Puddles*) took over the role in 1986 and stayed with the series until 1988.

Donovan became a huge star through his appearances on *Neighbours* during the late 80's, particularly thanks to his on and off screen relationship with co-star Kylie Minogue. The pair were not only married as Scott and Charlene in the series but also real life lovers for a spell.

Donovan won several awards during his time on *Neighbours* including the coveted Silver Logie in 1987 for 'Best New Talent' and in 1988 for 'Most Popular Actor'. He eventually left the show in March 1989 in a storyline involving Scott moving to Brisbane to be re-united with wife Charlene.

Donovan then signed a recording contract with Mushroom Records and, with the help of UK producers Stock, Aitken and Waterman, had his first top Five hit *Nothing Can Divide Us*. His pop career then shot into the stratosphere when he teamed up with screen-mate and fellow Hit Factory artist Kylie Minogue to record the ballad *Especially For You*. The song failed to reach its intended Christmas number One spot (*Mistletoe and Wine* was the festive chart-topper in 1988) but did eventually reach the top of the charts in January 1989 on its way to selling just under a million copies.

Donovan returned to the charts as a solo artist in March 1989 when his follow-up single *Too Many Broken Hearts* went to number One in the second week of release and spent five weeks in the top Two of the charts. Donovan-mania was now well and truly in effect and the fever for his next single was immense. His cover of the old Brian Hyland hit *Sealed With A Kiss* went straight into the Top Forty at number One (a rare feat indeed in the Eighties) and took revenge on Sir Cliff by denying him the number One spot (it was also Cliff's 100th single, *The Best Of Me*). Donovan's album *Ten Good Reasons* (recorded in a mere seven and a half days) also went to the top of the charts meaning Donovan became the first Australian to hold both number One positions simultaneously as well as being the youngest artist ever to enter the charts at number One.

A further single followed – the upbeat *Everyday (I Love You More)* - before Stock, Aitken and Waterman decided to write a festive song for Donovan to challenge for the coveted Christmas number One spot. The song, *When You Come Back To Me* wasn't quite the full Christmas shilling – it did feature festive bells and lyrics about presents and chills in the air, mind – but the video simply featured Donovan wandering about in a strange full-length salmon pink overcoat.

As with the previous year, Donovan was to be denied in his quest for a Christmas number One, although this time he only had himself and Stock, Aitken and Waterman to blame. They had decided to re-record the Band Aid classic *Do They Know It's Christmas?* and the heavily PWL influenced version kept *When You Come Back To Me* off number One. Donovan did however have the consolation however of appearing on the Band Aid II single – indeed he got to sing the iconic Bono line from the original Band Aid single alongside Matt Goss.

When You Come Back To Me, whilst perhaps not as instantly recognisable as some of Stock, Aitken and Waterman's other releases, remains one of their best songs. It would surely have been a certain number One were it not for the intervention of a Kylie and Bros filled version of the nation's second biggest selling record of all time. It also maintained Donovan's position as the number one teen idol of the time. His career continued to flourish with a further number One, *Any Dream Will Do* taken from his West End performance in *Joseph* before his pop career stalled in 1993.

Continuing to work in theatre and television throughout the intervening period, Donovan made a comeback to prime time TV in 2006 on ITV's daft *I'm A Celebrity, Get Me Out Of Here* which preceded a repackaged *Greatest Hits* package and UK tour in the autumn of that year. He has also returned to the West End in the musical version of *Priscilla, Queen Of The Desert*.

74 Altered Images
Happy Birthday

Released: 26 September 1981   **Epic EPC A 1522**
Highest UK Chart Position: #2

Famously, the traditional song *Happy Birthday* is the most recognised song in the English language. Eleven 'birthday' songs have reached the UK charts over the years by artists as diverse as Paul McCartney, Technohead and the Sugarcubes although it is Stevie Wonder's tribute to Martin Luther King Jr that is probably the best known of these. Wonder's 1980 hit *Happy Birthday* was part of a concerted campaign in the USA to make King's birthday a national holiday, an endeavour that was eventually successful as President Ronald Reagan approved the creation of such a day in 1983. The first national King day was celebrated on January 20th 1986 with an open-air concert where Wonder was the headline performer.

The charts had seen twenty-six years of action without a song called *Happy Birthday* ever appearing until the summer of 1981, when Wonder's hit climbed all the way to number Two on the UK charts. Bizarrely (in one of the many strange chart coincidences that seem to occur) the second hit with the title *Happy Birthday* entered the top Forty a fortnight after Wonder's song had dropped out and so, for a brief time, the top seventy-five singles contained two *Happy Birthday* tracks.

Formed in 1979 in Glasgow, Altered Images were a post-punk indie band featuring Michael 'Tich' Anderson, Tony McDaid, Johnny McElhone (later the guitarist in successful pop band Texas) and singer Clare Grogan. Having taken their name from a sleeve design on the Buzzcocks single *Promises*, the band began to gig around the Glasgow area, but it was Grogan's appearance in Bill Forsyth's 1981 film *Gregory's Girl* that helped raise the profile of the group. Grogan starred as Susan alongside John Gordon-Sinclair's Gregory in the successful British coming-of-age drama.

Having sent a demo tape of their work to successful band Siouxsie and the Banshees, Altered Images were invited to support the Banshees at their Glasgow show in June 1980 and then continued to provide support on their *Kaleidoscope* tour. They were spotted on this tour by influential DJ John Peel who offered the band two sessions (in October 1980 and March 1981) and this led to Grogan and the band being signed to CBS Records.

Their first single *Dead Pop Stars* failed to reach the top Forty and also caused controversy as it was released just three months after the death of ex-Beatle John Lennon (although the song was recorded before). Whilst most of their debut album *Happy Birthday* was produced by Banshees guitarist Steve Severin (who kept a more punky, guitar based sound) the record company employed Martin Rushent to produce the title track which had a more poppy feel thanks to Rushent's previous work on projects such as the Human League's seminal album *Dare*.

The more bubble-gum sound of *Happy Birthday* opened the band's top Forty account, eventually matching Stevie Wonder's success by reaching number Two for three weeks in November 1981. A combination of Dave Stewart and Barbara Gaskin's *It's My Party* and the Police's *Every Little Thing She Does Is Magic* prevented the Scottish foursome from securing a number One single.

After a successful headlining tour in 1981 and being voted NME's Best New Group, Altered Images followed up the success of *Happy Birthday* with the first single from their second album *Pinky Blue*. Continuing in a more poppy direction, *I Could Be Happy* became their second top Ten hit when it reached number Seven in January 1982, followed up by *See Those Eyes* which peaked at number Eleven later that spring. *Pinky Blue* was less warmly received by the critics who considered that the band had sold out for commercial gain and it also resulted in founding band member Tich Anderson leaving the band along with guitarist Jim McKinven. With Grogan as the band's main focal point a further top Ten hit followed – the well-known *Don't Talk To Me About Love* - but after the relative failure of third album *Bite* the group disbanded in 1983.

Grogan continued her acting career with a role in the BBC drama *Blott on the Landscape* before taking the part of Dave Lister's would-be love interest Kristine Kochanski in three series' of the cult BBC comedy *Red Dwarf*. She also appeared as Ian Beale's girlfriend Ros Thorne in the BBC soap *Eastenders* between 1997 and 1998.

In 2005 however Altered Images did re-form (in name only) as Grogan performed the band's hits on the UK *Here and Now* concert tour before taking to the road again in 2008 and 2009.

Whilst it may not be the best-remembered *Happy Birthday* track, this three minute pop gem is one of the catchiest and most infectious hits of the early 1980s. It may have belied the band's punk upbringing but there is no denying its rightful place in the annals of pop history.

75   Cliff Richard
I Just Don't Have The Heart

Released: 26 August 1989   **EMI EM 01**
Highest UK Chart Position: #3

Sir Cliff - The Peter Pan of Pop – has long been derided by many but it is easy to forget that the artist formerly known as Harry Webb is the UK's most successful chart act of all time.

Cliff has sold a record twenty one million singles, had fourteen chart-toppers and became the only artist to have a number one single in five different decades, a feat unlikely to be repeated.

It was at the Ivor Novello awards in April 1988 that Sir Cliff met the pop production team of Stock, Aitken and Waterman who were at the dinner to collect an award for penning the Rick Astley hit *Never Gonna Give You Up*. Sitting on the adjacent table, Cliff leaned over and told the producers "if you ever come up with another song like that, give me a call."

They told him that they would love to work with him and came up with the single *I Just Don't Have The Heart*. Pete Waterman admitted that they didn't know Cliff at all well, and that they therefore had to imagine they were Cliff when writing the song. Waterman came up with the title and what followed was a lyric which had Cliff falling in love with a girl and then meeting someone else. As Pete Waterman said, "What would he do? Well, he's such a spiffing chap he wouldn't have they heart to tell her, and that's where it came from."

The single was recorded at the PWL studios in February 1989 with the working title of *Harry* and included a sample of Cliff doing his vocal warm-up exercises. Despite not knowing whose voice it was, and arguing that it was just something he did before all his recording to ensure his voice was in tune, the sample sounded so good it was agreed it would be left in the recording.

Cliff's previous single, the monster Christmas number one *Mistletoe and Wine* was his 99th single release, and there was some conjecture in early 1989 as to what was going to be released as Cliff's milestone 100th single – the first artist to reach that number.

Although a guaranteed chart hit in the making, Cliff decided that *I Just Don't Have The Heart* wasn't a suitable or appropriate choice for his 100th single, and instead he released the somewhat predictable ballad *The Best Of Me*.

Despite being neither memorable or, indeed, much good at all (illustrated by the fact the gold single sleeve just contained the words "Cliff 100th Single", meaning he could have released anything and it would have sold by the thousands) the marketing machine ensured the record went straight into the top Forty at number Two, with teen-idol Jason Donovan's version of Brian Hyland's *Sealed With a Kiss* denying Cliff a fairytale number One record.

With Cliff back in the top Ten, *I Just Don't Want To Have The Heart* was the obvious next single and Cliff took the Stock, Aitken and Waterman penned track to number Three in September 1989.

It would be fair to say that *I Just Don't Have The Heart* is neither Sir Cliff's nor Stock, Aitken and Waterman's finest hour. It's catchy enough, but Cliff's vocals don't sit particularly well on top of the exaggerated female backing singers and, to be fair to the chart legend, the overproduction on this record makes it sound like his dulcet tones have been put through a series of voice alteration machines in order to crush every last element of Cliffness out of it.

Also, and I know this might sound somewhat obvious, *I Just Don't Have The Heart* is really quite repetitive. "Stock, Aitken and Waterman Single in "Quite Repetitive" Shock?" you say? Well, yes, but it wasn't always so. Some of their big hits were brilliantly crafted whilst others sounded like they had one idea for a chorus and knocked the rest of the tune out whilst waiting for Rick Astley to bring the tea and biscuits. I get the distinct impression that this was the latter.

Cliff continued to score major chart hits with the 1990 number One *Saviour's Day*, the 1999 smash hit *The Millennium Prayer* and the 2008 top Three hit *Thank You For A Lifetime*. In 1995 he became the first rock star ever to be knighted and in 2008 Sir Cliff reunited with The Shadows to celebrate their fiftieth anniversary in the music business.

76 Jellybean featuring Elisa Fiorillo
Who Found Who

Released: 28 November 1987   Chrysalis CHS JEL 1
Highest UK Chart Position: #10

One of the pioneers of disco DJ-ing and remixing, Jellybean was born Jonathan Benitez in New York in November 1957 to a Puerto Rican mother. He was nicknamed 'Jellybean' at an early age by his sister Debbie based on his initials 'JB' - she decided the J was for 'jelly' and the B for 'bean' - and the nickname stuck throughout his distinguished career.

Benitez relocated to Manhattan in the late 1970s where he became involved with the disco scene as well as studying marketing and promotions at Bronx Community College. He soon became a popular DJ and worked at famous New York clubs Funhouse, Electric Circus and Studio 54.

In the early 1980's, Jellybean began to start remixing singles and quickly became an in-demand producer and remixer for artists such as Rocker's Revenge and Afrikaa Bambaataa. He was also approached by Stephen Bray from the band The Breakfast Club to undertake a remix of their single and was introduced to Bray's bandmate Madonna who sang on the record. Not only did Benitez and Madonna begin a relationship at this time but the producer also remixed several singles from Madonna's debut solo album including well-known hits *Lucky Star, Borderline* and *Holiday*.

Benitez quickly became dance music's most sought-after remixer and worked with artists as diverse as Barbra Streisand, Billy Joel, Whitney Houston, Hall and Oates, Michael Jackson, Huey Lewis and Paul McCartney.

As well as being a well-respected producer and remixer, Benitez wanted to release records under his own name. Taking on an approach pioneered by 1970s producer Alan Parsons, Benitez did not write the songs, sing on them or - for the most part - play the music. His albums are collections of performances by other musicians and vocalists but that feature his name on the cover. Benitez has defended this tactic against detractors by arguing that as producer and visionary he supplies the creative backdrop on which the albums are based. "Jellybean is the artist - it's a concept" he explained in 1988. "It might be a little abstract for some people."

His first album was 1984's *Wotupski?!!* which contained the US top twenty hit *Sidewalk Talk* featuring none other than Madonna on vocals. His second album was 1987's *Just Visiting This Planet* which again featured a number of different vocalists and musicians. The biggest hit single from this album featured a little known up and coming vocalist who was a label mate at Chrysalis Records.

Elisa Fiorillo had been singing since the age of six and had shot to fame in America by winning the TV talent show *Star Search* aged just sixteen years. Her debut album Elisa Fiorillo was released on Benitez's label and after he heard a demo of one of her tracks in an A&R rep's office, he asked if Fiorillo would sing on the record.

Taking a song written by the British songwriter Paul Gurvitz (who had written a series of R&B hits for the likes of Five Star, Jermaine Stewart and Jody Watley) entitled *Who Found Who?* the song was recorded at Los Angeles' Larrabe Studios. An up-tempo track, *Who Found Who?* tells the story of a relationship going bad where the guy isn't treating the girl as well as he used to - which the girl can't understand considering the guy found and pursued her in the first place. Fiorillo embarked on a huge promotional tour for the record performing at the Montreaux Rock festival in Switzerland and being caught by the paparazzi leaving a London nightclub with Radio One DJ Gary Davies leading to press speculation that the pair were an 'item' when in fact they had met for the first time earlier that day.

The record was an immediate club hit with remixes by Little Louie Vega and it crossed over into mainstream chart success reaching number Ten in the UK in December 1987 and number Sixteen in the US. Jellybean had further hits in the UK - *The Real Thing* featuring Steven Dante, *Just*

A Mirage featuring Adele Bertei and his own *Jingo* all reached the UK top Twenty in 1987/1988.

Elisa Fiorillo went on to have minor solo success in the USA before working as a backing vocalist for acts as diverse as Prince (with whom she co-wrote her hit single *On The Way Up*), Belinda Carlisle and Savage Garden, the latter taking Fiorillo on their *Affirmation* world tour in 2000. Benitez has continued his work as a producer and remixer and was inducted to the American Dance Music Hall of fame in 2005 for his achievements as a DJ and producer.

77 Sheena Easton
9 to 5

Released: 19 July 1980　　　　　　　　EMI5066
Highest UK Chart Position: #3

For anyone who thought that pop singers emerging from TV talent shows started with *Pop Idol* and the *X-Factor*, I'd point you in the direction of the BBC series *The Big Time*. An early reality/documentary series, it ran from 1976 to 1980 and each episode followed a member of the public placed into the limelight as the result of their particular talent.

A young Scottish singer, Sheena Shirley Orr was told about the auditions for a 'pop singer' episode of the show whilst studying at the Royal Scottish Academy of Music and Drama in 1979. Producer Esther Rantzen wanted to make a show charting an unknown singer's rise to fame and fortune and the newly married Sheena Easton was coaxed into auditioning by one of her Academy tutors.

Easton was chosen for the show and despite EMI executives being reluctant to sign an unknown singer, they were impressed by Easton's talent and awarded her a contract. Christopher Neil was chosen as her producer and Dele Arkon as her manager before she spent most of 1980 being trailed by BBC camera crews following her quest to become a star. The footage included her EMI audition, discussions with other singers and the making, recording and promotion of her first single *Modern Girl*.

This first single was released prior to the show being aired and initially only reached a disappointing number Fifty-Six, providing cause for concern to the EMI executives who had been reluctant to sign her in the first place. They needn't have worried however as after *The Big Time: Pop Singer* aired, her second single, the Florrie Palmer penned *9 to 5*, rocketed up the UK singles chart climbing to number Three in August 1980. The popularity of the show was such that *Modern Girl* also re-entered the charts (eventually reaching number Eight) and gave Easton the honour of being the first artist since the 1950s to have two simultaneous top 10 singles.

The song was renamed *Morning Train (9 to 5)* when it was released in America to avoid confusion with the Dolly Parton song of the same name. Whereas Parton's song (and the film from which it was taken) was all about female liberation, the Easton *9 to 5* was the exact opposite - telling the story of a woman who sat at home bored all day waiting for her man to come home from work to provide her 'entertainment'. It also featured a video starring a green-jumpsuited Easton filmed on her bicycle and on the historic steam Bluebell Railway in Sussex.

As well as reaching the top Three in the UK, *Morning Train* was also a huge hit in the USA where it reached number One on the Billboard chart in 1981 and launched her hugely successful American career selling over a million copies. Easton became only the third British female artist (after Petula Clark and Lulu) to have a US number One hit.

Easton's transatlantic success prompted the producers of the new James Bond film to invite her to record the theme tune and her next project was the song *For Your Eyes Only* in which she became the only artist ever to appear in the opening credits of a Bond movie. The Oscar nominated song reached the top Ten on both sides of the Atlantic and earned Easton Grammy nominations. She duly won the Best New Artist Grammy in 1981.

Further success and award recognition followed for the Scottish singer throughout the 1980s, particularly in America. In 1984 she began collaborating with Prince, who contributed to her biggest selling album *A Private Heaven*. Easton also recorded single duets *U Got The Look* and *The Arms Of Orion* with the diminutive singer.

9 to 5 may not be an anthem of female emancipation in the Dolly Parton mould but it's an extremely likeable pop tune. Its lyrical content has made it popular with contemporary television series and it has been featured in shows as varied as *South Park, Not The Nine O'Clock News, Saturday Night Live* and *Seinfeld*. It has also been covered in various languages including Swedish (called *He Commutes Every Day*) and French (*Love Is Like A Cigarette*).

In a 2005 TV documentary it was also revealed that *9 to 5* was a favourite track of legendary British radio DJ John Peel. Amongst his estimated 100,000 strong vinyl collection, he kept a private wooden box containing 143 of his personal favourite records. Peel apparently loved the Easton record so much that he kept two copies of the *9 to 5* single in there.

78 Vanessa Paradis
Joe le Taxi

Released: 13 February 1988   FA Productions POSP 902
Highest UK Chart Position: #3

It wouldn't be unkind to say that the French haven't made the greatest contribution to world pop music over the last quarter of a century or so. Indeed, you'd probably struggle to name more than about two or three French artists that have gone on to achieve any sort of lasting fame in the UK or USA since the 1980's began.

Million sellers during the decade in France included a smattering of classics that were hits all over the world (*Beat It*, *Bette Davis Eyes* and *Woman In Love* to name three), the huge movie themes (*Flashdance* and *Ghostbusters*) as well as quite a number of French language hits.

The top five best sellers of the 1980's, however, don't make the classiest reading. Crooner Herbert Leonard's *Pour Le Plaisir* shifted a colossal one and a half million copies in 1981, and Les Forbans' *Chante* (a cover of the old 1960's Ernie Maresca hit *Shout Shout*) sold over 1.6million units a year later.

Alongside the UK famine relief single (*Do They Know It's Christmas?*) and the American effort (*We Are The World*) stood *Ethiopie*, a number One single by the French group Chanteurs sans Frontieres. This charity effort spent two months at the top of the charts in 1985 on its way to selling nearly one and three quarter million copies. At number Two (and creating *the* dance craze of 1989), French band Kaoma sold around five million copies of their *Lambada* single worldwide popularising this Brazilian dance and reaching number One across Europe (and number Four in the UK).

The best-selling single of the decade in France, though, created a different dance craze entirely – one more associated with school discos and wedding parties than with Rio de Janeiro.

Les Danse Des Canards – better known worldwide as either the *Chicken Dance* or the *Birdie Song* – is an oom-pah song written by Swiss accordionist Werner Thomas in the 1950's. Whilst the Tweets version reached number Two in the UK charts in 1981, the French version (JJ Lionel's *Les Danse des Canards*) sold over three million copies and is the best selling modern-day record in the country's history. Tucked down at number Thirty-Seven on France's 'best selling singles of the 1980s' list, however, is a song by one of the very few artists to achieve success in the UK with a French language single.

Having shot to fame on the TV show *L'ecole des fans* in 1980 (aged just eight) Vanessa Paradis was fourteen when she recorded the Franck Langollf and Etienne Roda-Gil song *Joe le Taxi* for her 1987 album *M&J*. The story of a Parisian taxi driver (the eponymous Joe) and his intimate knowledge of the streets of the capital shot Paradis to international fame and spent eleven weeks at the top of the French chart. Unusually for a foreign language record it was released in the UK where it also achieved success, peaking at number Three in March 1988.

A second French language album and a lucrative deal with perfumier Chanel followed and Paradis also won the Cesar Award for Most Promising Actress for her appearance in the 1990 film *Noce Blanche*.

In 1992 (now aged nineteen) Paradis recorded her first English language album in the US, written and produced by her boyfriend Lenny Kravitz. Her follow-up UK single, the brilliant and Motown-esque *Be My Baby*, reached number Six in 1992.

The French star appeared in several well-received movies in the 1990s, although it wasn't until 2000 that she released another record, *Bliss*, quickly followed by her second live album *Au Zenith*. A voice role as Florence in the French animated version of *The Magic Roundabout* and an appearance in the French children's album and concert *La soldat rose* followed before her 2007 album *Divinidylle* returned Paradis to the top of the French album charts.

Paradis is also well-known as the long term partner of acclaimed Hollywood actor Johnny Depp, who she met on a night out in Paris in 1998. They have two children, Lily-Rose and John and divide their time between their homes in Hollywood, France and, reportedly, the Somerset village of Timsbury.

It is unusual for a French artist to have a successful chart career in the UK – for example the great French legend Johnny Halliday never managed a single top Forty hit. Whilst musically we may have reasons to be annoyed at the French (the *Lambada* and the *Birdie Song* to name but two) I think we can safely thank them for this lovely, gentle piece of continental pop.

79

Charlene
I've Never Been To Me

Released: 15 May 1982   Motown TMG1260
Highest UK Chart Position: #1

There has been many a chart single that fails spectacularly initially, only to become successful (sometimes completely by accident) sometime after its original release. It took Danny Wilson three attempts to get *Mary's Prayer* into the top Forty and Climie Fisher at least two to score a hit with *Love Changes (Everything)*. In the case of this tearful karaoke staple, it took almost seven years for the song to finally become the monster hit Motown believed it would be.

Charlene Marilynn D'Angelo was born in California in 1950 and became the first white female vocalist to be signed by the legendary Motown label when she secured her first recording contract in 1973. Indeed, Motown created a label (Prodigal Records) especially for the singer on which her early recordings were released. Originally credited as Charlene Duncan (after her first marriage) and later as simply Charlene, the singer worked at Motown for several years recording solo records as well as providing vocals for the likes of Diana Ross and Michael Jackson.

It was during her time at Motown when lyricist Ron Miller approached Charlene with a song he had written. Miller had worked at Motown for several years and penned such soul classics as Stevie Wonder's *For Once In My Life* and *Yester-Me, Yester-You, Yesterday* and Diana Ross' *Touch Me In The Morning*. Originally written for a male vocal, Miller had re-written *I've Never Been To Me* from a female perspective specifically for Charlene's voice and invited her to his office to listen to the demo.

I've Never Been To Me is written as a conversation between a woman who has had a varied and exciting life and a 'bored' housewife. The fantasy world outlined by the woman is seen as exciting but ultimately unfulfilling as she has understood too late what the important things in life are (a loving husband, a child etc). The subject matter of the song did end up becoming mildly controversial with campaigners believing the lyrics were 'anti-feminist' in so much as they advocated the necessity of a husband to achieve a happy life.

What Miller hadn't realised as he played a demo version of the song to Charlene was that the lyrics of the record were painfully pertinent to the singers own life. She had married aged seventeen but the relationship had deteriorated into an abusive one by this time and so the lyrics struck a painful personal chord with the singer.

Charlene loved the song and she and Miller recorded a piano vocal demo of the song and played it to Berry Gordy, the legendary president of Motown. Gordy also loved the song and it was arranged that Charlene would record it in early 1976 accompanied by a thirty piece orchestra. On its release in 1977 (although as the old adage went '…records aren't released from Motown, they escape') the song failed to achieve success. With little promotion and a feeling that the song was too syrupy, it only reached number Ninety-Seven on the Billboard charts.

Charlene spent the next three years continuing to record with Motown but by 1980 had become disillusioned with the industry. Feeling that none of her work was of the standard of *I've Never Been To Me* the newly remarried Charlene Oliver left Motown and moved to the UK with her English husband where she started work in a sweet shop run by one of her husband's family.

It was at this time (early 1982) when Charlene received a call out of the blue one night from her mother telling her that an executive at Motown had been trying to find her. Thinking nothing of this the singer received a call a week later from Jay Lasker, president of Motown telling her that her song *I've Never Been To Me* was on the charts in the US. It had been picked up by Scott Shannon, a DJ on a Tampa radio station, and its popularity had spread across the US, propelling the song into the Billboard top Fifty.

A Motown executive quickly arrived in the UK to re-sign the singer who then returned to the US to promote the single. Appearances on US television and radio followed as the record eventually climbed to number Three in America. Its success was replicated around the world as *I've Never Been To Me* reached number One in Canada, Australia and in the UK, where it spent the week of 26 June 1982 atop the British charts.

Whilst Charlene failed to follow up the success of *I've Never Been To Me* (and is so generally considered a 'one hit wonder'), the song itself has lived on becoming both a gay anthem (following its appearance at the beginning of the cult 1994 film *Priscilla, Queen of the Desert)* and a staple with a younger generation thanks to its inclusion in the animated feature *Shrek the Third*.

80 Robin Beck
First Time

Released: 22 October 1988   Mercury MER270
Highest UK Chart Position: #1

There are many trained artists and musicians working in the industry but occasionally there is an instance of a Cinderella story where a singer with no vocal training strikes it lucky and goes on to have a giant Number One song.

Robin Beck is one such example. Born in Brooklyn, New York, Beck moved to Daytona Beach with her parents at a young age. Desperate to have a career as a singer, she was discovered by local musician Alex London who secured Beck her first professional job. Having toured with the band Deep South, she landed her first recording contract in the late 1970s and released the album *Sweet Talk*.

Living back in New York, Beck worked on various projects including the Broadway musical *Got To Go Disco*. Her long term boyfriend at the time, Will Lee, had contacts in the advertising jingle business and introduced Robin to a number of top executives and producers in the jingle industry. Jingle singers tended to be good readers of music but Beck used her recordings from her earlier career as a 'bridge' to introduce her as a different style of vocalist – more soulful and interpretive. Several firms were approached with Beck's recordings and she began a career as a professional jingle singer.

It was through this work that Beck was introduced to Tom Anthony, Gavin Spencer and Terry Boyle. The three writers wanted a rock vocalist for their new project and needed an 'artist' rather than a formulaic jingle singer. They had come up with an idea and song to be pitched to the Coca-Cola company and wanted Beck to record the vocals.

Turning up at the studio Beck heard the thirty-odd second jingle they had created and recorded a demo for the pitch. Coca-Cola loved the record and used it extensively in their well-known *Real Thing* advertisements in the UK and Europe in 1988.

Several weeks later Beck received a call from the writers asking her if she could come in and record a longer version of the song that had been requested for UK usage. Needing to head off to her paid day job, Beck went into the studio and quickly re-recorded a longer version of the track with some amended lyrics (the 'first time' replaced the Coca-Cola 'real thing' branding).

That was the last Beck had heard of the song until she received a phone call late one night several months later. A British voice was on the other end of the line, and Beck initially thought it was an English musician friend of hers playing a prank. In fact the caller was John Watson, head of Phonogram Records in the UK and when he finally convinced Beck who he was, he told her that her record *First Time* had reached number One in the UK and that she was needed to record that week's *Top Of The Pops* programme.

Having no knowledge that the record had even been released, Beck was convinced it was a wind-up until an entourage was arranged for her and she was flown to the UK to appear on the BBC flagship music show. *First Time* had reached number One on its sixth week on the chart and remained there for three weeks, largely on the back of its usage in the Coca-Cola commercial. The single cover didn't feature Beck's image, rather a still from the Coke advert that the song appeared in.

A whirlwind few weeks followed for Beck who made countless appearances throughout Europe as the record reached the top Ten across the continent, reaching number One in Austria, the Netherlands, Ireland, Norway, Germany and Switzerland. It was also a steep learning curve for Beck as having only ever appeared on television as the voice of a commercial, the singer had to also get used to performing live on TV. The sudden and unexpected success of the single in Europe had forced the singer into celebrity she really wasn't expecting or prepared for.

Beck is considered a 'one hit wonder' in most countries as she failed to follow-up the huge success for *First Time*. She did have a further top Ten hit in Germany with the Diane Warren song *Save Up All Your Tears* (later a hit for Cher) and despite a number of rock luminaries contributing to her album *Trouble or Nothin'* the record was not a widespread success. In 2006, Beck teamed up with the Swedish dance act Sunblock to re-record speeded-up vocals for their dance single *First Time* and following a further appearance on *Top Of The Pops* (eighteen years after the first) the single reached number Nine in the UK charts.

81

Kenny Loggins
Footloose

Released: 28 April 1984   CBS A 4101
Highest UK Chart Position: #6

Earworm: n : a song or tune that gets stuck in one's mind and repeats as if on a tape

A good friend of mine has spent the last couple of years recording, every week, a list of ten records that he (or a colleague or friend) have had stuck in their head at some time in the preceding seven days. You know the sort of thing - the songs you find yourself inexplicably humming on the bus on your way to work, or that you spend a day trying to shake after being the last thing you heard before you got out of the car in the morning.

The general term for these songs is an 'earworm' (from the German word 'ohrwurm') and it is used to describe any song (or portion of music) that becomes stuck in a person's head. A scientific study by James Kellaris at the University of Cincinnati found that music characterized by repetitiveness, simplicity and incongruity with listener's expectations is most likely to become stuck and, whilst differing people have varying susceptibility to earworms, almost everyone has been 'infected' at some point.

Having spent a couple of years reading a hundred or so 'earworm' lists, I'd say I was a reasonable authority on the concept, at least from a practical perspective. Over that time there have been songs which appear time and time again in people's lists (the theme from the 80s fruit drink commercials for Um Bongo and Kia-Ora feature disproportionately heavily). Current chart hits that are more likely to be heard on the radio at any given time are also pretty obviously a regular feature, but as we are considering the 1980s there is one song from that decade that gets lodged in the subconscious more than any other.

Footloose by Kenny Loggins is a weapons grade, nuclear powered behemoth of an earworm.

Clearly, there were catchier and more annoying records in the decade. There were also lots of better records, more repetitive records and records with dafter lyrics. There were louder, quieter, more anthemic and easier to remember records. However, our research (such as it is) has found that *Footloose* is (by a country mile) the 80's record most likely to become firmly embedded in your brain and stay there.

Kenneth Clark Loggins' most recognisable and biggest hit, *Footloose* was the title track from the 1984 motion picture of the same name. It was written in a hotel room in Lake Tahoe, Nevada during Loggins' recuperation from broken ribs and 'describes a young man who can't stop dancing and encourages others to do the same'.

The film, featuring a young Kevin Bacon, the film tells the story of Ren McCormack, a teenager who has moved to a small town where the town government has banned rock music and dancing. Wanting to stage a school prom, the kids have to find a way of circumventing the ban and bringing music and dance back to the town. Clips from the film feature heavily in the video (including quite a lot of extremely enthusiastic 80s dance moves, and an awful lot of leg warmers.)

The film soundtrack CD sold nine million copies in the USA and the single *Footloose* spent three weeks at number One. It fared less well in the UK although it did peak at number Six in May 1984. The song was also nominated for an Academy Award in 1985 but lost out to Stevie Wonder's *I Just Called To Say I Love You*.

So, then, why is this song such a severe earworm? It fits some of the scientist's definitions, I guess - it is repetitive and has a pretty straightforward structure. I've found, though, that it's the twangy introduction that's as likely to get stuck in my brain as the 'cut loose/footloose' chorus. It's not like it is a record you hear on the radio regularly or a film that gets much TV exposure and so, I suppose, it's just one of those songs that has something in its DNA that means it is destined to infect people like the aural version of influenza.

Remember, though, that earworms may not have a single cause. As the scientific study found "…an earworm may be like a stomach ache, for which there are many different possible causes. For example, just as overeating, excess acid, viral infection, spicy foods late at night, or emotional upset may cause the phenomenon people describe as a stomach ache, there may be many different causes of earworm episodes, such as stress, fatigue, over-exposure to music, hearing only half of a song before getting out of your car, or not being able to remember part of a song that surfaces in memory."

For reference, *Footloose* did not make it into Kellaris' 'top Ten' earworms list. How it managed to be omitted in favour of *The Lion Sleeps Tonight*, I will never know.

82

Wham
Young Guns (Go For It)
Released: 16 October 1982   Innervision IVL A2766
Highest UK Chart Position: #3

One of the 1980s most famous vocal artists and responsible for some of the decade's most recognisable pop records, there are not many George Michael recordings which could be considered 'forgotten'. Still, before Wham! were a worldwide sensation and George Michael the most talked about man in pop music, there were a few great records which continue to slip under the radar.

Georgios Panayiotou and Andrew Ridgeley met whilst students at Bushey Mead School in north London, forming their first band The Executive in 1979. They became Wham! in 1981 ('wham' being the sound they believed they made when they performed together), signing their first deal with Innervision Records.

The duo's debut single *Wham Rap* was one of the first by a British group to feature rapping, although it failed to chart (in part, thanks to Radio 1 refusing to playlist the song as the double A side mix contained a profanity). It would be their follow-up single, the George Michael penned *Young Guns (Go For It)* which would give the pair their first chart success.

Many of the band's initial releases displayed considerable political and social commentary even though they appeared to be frothy dance records and *Young Guns* was no exception. Michael wrote the lyrics from the point of a view of a teenager imploring his friend not to become too committed to a girl and to enjoy his teenage single life. It also featured a middle eight in which the girl tried to retaliate by getting her boyfriend to 'ditch' his best friend.

On release, the single was hovering just outside the UK top Forty when the pair received a call which would change their fortunes. The BBC's flagship music show *Top of the Pops* had an unexpected space in their line-up due to another artist pulling out of recording and as Wham!'s single was the climber nearest to the top Forty (it was number forty-two) they were invited to appear on the show.

The appearance is credited with propelling the pair into the public spotlight. Michael played the role of the imploring friend whilst Ridgeley and Shirlie Holliman (later of Pepsi and Shirlie who remained Wham!'s backing vocalists after the departure of previous singer Dee C Lee) 'played' the boyfriend and girlfriend. With a claustrophobic atmosphere that gave the appearance a nightclub-esque feel, the song instantly charted eventually peaking at number Three in December 1982 spending seventeen weeks on the chart.

Over the subsequent year the duo became one of the UK's biggest pop acts as their mixture of cutting-edge dance sound and powerful lyrics catapulted follow-up singles *Wham Rap!, Bad Boys* and *Club Tropicana* into the top Ten. Their debut album *Fantastic* reached number One on the UK album chart, although this prompted difficulties with their Innervision contract. Whilst a court battle raged over royalties the label released a further single against the wishes of the band – the *Club Fantastic Megamix* - which Ridgeley and Michael urged fans not to buy. Eventually, the pair signed to CBS ahead of the release of their second album.

Whilst Michael may have been the main songwriter and instrumentalist, Ridgeley is credited with defining the band's image, which was crucial to the success of their second album *Make It Big*. Sparking a huge pop revival, the duo's next single *Wake Me Up Before You Go-Go* saw them adopt a more adult 'sex symbol' image rather than remaining as the spokespeople for the teenage generation. The song was a huge international number One hit and remains one of the most recognisable pop records from the 1980s.

After a bizarre interlude in which Michael released his first solo single at the peak of the band's popularity (the timeless and multi-million selling *Careless Whisper*) the band continued their huge success with number One hits *Freedom* and *The Edge of Heaven* as well as the biggest-selling UK single never to top the charts – 1984's festive classic *Last Christmas*. After making history as the first Western band to tour China, Wham split on 28 June 1986 after a spectacular concert at Wembley Stadium entitled *The Final*.

Whilst Ridgeley's solo career never took off, Michael went on to become one of the biggest selling male vocalists of the last quarter century. Hits including *A Different Corner*, *Faith*, *Outside* and *Jesus To A Child* and number One duets with Aretha Franklin, Elton John and Queen sustained Michael's success, even in light of some unusual and adverse publicity.

It is easy to forget that before the slick, soulful pop of his later career that Michael began as the mouthpiece of a disaffected generation. It is also important not to understate Ridgeley's influence on the direction of the band and the pair's early work was spikier and more cutting edge than their better remembered mid 80s output. *Young Guns (Go For It)* is a terrific song and in many ways a base point from which much of the later 80s pop developed.

83   Go West
We Close Our Eyes

Released: 23 February 1985   Chrysalis CHS2850
Highest UK Chart Position: #5

Peter Cox and Richard Drummie met in Twickenham, London and formed their band Go West in 1982. They took a surprisingly common route into the industry when they were signed initially on a publishing, songwriting contract with ATV Music and during that time the pair wrote a number of songs and were re-signed in 1983 and 1984.

Vocalist Cox had been inspired by the likes of Free and Paul Rodgers and was introduced to the West Coast American sound (artists such as the Doobie Brothers) by bandmate Drummie. Having hired a studio to record some demos, the duo were eventually signed to Chrysalis Records in 1984 mainly on the strength of what the label considered the knockout single. (Interestingly, this wasn't the band's first release and biggest hit, but their later single *Call Me*.)

Whilst recording their debut album *Go West*, the pair came up with a slow song entitled *I Need Your Love*. The pair were never happy with the title however and despite the production team The Quick hating the idea of changing the lyrics, changed they were and the record became *We Close Our Eyes*.

Originally a slow, guitar based record, ATV wanted *We Close Our Eyes* for soul artist Phil Bailey's album (which was being produced at the time by collaborator and general music legend Phil Collins). Go West were keen to record the song themselves however and with the help of producer Gary Stevenson the record took shape. The first thing Stevenson did was to speed up the track (as he also did with *Call Me*) and keyboard programmer Dave West gave the song its brilliant and memorable synthesizer solo.

Chrysalis invited Cox and Drummie to choose which song they wanted to release as their debut single and whilst their record deal had been on the strength of *Call Me*, the pair chose *We Close Our Eyes*. Chrysalis spared no expense with the video for the single, bringing in the fantastically successful and respected team of Kevin Godley and Lol Creme to oversee the project. The result was one of the most famous videos of the era and, in the early days of MTV, it helped get the song valuable airplay.

Turning up for the recording, Cox didn't have any idea of the content of the video. He was quickly dressed in a classic Marlon Brando 'mechanic' image, and, with absolutely no prior warning, was asked to spend a day filming in a white vest and jeans working out with a giant wrench. It was a hot and tiring day, and the end result shows the fine figure of Cox singing the song whilst sweatily swinging a huge metal spanner. Drummie had the less energetic but odder task of parrying attacking wooden artist's mannequins with the end of his electric guitar. Odd it may have been, but striking it was also (and ended up costing more than the recording of the whole album.)

We Close Our Eyes was released in February 1985 and eventually peaked at number Five, spending fourteen weeks on the chart. It also made the Billboard top Fifty as well as being a number One single in New Zealand. The band became instant stars, and their 'modern Motown' sound was well-received, leading to further hit singles *Call Me* and *Don't Look Down* from their self-titled debut album, which sold in excess of one and a half million copies. The duo also won the BPI Award for Best New Act in 1986.

Whilst they had always imagined themselves as a rock band, their success was largely based on the ability of their songs to be played in dance clubs, particularly in the USA. This was far from what the band expected and perhaps the reason why their less synthesized subsequent recordings were slightly less successful. After further chart hits with the likes of *Goodbye Girl*, the duo wrote the song *One Way Street* for the film *Rocky IV* (at the request of Sylvester Stallone) before returning to the charts in

1990 with the terrific *King Of Wishful Thinking* from the soundtrack of the smash Richard Gere and Julia Roberts film *Pretty Woman*.

Some minor hits followed but the duo's fame diminished until Peter Cox's appearance on the 2003 ITV show *Reborn in the USA*. The show became the perfect showcase for Cox's significant vocal talents and only a blunder in the semi-final (he forgot the lyrics to the Norah Jones record *Don't Know Why*) cost Cox the chance of winning the series. He was firmly back in the public eye, however, and regular tours in the UK (often with friend and fellow 80's star Tony Hadley) have followed since.

84 George Harrison
Got My Mind Set On You

Released: 24 October 1987 **Dark Horse W8178**
Highest UK Chart Position: #2

Still the most famous band in the history of popular music, it is a little known fact that the Beatles actually had four top Forty hits in the 1980s, a full decade after their split. The biggest of these was a re-release of their debut single *Love Me Do* which reached number Four in the UK in 1982 and their 'movie medley' single also reached the top Ten that year.

The various constituent parts of the band (with the exception of Ringo Starr who was absent from the UK charts between 1974 and 1992) also had hits in the Eighties with varying degrees of success. Paul McCartney was a solo artist by the turn of the decade and scored a number of huge hits in the UK with the likes of *No More Lonely Nights*, *Coming Up*, *Once Upon A Long Ago* and his 1983 chart-topper *Pipes of Peace*. He also teamed up with artists as diverse as Stevie Wonder (*Ebony and Ivory*), Michael Jackson (*Say, Say, Say* and *The Girl Is Mine*), The Christians, Gerry Marsden and Holly Johnson (*Ferry Cross The Mersey*) and, of course, the Frog Chorus (*We All Stand Together*).

John Winston Lennon had the biggest chart success of any of the former Beatles in the 1980s but for all the wrong reasons. His 1980 single *(Just Like) Starting Over* had peaked at number Eight and was heading down the UK charts when news broke in New York of his untimely death having been shot four times in the back outside the city's Dakota building. Whilst Mark Chapman was being held in custody for the singer's murder, *Starting Over* shot to the top of the UK charts. Although the single was knocked off the top of the charts (somewhat unbelievably by the St Winifred's School Choir's *There's No-One Quite Like Grandma*) the re-release of Lennon's 1976 classic *Imagine* gave the singer a second posthumous number One single. His third chart-topper followed immediately as

Woman spent a fortnight at the top of the UK charts and in March 1981 a cover of the Lennon song *Jealous Guy* (recorded as a tribute to the singer) became Roxy Music's only UK number One hit.

Whilst Lennon and McCartney were spending many weeks in the upper echelons of the UK charts, the same success was not being enjoyed by the third ex-Beatle. Guitarist George Harrison was the first of the band to achieve a number One single when his song *My Sweet Lord* topped the charts for five weeks in early 1971 (it returned to number One after news of Harrison's death in January 2002), but his chart action in the 1980s was initially limited to his number Thirteen hit *All Those Years Ago* in 1981. His 1982 album *Gone Troppo* was met with general indifference and as a result Harrison disappeared from the music scene for five years.

When he returned in 1988 it was with the acclaimed album *Cloud Nine*, which was co-produced by the Electric Light Orchestra's Jeff Lynne. Recorded at Harrison's own Friar Park studio, the album featured a number of Harrison's longstanding musical friends, including the likes of Ringo Starr, Eric Clapton, Elton John and Lynne himself. The debut single from the album was chosen as a cover of an obscure 1962 song *Got My Mind Set On You*, written by little known American Rudy Clark.

Clark was an ex-New York postman who wrote a number of songs in the 1960s and 1970s for the likes of the Young Rascals, the Olympics and Betty Everett. As well as *Got My Mind Set On You* which was a minor hit for vocalist James Ray in 1962, Clark wrote Everett's 1964 hit *The Shoop Shoop Song (It's In His Kiss)* which became a huge worldwide hit for the actress Cher in 1991.

Harrison's version of the song was a surprise smash, reaching number One in the USA and number Two in the UK charts. The video featured Harrison sitting in a study with random knick-knacks moving and dancing to the song and the singer performing an athletic back-flip from his chair as part of a dance routine. It was a big hit on MTV and was nominated for three Video Music Awards.

Harrison followed up the success of *Got My Mind Set On You* with the Beatles tribute *When We Was Fab*, before deciding to team up with Lynne and old friends Bob Dylan, Roy Orbison and Tom Petty to form the Travelling Wilburys.

Whilst not an original single (is is believed Harrison wanted the Beatles to record *Got My Mind Set On You* in the early days), it firmly re-established Harrison as a credible artist after many years in the wilderness. Whilst further chart success eluded Harrison until his posthumous number One in 2001, *Got My Mind Set On You* is a brilliant, catchy pop single. If imitation is the sincerest form of flattery, Weird Al Yankovic's parody *(This Song's Just) Six Words Long* must be the ultimate compliment.

85 Sonia
You'll Never Stop Me Loving You

Released: 24 June 1989 **Chrysalis CHS3385**
Highest UK Chart Position: #1

From 1989 to 1992, celebrities as varied as Chris Eubank and Kenny Everett were subjected to an automated personal examination on the Channel 4 series *Star Test*. The idea of the show was that a celebrity would sit on a chair in a large room and select categories ('sweet and sour', 'power and glory', 'health and happiness' and the like) before picking numbers, behind which were hidden random personal questions. Delivered by a slightly snooty female computer, the guests were effectively interviewed by the machine before the show ended with the celebrity choosing from a selection of adjectives to describe themselves.

Of course, the format of *Star Test* provided a perfect backdrop for parody and no-one took better advantage of this than the much loved British comedy double act of Dawn French and Jennifer Saunders. The pair used the *Star Test* format often in their early series to impersonate pop stars, actors and television personalities (often utterly convincingly) as it allowed them to both exaggerate elements of the celebrity's personality and to spoof them doing their actual 'job'.

The most famous of these sketches featured Dawn French as the young Liverpudlian starlet, Sonia Evans.

Born in Skelmersdale in February 1971, Evans spent much of her childhood studying at drama school and her first taste of fame came through appearances in Channel Four soap opera *Brookside* and as Billy Boswell's girlfriend in the popular TV sitcom *Bread*. During that period, record svengali Pete Waterman presented a weekly radio broadcast from Evans' home city of Liverpool and was badgered outside the studio one weekend by the singer to listen to her demo tape. Waterman called Sonia's bluff and asked her to sing live on his show and after this impromptu audition she was signed to a recording contract with Simon Cowell's BMG.

Aged just eighteen, Sonia (Waterman had the idea to just use the singer's first name) recorded her debut single with the Hit Factory team, mixed by Phil Harding. *You'll Never Stop Me Loving You*, a typically up-tempo Stock, Aitken and Waterman creation reached number One in the UK in just its fifth week of release, spending two weeks at the top of the charts.

With her curly red hair, and chatty, effervescent Scouse demeanour, it was easy to paint the singer as a naïve, bland singer from the Hit Factory production line. It was precisely this image that Dawn French exaggerated in her parody as she portrayed Evans in a giggly Scouse stereotype with a permanent beaming smile. ('What's your favourite drink?' 'The Mersey!') Evans was initially upset by the sketch, but had acknowledged the flattery of the imitation by the time French hid from her at a charity dinner some years later.

Having sold over three hundred and fifty thousand copies of *You'll Never Stop Me Loving You* and becoming the youngest Briton to have a number one hit since Mary Hopkin over two decades earlier, the flame-haired Liverpudlian followed up this success with further top twenty singles *Can't Forget You* and *Listen To Your Heart*. She also made the top Twenty alongside fellow PWL artists Big Fun on their 1990 Childline charity single *You've Got A Friend* as well as spending Christmas 1989 as Number One as part of Band Aid II's remake of *Do They Know It's Christmas?* Her debut album *Everybody Knows* also reached the top ten selling half a million copies.

The singer's relationship with Stock, Aitken and Waterman deteriorated quickly, however, and Evans left the label after just one album. Her chart success continued, with the hits *Only Fools (Never Fall In Love)* and *Be Young, Be Foolish, Be Happy*, although her self-titled second album was only a minor hit.

Sonia returned to the charts in 1993 after she was chosen to represent the UK in the 1993 Eurovision Song Contest. Having performed eight songs in the Song for Europe national final, the song *Better The Devil You Know* was chosen by the UK public and Evans finished a narrow second in the Contest proper, pipped to the title by the Irish hosts – Niamh Kavanagh's *In Your Eyes* was triumphant on the night. *Better The Devil....* would, however be Sonia's last top Forty hit.

You'll Never Stop Me Loving You capped a stunning summer for Stock, Aitken and Waterman, becoming the sixth number One single they had been involved with in 1989 and their penultimate number One of the 1980's. Whilst Sonia was a talented singer (her later West End performances showed this), her material was the aural equivalent of the character Dawn French so carefully parodied – frothy, effervescent and ultimately difficult to dislike.

86 Stefan Dennis
Don't It Make You Feel Good

Released: 6 May 1989 Sublime LIME 105
Highest UK Chart Position: #16

The path from *Neighbours* to *Top Of The Pops* in the heyday of the Australian soap was a well-trodden one, as Antipodean star after Antipodean star followed the trail blazed by diminutive pop icon Kylie Minogue. Her on and off-screen boyfriend Jason Donovan followed her into the UK charts, as did her on-screen brother Henry (Craig Maclachlan and Check 1-2's *Mona* reached number Two in 1990). Delta Goodrem, Gail and Gillian Blakeney (the Alessi Twins), Natalie Imbruglia, Alan Fletcher (Dr Karl Kennedy) and Holly Valance are amongst the other *Neighbours* alumni to have released singles in the UK (with varying degrees of success). Even Madge and Harold made an assault on the charts with their 1989 festive effort *An Old Fashioned Christmas* which (some would say 'thankfully') failed to chart.

One man, though - both an ex and current *Neighbours* star - has a special place in the heart of Eighties pop fans with a record that achieved a cult status the other Ramsey Street crooners can only dream of.

Born in October 1958 in the Victoria town of Tawonga, Stefan Dennis moved to Queensland with his family at an early age and began performing on stage well before his teens. He became involved with the amateur theatre in Queensland at the age of eleven, appearing for the first time in a production of the musical *Oliver!* After qualifying as a chef, Dennis moved to Melbourne where he gained acting experience whilst working in the city's restaurants.

His first TV roles were bit parts in popular Australian shows including *The Sullivans* and *Cop Shop* before this work developed into guest roles on numerous drama series such as *The Young Doctors*, *Skyways* and alongside Kylie and Jason as Terry in *The Henderson Kids*. Whilst waiting for a role in a feature film, Dennis' agent encouraged the actor to attend an audition for a new Channel Seven drama series *Neighbours*. Dennis originally auditioned for the role of Shane Ramsay (ultimately played by Peter O'Brien) but was instead offered the role of Paul, the eldest of the Robinson family children.

Dennis appeared in the very first episode of *Neighbours*, which aired in Australia in March 1985 and in the UK in October 1986. He stayed in the soap as ruthless businessman Paul Robinson (the manager of the Lasseters complex) for seven years featuring in storylines as bizarre as being shot by his first wife Terry, faking a wedding to Gail to secure a business deal with Mr Udagawa and having an affair with each of a pair of twins before leaving the show in 1992 when his character was imprisoned for fraud. Dennis was the third longest running cast member at the time of his departure and has appeared in over two thousand episodes of the show.

It was during the major success of *Neighbours* in the UK in the late 1980s that Dennis decided to pursue a sideline music career. In the spring of 1989 his debut single *Don't It Make You Feel Good* was released on an unsuspecting British public accompanied by a now cult video featuring Dennis attired in a leather jacket alongside some strange mannequin brides.

The song itself was a rock-tinged affair punctuated with a driving synthesised beat and a screaming electric guitar solo and featured Dennis', growly vocals. *Don't It Make You Feel Good* spent seven weeks in the UK Top Forty peaking at number Sixteen in May 1989.

Dennis followed up *Don't It Make You Feel Good* with a further single *This Love Affair* in October 1989 but this spent two weeks in the lower reaches of the top Seventy Five making him, effectively, a 'one hit wonder'.

Dennis moved to the UK in 1992 after leaving *Neighbours* and appeared in many stage productions including the *Royal Variety Performance* and a national tour of the musical *Blood Brothers*. He also appeared in a number of popular UK TV shows, including *Casualty*, *River City* and the Sky One football drama *Dream Team*. In 2004 he returned to *Neighbours*, initially on a short-term contract for the twentieth anniversary celebrations but this was quickly extended and Paul Robinson remains the only current *Neighbours* character to have appeared in the show's first episode. Dennis' recent storylines have included an air crash, another wedding and having his leg amputated after a fall from a cliff.

Despite Dennis being much better known for his two long stints in *Neighbours*, his contribution to the pop music legacy of the Eighties – albeit on something of a cult basis – should not be ignored. Whilst on the face of it he might not be the finest vocalist to grace the charts, *Don't It Make You Feel Good* is a great, classic slice of 1980s nostalgia and, in truth, not a bad record.

87 Bucks Fizz
The Land Of Make Believe

Released: 28 November 1981　　　RCA163
Highest UK Chart Position: #1

There haven't been many Eurovision winners who have gone on to have a long and successful career in the music business. Sure, some have had a hit or two (primarily with their winning song), but sustaining a long-term career after Eurovision success has proved elusive for most.

The United Kingdom's penultimate winners (at the time of writing, and, if recent results and voting patterns are anything to go by, 'forever') did, however, manage to sustain their success. They scored a number of further chart hits over the remainder of the decade and are still going today.

In early 1981, writers Nichola Martin and Andy Hill went in search of singers for a new four piece vocal band. Following the successful 'two girl, two boy' Euro-pop formula made famous by seventies legends Abba, four blond singers were recruited - Bobby Gee and Mike Nolan and girls Jay Aston and Cheryl Baker. The intention was to enter the group in the UK's *Song for Europe* competition to determine who would represent the United Kingdom at the 26th Eurovision in Dublin.

On 11th March 1981, the virtually unknown band Bucks Fizz beat seven other artists with their ninety-seven point tally to win the honour of representing the UK in the Contest proper. Less than four weeks later in one of the closest finishes in the history of the Eurovision, the UK entry won the Contest by a mere four points. Bucks Fizz's performance of *Making Your Mind Up* that night has become part of competition folklore and the 'skirt ripping' dance routine remains one of the iconic memories of the Eurovision and was voted the 'best Eurovision moment' in a BBC poll in 2005.

Making Your Mind Up sold almost five million copies worldwide and was a smash hit single across the globe. However, unlike many a Eurovision winner, Bucks Fizz successfully followed up their wining sing with the further top twenty hits *One Of Those Nights* and *Piece of the Action*.

In the autumn of 1981 at Mayfair Studios in London, the band was given a further song to record by their production company. Ex King-Crimson member Pete Sinfield had come up with some lyrics of what appeared to be a sugar-coated fairytale song called *The Land Of Make Believe*. Band founder Andy Hill wrote the music.

Sinfield had already had writing success with bands like Crimson and Roxy Music as well as writing the Greg Lake festive standard *I Believe In Father Christmas*. Whilst *Land of Make Believe* was apparently in the same festive, Christmassy vein, the lyrics for the Bucks Fizz song are actually intended as an anti-Thatcher message. The song was a subtle attack on the Iron Lady and her policy at the time, a fact that went largely unnoticed amongst the fairytale image the song portrayed. The video (costing an unprecedented £50,000, a fortune in 1981) featured a parody of many childhood stories including Cinderella, The Wizard Of Oz and the Lion, the Witch and the Wardrobe and these images only served to reinforce this interpretation.

The general festive sound of the record led RCA to release the record in November 1981 with the intention of having a tilt at that year's Christmas number One. Despite climbing quickly, the song only reached number Five at Christmas and had to wait a further three weeks before reaching number One, dislodging what is generally regarded as one of the decade's finest records, the Human League's *Don't You Want Me*.

The Land Of Make Believe's climb to number One established Bucks Fizz as a credible band and they followed it up with a string of other hits including a further number One (*My Camera Never Lies*) and further Eighties smashes including *Now Those Days Are Gone*, *New Beginning* and *If You Can't Stand The Heat* over the next seven years.

Since 1989, membership of the band has been something of a revolving door with a total of fifteen band members having been part of Bucks Fizz since 1981 (including, for a spell, Dollar frontman David van Day). Whilst *Making Your Mind Up* remains Bucks Fizz's biggest selling single, *The Land of Make Believe* remains their longest chart hit, spending four months on the hit parade. Pete Sinfield went on to write Celine Dion's mammoth chart-topper *Think Twice*, a song he described as his 'lottery win'.

The Land Of Make Believe made a comeback in 2002, when CITV 'band' allSTARS* took a faster, euro-pop version of the song to number Nine in the singles charts – the group's biggest hit.

88   Dollar
Mirror, Mirror (Mon Amour)

Released: 14 November 1981   **WEA BUCK2**
Highest UK Chart Position: #4

There are few bands that have had more ups and downs over their thirty year careers than the ex-cabaret act Dollar. Engagements, label changes, hits, misses, break-ups, drugs, burgers, reformations, the Australian outback and a court case have all contrived to shape the careers of Thereza Bazar and David van Day since they first encountered each other in 1974.

Bazar and van Day first met aged seventeen when they were both successful at the auditions for the club act Guys'n'Dolls. After eighteen months of cabaret performances the pair decided that they wanted to pursue a more contemporary music career and so left Guys'n'Dolls and eventually signed a contract with French label Carrere Records.

Their first two singles. *Shooting Star* and *Who Were You With In The Moonlight?* both reached number Fourteen in the UK charts before singing duties were handed to Bazar for their third single *Love's Gotta Hold On Me* which became one of their biggest hits, reaching number Four in September 1979.

The duo moved to WEA Records in 1980 and penned all the songs for their second album. *The Paris Collection* was a commercial failure however and none of the three singles reached the UK top Forty. In an attempt to generate record sales, the pair announced their engagement at a lavish party at London's Savoy hotel, a move later acknowledged by both singers as a publicity stunt.

In 1981 Bazar approached the British producer Trevor Horn to work with the duo on their third album. This collaboration was immediately successful and returned the pair to the charts when *Hand Held In Black And White* reached the top Twenty in the summer of 1981. It was to be the follow-up single, *Mirror Mirror*, also co-written and produced by Horn that would give Dollar their biggest hit, however. The up-tempo song (subtitled *Mon Amour*) reached number Four in January 1982 and spent seventeen weeks on the UK charts.

The Horn collaboration represented the peak of the duo's career with further hits *Videotheque* and *Give Me Back My Heart* also reaching the top Twenty. This work brought Horn to the attention of other bands and he went on to become one of the 1980s most successful producers, working with the likes of ABC and Frankie Goes To Hollywood.

Tensions within Dollar had also reached breaking point by this time and the pair spent the next three years pursuing unsuccessful solo projects. Van Day's solo single *Young Americans Talking* failed to make the top Forty, as did Bazar's singles and solo album *The Big Kiss*.

In late 1985 the pair decided to reform Dollar and in August 1986 they released the first Dollar record in almost four years. The Arista singles *We Walked in Love* and *Haven't We Said Goodbye Before* both failed to chart and it was only on their move to London Records in 1987 that the duo returned to the top Forty. Their cover of the little known Erasure track *O L'Amour* peaked at number Seven in February 1988 but was to be their last chart success and in late 1988 Dollar disbanded again.

Van Day tried unsuccessfully to relaunch a solo career and in the 1990s he joined a rival Bucks Fizz band with original member Mike Nolan. This venture resulted in a High Court appearance for Van Day when another original Bucks Fizz member, Bobby G, took Van Day to court over usage of the Bucks Fizz name. In an out-of-court settlement, it was resolved that Van Day would tour under the name 'David Van Day's Bucks Fizz Show'.

It was also revealed at this time that van Day was working in a burger van in his home town of Brighton whilst also travelling the UK in his Bucks Fizz show. Bazar, meanwhile, had turned her back on the music industry, moving to Australia where she married a barrister.

The band reformed once more in 2002 for the ITV prime-time show *Reborn In The USA*, but were voted off the show in the first week. The publicity helped them secure a place on the nostalgia *Here and Now* 80s tour and they performed alongside the Pet Shop Boys and ABC at Wembley Arena in 2004 in a show celebrating the work of Trevor Horn.

Van Day returned to reality television in 2008 when finishing fourth in the ITV show *I'm A Celebrity…Get Me Out Of Here*, an appearance which incensed his former band partner who had no idea he was starring on the show in her native Australia. Whilst Bazar vowed never to work with him again after his appearance, the pair have since put aside their differences and so perhaps a fourth incarnation of Dollar is on the cards….?

89 Irene Cara
Flashdance....What A Feeling

Released: 4 June 1983   Casablanca CAN 1016
Highest UK Chart Position: #2

Responsible for some of the 80's and early 90's biggest and most successful action movies, it is a little known fact that Don Simpson and Jerry Bruckheimer first teamed up on a 1983 low budget movie about an eighteen year old steel welder who dreams of winning a place at a prestigious dance school. Before their success with the likes of *Top Gun*, *Days of Thunder*, *Beverley Hills Cop* and *The Rock*, the pair collaborated with director Adrian Lyne (later an Oscar nominee for *Fatal Attraction*) on the musical romance *Flashdance*.

Despite poor reviews, *Flashdance* was a huge success on its release in April 1983. Starring Jennifer Beals as the welder-cum-dancer and Michael Nouri as her boss/lover it is estimated that the film grossed $150million worldwide. The success of the film has been attributed in parts to the popularity of the recently launched MTV channel in the USA, as sequences from the film were used as music videos for the new channel. Whilst not a musical in the traditional sense, the film featured a popular and successful soundtrack, which was used to provide musical accompaniment to certain scenes in the film.

The film's soundtrack was an unprecedented success, selling over 700,000 copies in its first two weeks of release and over six million copies in the USA alone. Containing the US number One hit *Maniac* by Michael Sembello, the soundtrack also featured songs by Joe Esposito, Laura Branigan and Kim Carnes as well as Irene Cara's title track.

Although she had been a child star, Cara had first shot to stardom in the aptly titled 1980 film *Fame*. As her character Coco Hernandez she sang both the theme song and the follow-up single *Out Here On My Own*, which were both nominated for an Oscar (*Fame* eventually won the

Academy Award). Declining the opportunity to reprise her role in the subsequent television series to pursue her acting or recording career, she appeared in several films and TV movies before being asked to collaborate with Keith Forsey and Giorgio Moroder on the soundtrack for the film *Flashdance*.

Cara was initially reluctant to work with Moroder to avoid comparisons with Moroder's previous collaborator Donna Summer, but eventually agreed to the project. Moroder wrote the music for the song and Forsey and Cara co-wrote the lyrics in the back of a car on the way to record the song in a New York studio. The song was eventually called *Flashdance... What A Feeling!* even though the word 'Flashdance' doesn't appear in the lyrics. The song itself appears over the title sequence of the 1983 movie as well as providing the backing for the main character's dance audition routine at the end of the film.

Released in early 1983 alongside the film, the song was a huge worldwide hit. It reached number One on the US Billboard charts in May 1983 and was the third biggest selling single in America that year. It reached number One in countries as diverse as Italy, Japan, Sweden and New Zealand but peaked at number Two in the UK, being held off the top spot by Rod Stewart's hit *Baby Jane*. It was the UK's 25th biggest selling single of 1983 spending fourteen weeks on the charts.

The song also earned Cara her second Academy Award, winning the Oscar for Best Original Song in 1984. It also won the equivalent Golden Globe and Cara won the Grammy for Best Pop Vocal Performance in the same year.

Flashdance proved to be the zenith of Cara's career, as her subsequent releases failed to reach the top Forty in the UK. She appeared in the 1985 film *City Heat* alongside Burt Reynolds and Clint Eastwood before spending the 90s scoring several moderate European dance hits and touring in Europe and Asia. She did however team up with the Swiss/German rapper DJ Bobo in 2001 to record a dance remix of *Flashdance*, which reached the top three in both Switzerland and Germany.

The song itself has been covered on several occasions. Abba tribute act Bjorn Again released *Flashdance* as a single in 1993, but it spent just one week at number sixty-five on the UK charts. Australian 'supergroup' the Young Divas recorded *What A Feeling* as the opening track to their 2006 self-titled album and the song has also been covered by Serbian metal band Alogia and punk band Six Pack. I has also been parodied and imitated on countless occasions including the video for Geri Halliwell's cover of the 80s classic *It's Raining Men*.

Whilst not as well-known in the UK as Cara's number one hit *Fame*, *Flashdance* capitalised on the burgeoning popularity of the music channel MTV and became a multi-million selling, Oscar winning success. It is a terrific feel-good pop record and certainly deserves its place at number twenty-six on Billboard's Hot 100 All Time Top Songs.

90 Laura Branigan
Gloria

Released: 18 December 1982 **Atlantic K 11759**
Highest UK Chart Position: #6

Laura Branigan was born in 1957 in the north New York town of Brewster. She grew up in the nearby town of Armonk, but it wasn't until she took the lead role in a school musical in her high school senior year that she considered a career in the entertainment business. After graduation, Branigan moved to New York City to study at the American Academy of Dramatic Arts and, having completed her studies, she secured work as a backing vocalist for legendary singer-songwriter Leonard Cohen on his European tours.

With ambitions to be a solo performer, Branigan signed a contract in 1979 with Ahmet Ertegun, the founder of Atlantic Records. Once signed, Atlantic had a dilemma as to how to position Branigan with the record buying public as her powerful alto voice (she had an unusual four octave range) was difficult to categorise. It took a couple of years before the label decided what sort of material they felt most appropriate for the singer and it wasn't until 1982 that her first solo album *Branigan* was released.

Deciding to position Branigan as a straightforward pop artist, her debut single *All Night With Me* was moderately successful on the Billboard chart in early 1982. It was to be her follow-up single from *Branigan* however - the Eighties classic *Gloria* - that would catapult the singer to international stardom.

Gloria wasn't an original Branigan song but actually a cover of a 1979 Italian love song written by Umberto Tozzi and Giancarlo Bigazzi. Tozzi had achieved success in his home country as both a singer and songwriter in the mid 1970's and then across Europe with his 1977 hit *Ti-Amo*. *Gloria* was a hit for Tozzi in Italy in 1979.

Whilst Tozzi's single was a slow paced love song, Branigan's version was reworked with the Italian's own arranger, Greg Mathieson. Alongside fellow producer Jack White, they updated the production and turned the song into a powerful, medium paced pop record (as Branigan said – with 'an American kick'). With re-written lyrics (not a literal translation of the Italian original) the song was initially popular in dance and gay clubs before crossing over onto mainstream American radio.

Gloria was one of the biggest American hits of the decade, spending a record thirty-six weeks on the chart. It climbed to number Two in the Billboard chart and number One in Canada and Australia as well as reaching number Six in the UK in February 1983. It also earned Branigan a Grammy nomination for Best Female Pop Vocal Of the Year, although the singer lost out to fellow American Melissa Manchester.

Gloria also featured in the 1983 smash hit movie *Flashdance* and featured on the soundtrack along with a new Branigan song, *Imagination*. The soundtrack reached number One on the album charts selling over six million copies in the US alone as well as winning the 1983 Grammy award for Best Soundtrack.

Many covers of *Gloria* have been recorded in foreign languages but, interestingly, the lyrics are not always literal translations. It is also reported that the British guitar band Pulp used the guitar line from *Gloria* for their 1995 hit *Disco 2000* and that singer Jarvis Cocker changed the girls name in the song from Gloria to Deborah to avoid litigation and drawing obvious attention to the borrowed riff.

Branigan's success continued with her two follow-up albums, *Branigan 2* in 1983 and *Self Control* in 1984. The former featured the hit singles *Solitaire* (the first chart hit for legendary lyricist and songwriter Diane Warren) and the ballad *How Am I Supposed To Live Without You?* (which later became the debut hit for its co-writer Michael Bolton). The latter album featured the huge title track *Self Control*, which became Branigan's biggest hit in the UK, reaching number Five in August 1984 in a seventeen week chart stay.

Branigan continued to record albums throughout the 1980s and 1990s as well as recording television and radio advertising campaigns (for the likes of Dr Pepper and Chrysler) and making guest appearances on various television shows including *CHiPS* and *Knight Rider*.

Sadly, on 26th August 2004 (shortly after re-recording updated versions of her two biggest hits (*Gloria* and *Self Control*) alongside some of Europe's top remixers) Branigan died suddenly of a brain aneurysm. Her loyal fans (affectionately referred to by the singer as her 'other half') arranged a memorial service on the first anniversary of her death in Long Island and campaigns by fan groups also led to the re-release of some of Branigan's early albums and a *Greatest Hits* package in 2007.

91 Duran Duran
Girls On Film

Released: 25 July 1981   EMI5206
Highest UK Chart Position: #5

One of the most popular and biggest selling bands of the 1980s, Duran Duran were formed in Birmingham by school friends Nick Rhodes and Andy Taylor in 1978. Named after a character from the Jane Fonda science-fiction film *Barbarella*, the make-up of the band changed several times in the early years before the quintet settled on their line-up after the addition of vocalist Simon le Bon in 1980.

By the end of 1980 the band had been signed to EMI Records and they were a popular part of the burgeoning New Romatic movement alongside bands such as Spandau Ballet and Ultravox. Their debut single *Planet Earth* was released in February 1981 and made the top Twenty in the UK before record company EMI decided to select their next single for release, *Careless Memories*, which reached the lower echelons of the top Forty in May 1981.

The next single to be chosen (this time by the band) was a song written in 1980 by the band and their previous lead vocalist Andy Wickett. Wickett wrote the melody for *Girls On Film* and it was first recorded by the band for their original demo at a studio in Moseley, featuring a lyrical message about fashion model exploitation. Wickett left Duran Duran shortly afterwards for personal reasons, but the band liked *Girls On Film* and wanted to use it for their debut album. Wickett was paid £600 and asked to sign a waiver removing his rights to the song, something his solicitor later admitted that he wouldn't be able to fight as EMI would 'buy him out of court'.

With the album and single version sounding very different to the original demo (the single version begins with the famous camera motor drive sounds), *Girls On Film* was released as Duran Duran's third single in July 1981. It climbed to the top Thirty in the UK before the band recorded their now infamous video for the song. Produced in early August 1981 and directed by the esteemed video artists Kevin Godley and Lol Crème the video featured topless women mud wrestling and depictions of other sexual fetishes. The intention was for the video to be played on screens in the newer nightclubs and on adult pay-TV channels in a deliberate attempt to get the band noticed and to get people talking about the song.

The video was released just two weeks after the music station MTV launched in the US and a heavily edited version of the video was an early favourite on the channel. The BBC banned the video, which again generated huge publicity that the band unashamedly capitalised on. The song itself, fuelled by the coverage the video had generated, reached number Five on the UK singles chart in August 1981 and propelled the band's eponymously titled debut album to number Three on the album charts where its run lasted for over two years.

After the success of *Girls On Film* Duran Duran's popularity soared and they quickly became one of the most successful artists of the early 1980s. Their second album *Rio* spawned the hit singles *Hungry Like The Wolf, My Own Way, Save a Prayer* and the title track *Rio* and the band cleverly used the promotional videos for these songs to generate interest in their music. Exploiting the huge success of MTV, the band made iconic and memorable videos often featuring exotic foreign locations – the films for *Hungry Like The Wolf* and *Save a Prayer* were filmed in Sri Lanka and *Rio* on a yacht in the Caribbean.

Further success came with the release of their 1983 single *Is There Something I Should Know?* which achieved the rare feat of entering the UK singles chart at number One (only The Police, the Jam and Adam and the Ants had managed it since the turn of the decade). *Union of the Snake* and *New Moon On Monday* both reached the top Ten before their 1984 release *The Reflex* returned the band to the number One spot. It was also the first of their two American number Ones (*A View To A Kill* was the other).

1985 saw the band splinter into separate projects. John and Andy Taylor teamed up with Robert Palmer to form Power Station scoring hits with the songs *Some Like it Hot* and their cover of the T-Rex classic *Get It On*. Le Bon and Nick Rhodes formed Arcadia whose single *Election Day* also made the UK top Ten. Roger Taylor provided drums for both bands.

Despite a short reformation (to record the brilliant Bond theme *A View To A Kill* and to perform at 1985's Live Aid) the band had effectively split. Rhodes, Le Bon and John Taylor continued as Duran Duran with the albums *Notorious, Big Thing* and *Duran Duran* achieving minor success including the superb top Ten hit single *Ordinary World*.

In 2001 the band announced they were reforming with their original line-up and a series of sell-out tours followed and a return to the top Ten with the single *Reach Up (For The Sunrise)* in 2004. Andy Taylor left the band for a second time in 2006 but, with over seventy million records sold worldwide and new material in the pipeline, Duran Duran continue as one of the most instantly recognisable artists in British music.

92

Jermaine Stewart
We Don't Have To (Take Our Clothes Off)

Released: 9 August 1986   10 TEN 96
Highest UK Chart Position: #2

Whilst it is easy to recall the colourful and lighthearted legacy of the 1980s, there was of course a darker side to the decade that is often easily forgotten. The Falklands War, miner's strikes, inner city riots and African famine dominated the headlines and, whilst the latter part of the decade may have brought us Kylie and Jason, it also brought on the very real dangers of AIDS.

Acquired Immune Deficiency Syndrome was first reported in America on the 5th of June, 1981. Initially, the disease did not have an official name and it was often referred to by way of the diseases associated with it or as 'GRID' (Gay Related Immune Deficiency). It was not until July 1982 that the name 'AIDS' was adopted to describe the disease, once it had been established that it was not isolated to the homosexual community.

By 2007, an estimated 33.2 million people lived with the disease worldwide and it had killed an estimated 2.1million people. Although treatments from AIDS and HIV can slow the course of the disease, there remains no cure.

Despite its impact on the sexual landscape of the late 1980s there remain relatively few songs written directly about the disease. The most famous is Bruce Springsteen's 1993 hit *Streets of Philadelphia* – as much for the context of the movie from which it was taken as the lyrics themselves.

One of the earliest and most commercially successful hits to tackle the early AIDS scare was this great up-tempo dance smash of 1986 in which Jermaine Stewart made it clear that sex wasn't the only way two people could have fun together. No, they could dance, party or even drink cherry wine....

Stewart was born in Columbus, Ohio in 1957 and started dancing and performing from an early age. At school he charged other kids $1 for dancing lessons and, following his family's move to Chicago in 1972, Stewart got a job on hit TV music show *Soul Train* as a dancer.

From there, he began singing backing vocals for great soul artists including the Staple Singers, the Chi-Lites and Shalamar (*Jody* – a tribute to Shalamar singer Jody Watley would later be a hit for Stewart). In 1983, he sang on Culture Club's second album *Colour By Numbers* and it was the band's contacts that helped Stewart secure his first solo recording deal with Arista Records.

After success with his debut album *The World Is Out*, Stewart teamed up with two of the 1980's most famous and respected music producers, Narada Michael Walden and John 'Jellybean' Benitez to record the follow-up *Frantic Romantic*.

The first single from this album ended up being Stewart's biggest international hit. Written by Narada Michael Walden and Preston Q Glass, *We Don't Have To* rocketed into the top Ten across the world including making the US Billboard top Five. Its chart progress was certainly helped by an appearance on the popular US series *Miami Vice*. In total it spent almost four months on the UK singles chart, including a month inside the top Three in September 1986. Indeed, it took the UK's biggest selling single of that year (*Don't Leave Me This Way* by the Communards) to keep it off the number One spot.

The AIDS awareness message of the song was clear – Stewart urging his date to 'show some class' by them getting to know each other better before jumping into bed together. Stewart wanted the song to be used as a theme for people to be able to say 'no' to the pressures society forced on them – drink, drugs and in this case, sex.

The song itself has proved particularly enduring and remains a well-known disco anthem. A number of cover versions having been recorded, including those by British artists Clea and Lil' Chris, who had limited single success with their versions of the song. The tune also returned to the UK top Five in August 2007 as US hip-hop artists Gym Class Heroes used the main hook from the song as the basis for their hit *Clothes Off!*

After *We Don't Have To* several more hits followed for Stewart (1988's *Say It Again* made the UK top Ten) and he also had the somewhat dubious pleasure of providing the song *Hot and Cold*, performed over the closing credits of the 1989 comedy *Weekend At Bernie's*. Sadly, after a long illness, Stewart died in 1997 from liver cancer, ironically caused by AIDS. He was just 39 years old.

93 Blancmange
Living On The Ceiling

Released: 30 October 1982 **London BLANC3**
Highest UK Chart Position: #7

Neil Arthur and Stephen Luscombe formed their first band in 1978 following a chance meeting at the art college in London where Arthur was studying. Sharing a love for experimental sound, the pair met when Arthur's band the Viewfinders and Luscombe's group Miru were rehearsing in the same art college building. Their music wasn't their primary concern for the first couple of years as Arthur was completing his college course whilst Luscombe held down a job as a graphic designer at a printing company.

The pair spent months writing and recording a lot of material, capturing this work on old tape machines (the pair recorded everything they wrote). These tapes were then often used to manipulate the sounds they had recorded with instruments as strange as old washing machines and vacuum cleaners. The pair got their first break when a friend of Arthur's, David Hill (who also worked as a life model at the art college) asked the pair to record an EP.

Having to come up with a name for their band, the decision was ultimately made at a party at Luscombe's in 1980. Fed up with eating the party food, Arthur bought a takeaway from the local curry house but dropped the meal as he re-entered the flat. Scooping up the remains into a pint pot, Luscombe appeared carrying a rabbit shaped blancmange mould and so the pair decided to choose between the possible names 'pint of curry' or 'the blancmange'. The latter was chosen, and the 'the' only dropped in a nod to London Records when they asked the pair if they'd consider changing their moniker.

A thousand copies of the *Irene and Mavis EP* were pressed and this led to their track *Sad Day* being used on a Some Bizarre compilation album of new, unsigned artists. Support slots with the popular new wave bands Depeche Mode and Japan followed, whilst ex-Human League writer Martyn Ware also produced four tracks for the duo.

London Records eventually signed Blancmange in 1982 at which time the pair began working as musicians full-time. Their first two singles *God's Kitchen* and *Feel Me* reached the top Seventy-Five, the latter peaking just outside the top Forty.

Their third single was to be a song that the duo had written and recorded a couple of years previously. *Living On The Ceiling* originated in 1980 and was written in Arthur's housing association squat in North London. Starting to play a melody he had written, the singer made a mistake - but when the pair played back the recording they realised that the incorrect tune actually sounded much better. Arthur had also scribbled some lyrics for the tune in his diary about the ups and downs of a relationship where the two parties are never quite sure where they stand with each other.

The use of the line 'up the bloody tree' in the lyrics caused some consternation with London Records, who believed that the inclusion of such a swear word would limit its radio airplay. An alternative version was recorded, with Arthur using the line 'up the cuckoo tree' although the original was the one most commonly played on radio and television.

During the recording of their debut album *Happy Families*, the duo were introduced to musicians Dinesh and Deepak who provided both percussion (tabla) and sitar on the song which transformed it from the demo into the version that was ultimately released. An Eastern/Indian influence is clear throughout the band's work and the use of Indian instrumentation gave their synthesised pop sound a unique identity. The Indian pair also contributed on a number of other Blancmange songs both on *Happy Families* and their subsequent releases.

Living On The Ceiling was released in October 1982 and quickly reached the top Ten. It spent three weeks at number Seven in the UK top Forty, eventually spending over three months on the chart. It launched the pair's successful career and the follow-up single *Waves* reached the UK top Twenty whilst their debut album *Happy Families* spent nine months on the chart.

Second album *Mange Tout* was also a commercial success, as were the singles *Blind Vision*, *Don't Tell Me* and their cover of the Abba hit *The Day Before You Came*. Third album *Believe You Me* was less successful, and the band officially announced their split in 1987.

Arthur and Luscombe spent the next two decades working on their own solo projects before announcing in 2008 that they have reformed and are working on new material. *Living On The Ceiling* also made a reappearance in 2008 when it was featured on a long-running television advertisement for Berocca vitamin tablets.

94 Strawberry Switchblade
Since Yesterday

Released: 17 November 1984   Korova KOW38
Highest UK Chart Position: #5

Strawberry Switchblade's story is topsy-turvy in all sorts of ways. They had a name before they had a band, formed a band and arranged a gig without having any songs and recorded radio sessions without having a demo tape. Still, this slice of mid 80's breezy pop ended up selling almost a quarter of a million copies despite their unorthodox route to fame.

Jill Bryson and Rose McDowall met in Glasgow during the fledgling punk scene in 1977. Bryson was an art school student and McDowall worked in a local cake shop by day and performed in the band The Poems by night. The girls socialised with many of the up and coming local artists of the time who encouraged them to start a band of their own. Whilst on a bus one day, James Kirk (the guitarist from Scottish band Orange Juice) had told Bryson about a new fanzine he had come up with called *Strawberry Switchblade*. Bryson loved the title, and Kirk was happy for her to use it as the name of her and McDowall's new project.

They organised a gig before they had written more than a couple of songs and had two months to come up with enough material for their first live performance at the Spaghetti Factory in Glasgow in December 1981. They continued to play live in their home town and secured a radio session with Kid Jensen somewhat by accident, after fellow Glaswegian Jim Kerr (of Simple Minds) had namechecked the band in a radio interview when asked who was currently big on the Glasgow music scene.

John Peel's producers also requested a session and the girls recorded two four song sessions for Jensen and Peel three days apart in October 1982. Bill Drummond (Echo and the Bunnymen's manager and the main man behind 1990s band the KLF) heard the Jensen session and signed the girls, and their first single *Trees and Flowers* was released on the

92 Happy Customers indie label. The record features several friends of Drummond, including the Madness rhythm section and Aztec Camera's Roddy Frame.

Although *Trees and Flowers* came out in 1983, the recording of their debut album took over a year. Their original recordings were deemed too gentle and delicate, and both their new label Warner and the girls themselves wanted a more poppy sound. David Motion was brought in to produce the album and introduced a more synthesized electronic feel to the recordings.

The most prominent song on the album was the upbeat pop tune *Since Yesterday*. With lyrics re-written late on (Motion thought the original words were somewhat repetitive) and the fanfare from Sibelius' 5th Symphony added to the start of the song, it was released as the first single from their eponymously titled album.

Released in October 1984 with a mainly black and white video directed by Tim Pope (with help from the animators from *The Magic Roundabout*), *Since Yesterday* spend a couple of months bubbling around the lower reaches of the top Seventy-Five chart before the record company decided to focus their efforts on it over the Christmas period.

This promotion kicked in and the record slowly climbed in the New Year of 1985, eventually reaching number Five at the end of January. Their trademark black and white gothic look (featuring polka dot rah-rah skirts as on the sleeve of the single) also attracted much attention.

Despite the success of *Since Yesterday*, their two follow-up singles failed to reach the top 40 and then a cover of the Dolly Parton song *Jolene* (a compromise reached with the record company) also failed to chart. WEA began to lose faith in the girls who themselves became disillusioned with the industry and the compromises they were being asked to make. They therefore split up after one album, and have the unenviable 'one hit wonder' tag as *Since Yesterday* was their only UK top Forty hit.

Whilst *Since Yesterday* was a nice breezy mid-80s pop record, and the girls toured with the likes of Howard Jones, their influences, look and approach were not particularly from the pop mainstream. From their punk beginnings to their desire for interesting instrumentation in their records, it is clear that the duo were somehow hijacked into the pop world around the time of their hit single. Their sound lives on, however, providing inspiration for the likes of the Cranberries and Belle and Sebastian.

95

Edelweiss
Bring Me Edelweiss

Released: 29 April 1989   WEAYZ 353
Highest UK Chart Position: #5

Austria hasn't historically provided the world with many pop stars. Historically, of course, it has provided the world with some of the greatest names in music as Mahler, Mozart, Strauss, Haydn, and Schubert all hail from the country. In the 21st century, however, Austria's general contribution to the world of music has been virtually non-existent. (Some would say their contribution to the world in general has been largely non-existent – Niki Lauda, Adolf Hitler and Arnold Schwarzenegger are probably Austria's three most famous 21st century sons, and we'd happily have done without at least two of them).

Falco, of course, was Austrian and was inspired by the biopic of his country's most famous musical son to write the number one hit *Rock Me Amadeus* in 1986. Beyond that, though (whilst tipping a nod to Penny McLean, singer of disco combo Silver Convention) Austria hasn't exactly been a hotbed of 20th century pop talent.

The one bright contribution the Republic made to the chart scene of the late 1980s came from a bizarre borderline novelty pop trio who crowbarred as many Austrian clichés into their songs and stage act as humanly possible....

In 1988, Austrian musicians Walter Werzowa and Martin Gletschermayer had an idea for a side-project involving making a pop record including some traditional Tyrolean yodelling. Calling this project 'Edelweiss', they loosely followed the advice of Bill Drummond and Jimmy Cauty's book *The Manual*, a tongue in cheek guide to achieving a number One record. The authors (better known as the KLF) had done exactly this with *Doctorin' The Tardis* as the Timelords the previous year. Over the course of two to three weekends, the duo (along with friend Matthias

Schweger), and with the help of amazing yodeller Maria Mathis came up with a song called *Bring Me Edelweiss* which sounded great but was missing a traditional chorus. Sitting in their studio drinking schnapps, the writers heard the old Abba classic *SOS* and used that melody to fit their lyric 'bring me edelweiss'.

The song was passed to their friend, record company owner Marcus Speigl (he had discovered fellow Austrian star Falco) who loved it and turned it into a single. Intending the song to be a fun and humorous mickey-take of Austrian ski resort life, it was number One in Austria two weeks after release. A fortnight later it had made number One in Germany and its success spread across Europe like wildfire. The song made number Five in the UK in May 1989.

Bring Me Edelweiss was one of the biggest hits in Europe of 1989. Promotion and appearances for the record took the band from country to country and their novelty and unusual stage act went with them. The show tended to include rubber chickens, lederhosen, weird and wonderful costumes and stage decoration and often they left the stage a complete mess. At the MTV awards, the Fine Young Cannibals even refused go on after Edelweiss as the stage was such a state.

The costumes and general accoutrements making their way from country to country also made the band well known to airport staff and customs officers across the continent. Their hand baggage frequently included chicken costumes or ski poles and the customs officials ended up getting to know them and letting them through with their strange luggage.

After huge success across Europe, the band was taken to America in search of a record deal and Sire/Mute records were keen to sign them. As part of the negotiation, Walter and the boys had the surreal experience of having two record company executives standing in front of different stereo speakers with telephones playing *Bring Me Edelweiss* to none other than Madonna (who was Sire's biggest artist at that time). Atlantic Records ended up signing the band.

Although *Bring Me Edelweiss* sold five million copies worldwide, the band failed to successfully follow-up the single and so they are generally regarded as a 'one-hit wonder'. After Edelweiss, Walter Werzowa moved to the US where he has subsequently had an acclaimed and successful career as a composer. He won an Emmy in 2006 for his work on *Superbowl XXXIX* and has composed music for film scores including *Eraser*, *Mimic* and *Mercury Rising*.

Most famously, however, in 1994 Werzowa wrote a four note piece of music which is played somewhere on the planet every five minutes. What has become known as the *Intel Bong* is one of the most recognised and used 'jingles' in the world today and is only marginally less catchy than the 1989 hit he helped to create.

96 Bee Gees
You Win Again

Released: 26 September 1987   **Warner Bros W8351**
Highest UK Chart Position: #1

Including a number One single by one of music's all time biggest selling artists might not sound all that appropriate for a book about 'forgotten pop hits', but if the purpose here is to celebrate the brilliant pop singles of the decade that don't get played to death in clubs, at weddings or on the radio, then this song falls squarely into that category.

The Bee Gees (not named after anything to do with the 'Brothers Gibb', incidentally, but rather as the initials of radio DJ Bill Gates and promoter Bill Goode who helped launch the brothers' career) had been performing and recording for over a quarter of a century by the time *You Win Again* was released.

They first hit the charts in 1967 and spent a successful early part of their career as a harmonic soft-rock outfit, scoring bit hits in both the UK and US with songs like *Massachussets*, *Words* and *I've Gotta Get A Message To You*. As their career declined in the 1970's, the brothers were forced to change their style and moved towards making funkier disco records.

Their career was already on the rise again by the time they agreed to participate in the writing of the *Saturday Night Fever* soundtrack and it was this album that propelled the band back to the top of the charts. In a thirty two week period around the end of 1977, records written by the Gibbs spent twenty five of those weeks at number One in the US. Their own *How Deep Is Your Love*, *Stayin' Alive* and *Night Fever*, brother Andy's hits *Love Is (Thicker Than Water)* and *Shadow Dancing* and Yvonne Elliman's *If I Can't Have You* (from the *Saturday Night Fever* soundtrack) all topped the Billboard charts in an astonishing eight month period.

The 1980s saw another decline in the band's popularity, and the brothers embarked on a number of solo projects as well as writing and producing successfully for other artists including Barbra Streisand, Kenny Rogers and Diana Ross (her mammoth hit *Chain Reaction* was a Bee Gees creation). After the release of their fourteenth studio album *Living Eyes* in 1981, it took six years before the brothers went back into the studio where they reunited with producer Arif Mardin to record the *ESP* album.

The key track for this album had a title based on an old Hank Williams song (although Robin Gibb had not heard that track), a Barry Gibb melody and an instantly recognisable drumbeat created by Maurice Gibb and Rhett Lawrence. *You Win Again* took over a month to edit and mix before the band were happy and it was released on 26 September 1987 with the band convinced that it was going to be a big hit.

As predicted by the band, but still somewhat unexpectedly (considering the critics' assertion that their careers were pretty much over) the Bee Gees 1987 return was spectacularly successful. *You Win Again* was a huge hit around the world (with the exception, somewhat surprisingly, of the US) and spent four weeks at number One in the UK in October 1987. Keeping hugely successful current artists like George Michael and Rick Astley off the top spot, *You Win Again* was the band's fifth UK number One and their first since 1979. It was the UK's fourth biggest selling single of 1987.

Despite their follow-up singles failing to make the top Forty, the Bee Gees had announced their return to form in style. Over the next decade they would have further top Five hits in the UK (with the likes of *Secret Love*, *Alone* and *For Whom The Bell Tolls*), win countless awards (including the 1997 Brit award for 'Outstanding Contribution to British Music') and were awarded the CBE in the 2002 New Years Honours list.

Their last album was 2001's *This Is Where I Came In,* as in January 2003 Maurice Gibb died suddenly from a strangulated intestine. Initially, Robin and Barry were going to continue writing and recording under the band name but as time has passed they have decided to retire the 'Bee Gees' name having sold almost seven million singles in the UK alone.

The Bee Gees remain one of the biggest selling artists of all time with an estimated 220 million record sales. In 1997, it was suggested in their 'Rock and Roll Hall of Fame' citation that only the Beatles, Elvis, Garth Brooks, Paul McCartney and Michael Jackson had sold more records, and this does not include the countless million sales achieved by songs written and/or produced by the band.

You Win Again is one of the biggest selling songs that you hardly ever hear. Its driving drumbeat, harmonic vocals and brilliantly catchy melody make it one of the most perfect pop creations of the generation. The best British number One single of the 1980's? No arguments from me.

97 Nick Berry
Every Loser Wins

Released: 4 October 1986   BBC RESL 204
Highest UK Chart Position: #1

The path from 'appearing in a rubbish TV series' to 'the top of the hit parade' is a long and well-trodden one. Every aspiring singer in the current era who takes a part in a hopeless TV drama or soap opera in the hope that their pop star ambitions will then be fulfilled has, pretty much, one man to thank.

Eight months after the launch of the BBC's new flagship drama series *Eastenders* the scriptwriters were forced to come up with a 'young' character after the sudden departure of David Scarboro, the original Mark Fowler. The flash womaniser Simon Wicks ('Wicksy' to his mates, and fifteen million viewers) played by Nick Berry was created and became an instant audience favourite.

In the summer of 1986 scriptwriter Tony Holland and producer Julia Smith decided to build in a storyline involving 'an important and complicated story about the ups and downs of a pop group'. The Walford band (called *Dog Market*) included not only Wicksy and Eddie Hunter but also, alarmingly, Sharon Watts and Ian Beale. Scheduled to make their debut in the Queen Vic (of course) in August 1986, their amplifier fused the electrics in the pub and landlord Den Watts threw them out, at which point they changed their name to *The Banned*. You see what they did, there?

Entering a young musicians competition, The Banned wanted to perform Wicksy's composition *Something Outa Nothing* but after fellow band-member Harry Reynolds disagreed, Wicksy left the group. Retaining his dream of becoming a musician, Wicksy wrote the ballad *Every Loser Wins* and performed this song (accompanied by a piano) on *Eastenders* in October 1986.

Whilst the *Eastenders* band storyline may not have been a success (Holland and Smith thought it lacked credibility) the single certainly was. Released whilst the storyline was still running, and with a single sleeve shamelessly including the line 'the song performed by Wicksy in *Eastenders*'' the BBC banked on the show's audience to buy the record.

Buy it in their tens of thousands they did, and *Every Loser Wins* held a record that stood for fifteen years for the 'highest ever climbing chart single' with its sixty-two place leap on 11 October 1986 (Steps' *The Way You Make Me Feel* climbed seventy places in January 2001). It spent three weeks at number One in the UK and sold over a million copies, becoming the years' second biggest selling single (behind the Communards' *Don't Leave Me This Way*). It also won composer Simon May an Ivor Novello award.

Every Loser Wins was actually May's third TV theme success in 1986. The vocal version of the Eastenders theme tune, *Anyone Can Fall In Love* reached number Four for Queen Vic landlady Anita Dobson in August 1986 and his song *Always There* (the theme to the BBC boating drama *Howard's Way*) reached number Thirteen for Marti Webb at the same time *Every Loser Wins* was at number One.

The song that Wicksy's fellow Banned members performed at the young musician's contest (before Harry Reynolds sabotaged their stage performance resulting in the band being booed off stage), *Something Outa Nothing* was eventually recorded by Letitia Dean and Paul Medford and reached number Twelve in the UK charts in November 1986. The Guardian voted the Banned the 9th worst soap star 'artist' of all time (just ahead of Coronation Street's Jack Duckworth.)

Nick Berry, of course, went on to have a successful TV career throughout the 1980s and 1980s with shows such as *Heartbeat* and *Harbour Lights*. His re-recording of the Buddy Holly classic *Heartbeat* (used as the theme to the series) made number Two in the UK charts in June 1992.

Every Loser Wins is one of those records that, whilst it was unbelievably popular at the time, is now considered rather naff. For a million seller, it gets precious little airplay and I think is seen as something of a novelty. Clearly its appearance on *Eastenders* did its sales no harm at all, but that won't automatically catapult a rubbish song to number One (take the Anita Dobson hit as a case in point – it effectively got four plays a week on the BBC but only made number Four.)

The truth is that whilst it may not be the finest ballad of the decade, it actually stands up pretty well as a gentle piano-led paean. It's clearly a better song than, say, *Anyone Can Fall In Love* and Berry is a talented enough performer. I think I'd file this one under 'unfairly consigned to the nostalgia dustbin'.

98 Bobby McFerrin
Don't Worry, Be Happy

Released: 24 September 1988   **Manhattan MT56**
Highest UK Chart Position: #2

Originally intended as a way of differentiating Renaissance polyphony and Baroque concertato style (no, me neither), 'a cappella' (literally: 'from the chapel/choir') has come to mean an all-vocal performance unaccompanied by any musical instruments. Originally, and most commonly, a religious style (Gregorian chanting remains one of the most well-known examples), a cappella has in the last few decades also been increasingly associated with modern pop and rock music.

The UK saw a couple of a cappella number One singles (its first) in the 1980's. The most famous was the Flying Pickets' cover of Yazoo's classic *Only You*, which spent five weeks at the top of the charts over the Christmas of 1983. Three years later, the Housemartins' unaccompanied version of the Isley Jasper Isley standard *Caravan Of Love* also made number One.

It took a further two years though for the Billboard charts to see its first a cappella number One single and when it did, it was a song that has become one of the most popular/annoying* (*delete as applicable) pop records of all time.

In 1988, well-known and well-respected jazz musician Bobby McFerrin noticed a poster in the apartment of San Francisco jazz band Tuck and Patti featuring the spiritual master and self-declared 'avatar of his age' Mehar Baba. It contained the expression 'don't worry, be happy', a phrase regularly used on Baba's inspirational cards and posters of that era.

McFerrin was recording his *Simple Pleasures* album at the time and he already had a roster of songs to be included on the record. One morning when walking into the Fantasy Studios in Berkeley, California, the singer and producers walked through doors saying 'Stu Dios' and began singing and playing in dreadful Spanish accents. Sitting at the piano singing as 'Juan', McFerrin sang the riff to a song he had come up with based on the Baba mantra 'don't worry, be happy'.

Encouraged by producer Linda Goldstein and engineer Chris Terguson to write some verses for the song, *Don't Worry, Be Happy* was created in an hour or so in the studio and recorded as an a cappella eight-track with McFerrin providing both the vocals and the backing accompaniment.

Included in the Tom Cruise film *Cocktail* and then released as single, *Don't Worry, Be Happy* became the first a cappella American number One single in September 1988, sandwiched between chart toppers from rock legends Guns N'Roses and Def Leppard. The song climbed to number Two in the UK charts, narrowly missing out on the top spot thanks to Whitney Houston's Olympic anthem *One Moment In Time*.

The song became a mammoth hit all over the world, selling several million copies. Its video, featuring McFerrin alongside vaudeville clown Bill Irwin and Oscar-winning actor and comic Robin Williams, helped it gain much MTV coverage and McFerrin won three Grammy awards in 1989 for Best Pop Song, Record of the Year and Best Male Vocal Performance. The song was also used in George Bush Sr's Presidential election campaign until McFerrin (a Democrat) objected.

The song itself has become something of a everyday mantra and a feel-good song – McFerrin himself admitted that 'don't worry, be happy' was a pretty neat four-word philosophy. However, its over simplicity and denial can also be pretty irritating, and as anyone who has suffered from clinical depression will tell you, it generally requires more than the adoption of a Pollyanna attitude to get over your troubles. Rap group Public Enemy used the line in their song *Fight The Power* to criticize those people with a rosy outlook on the world.

Indeed, for several years following the success of the single it was believed that McFerrin himself had failed to take his own advice and had committed suicide. The tale was justly ironic and therefore much believed, although there was clearly no evidence of truth in it. McFerrin has admitted to being dismayed that people believe him to be a '"one hit wonder' when the reality is that he has had a long and distinguished recording career over several decades. He has described *Don't Worry, Be Happy* as being like '...one of his children. Some you want around and some you want to send off to college as soon as possible…..'

Love it or hate it, *Don't Worry, Be Happy* was an interesting, catchy song, and whether you believe in its happy-clappy message or not, it's practically impossible not to sing along.

99   Tears for Fears
Everybody Wants To Rule The World

Released: 30 March 1985   Mercury IDEA9
Highest UK Chart Position: #2

Roland Orzabal and Curt Smith met aged thirteen in Bath in the late 1970s. They formed a series of bands as teenagers, culminating in their band Neon, featuring future Tears for Fears drummer Matty Elias as well as Pete Byrne and Rob Fisher (who would go on to form Naked Eyes and Climie Fisher).

After a 1980 album as the band Graduate, the duo formed the band Tears for Fears, a name taken from Dr Arthur Janov's influential 1970 book *The Primal Scream* (the notion of 'tears as a replacement for fears'). Whilst Orzabal and Smith were the public face of the band, Tears for Fears also included keyboardist Ian Stanley and drummer Elias and they were signed to Phonogram Records in 1981, releasing their first single *Suffer The Children* in late 1981.

It was to be their third single which was their first major hit, as the haunting *Mad World* reached number Three in November 1982 (later becoming a Christmas number One single for Michael Andrew and Gary Jules twenty one years later.)

After the number One success of their debut album *The Hurting*, the band went back into the studio and originally planned the release of their next single *Mothers Talk* in early 1984. However the duo were unhappy with new producer Jeremy Green and brought Chris Hughes (producer of *The Hurting*) to oversee the second album *Songs From The Big Chair*. Orzabal and Smith believed that each of the songs on the album had a personality of their own, and the title was taken from the TV miniseries *Sybil* about a woman with multiple personality disorder who took refuge in her analyst's 'big chair'.

Whilst the song *Everybody Wants To Rule The World* became the band's biggest international hit, it was in fact the last song recorded for the album. Orzabal and Smith felt that they needed a more up-tempo song for the album and came up with the rhythm for …*Rule The World*. The lyrics were in fact 'everybody wants to go to war' but they were changed as it was felt they were a little too depressing. Written and recorded in two weeks, the song has a serious message about 'everybody wanting power and warfare and the misery that it causes' – as Smith says 'clueless blowhards who shoot first and ask questions later'.

Whilst *Mothers Talk* was a top Twenty hit, it was the follow-up *Shout* which returned the band to the top Five and began their period of huge international success. Interestingly, the final lyrics of *Everybody Wants To Rule The World* ('so sad they had to fade it') are a veiled insult against their record company executives who, at the time, had insisted on five seconds being cut from the end of the earlier single *Shout* as they felt that it would be the difference between it being a hit or not.

Despite the band not believing that …..*Rule The World* was a single, the record company disagreed and released it as the lead single from the album in the US and the third single in the UK and Europe. It was a massive international hit, reaching number Two in the UK and Ireland in April 1985. Its video, featuring vocalist Smith driving around Southern California in an Austin-Healey sports car, also helped it reach number One in the USA thanks to music television station MTV featuring the song heavily.

At the height of their international success in the summer of 1985, the band were scheduled to perform at the Philadelphia leg of Live Aid, however it was announced on the morning of the show that they had withdrawn. The official reason given was that two of their backing musicians had failed to appear for the show after the expiry of their contracts. This non-appearance meant Live Aid organizer Bob Geldof 'gave us [the band] so much gip for not turning up' that they agreed to re-record their hit for 1986's *Sport Aid* campaign. Renamed *Everybody Wants To Run The World* and with all proceeds going towards famine relief in Africa, the song was a hit all over again, reaching number Five in the UK charts in July 1986.

Whilst the duo failed to achieve subsequent international success on the scale of ...*Rule The World*, their superb follow-up album *The Seeds Of Love* spurned hit singles *Sowing The Seeds Of Love* and *Woman in Chains*. The duo split acrimoniously shortly after, although Orzabal kept the band name for output throughout the 1990's. The pair patched up their differences in 2000 and released their most recent album, the appropriately titled *Everyone Loves A Happy Ending* in 2004.

100 Shakin' Stevens
Green Door

Released: 25 July 1981 **Epic A 1354**
Highest UK Chart Position: #1

So, then – who is the biggest selling male UK singles artist of the 1980's? Rick Astley? George Michael? Paul Young? Nope – all wrong. Helped by twenty-eight top Forty hits during the decade, the Welsh Elvis, Shakin' Stevens holds that distinction.

Born Michael Barrett in 1948 in Ely, south Cardiff, Stevens was far from an overnight sensation. He formed his band Shakin' Stevens and the Sunsets in 1969 and spent eight years touring the UK and Europe and recording relatively unsuccessful albums and singles with EMI and CBS. It was whilst performing at a gig with the band, however, that Shaky got his big break. Spotted by theatre producer Jack Good, Stevens was invited to attend an audition for his new musical *Elvis!* and the singer landed one of the lead roles, playing the 'army and movie star' incarnation of Presley in the West End production.

The show ran successfully for almost two years and during that time Stevens came to public prominence through his performances on various TV shows including *Oh Boy* and *Let's Rock*. He left the Sunsets, signed a solo contract and finally had his first top Forty single, *Hot Dog*, in 1980. Six months later, his follow-up single *Marie, Marie* gave Shaky his first taste of European success before his re-working of the song *This Ole House* topped the UK charts and became a huge international hit.

Shaky's second UK number One single was another cover, this time of a popular 1956 Jim Lowe American hit. With music written by Bob Davie and lyrics by Marvin Moore, *Green Door* describes a nondescript establishment with a green door behind which a 'happy crowd' play piano and 'laugh a lot' - and a place in which the singer is not allowed.

The lyrics are apparently inspired by a popular music club in Dallas, Texas where kids were not allowed in and so hung around outside its yellow door. The colour was supposedly changed to green as it 'sounded better'. There was also some speculation that the song referred to the 1930's lesbian *Gateways* club in Chelsea (which had a green door) but this has since been disproved.

Jim Lowe's version (originally called *The Green Door*) spent three weeks at number One in the US in 1956 and reached number Eight in the UK. A more popular version of the song was recorded by English singer Frankie Vaughan and this reached number Two, also in 1956.

The Shaky version was an instant hit, reaching number One in the UK in only its second week of release (it jumped from number Twenty-Two to number One in the charts, toppling the Specials' *Ghost Town*). It stayed at the top of the charts for a month in August 1981.

Stevens career continued to flourish after *Green Door* including two further UK number One singles – the self-penned *Oh Julie* and the 1985 festive classic *Merry Christmas Everyone* (the release of this song was delayed for a year so as not to clash with the release of Band Aid's *Do They Know It's Christmas?*) He also achieved a string of other top Twenty hits including *Cry Just A Little Bit* and *What Do You Want To Make Those Eyes At Me For?*

Shaky's recording career halted in 1993, although he continued to tour and perform live shows for a further decade before finally recording new albums which were released in 2005 and 2007. He also won the hit ITV series *Baby One More Time* in 2005 and the subsequent re-release of *This Ole House* backed with his cover of Pink's *Trouble* made the top Twenty.

Stevens also opened the Saturday bill on the Pyramid stage at Glastonbury in 2008 performing many of his hits but, to the dismay of the large audience, not *Green Door* (despite some loyal fans carrying a full sized green front door to the stage....)

Whilst he might not have been pushing the musical boundaries with his brand of Fifties inspired rock and roll, it is impossible to ignore Shaky's popularity. He has had thirty-three top Forty hits in the UK including four number One singles and has spent over five years on the singles chart. In 2002, Stevens was ranked as the 16th highest selling artist in the UK of all time.

Green Door might well be over fifty years old but it remains a great record and the 'secret' of what is behind the door has perplexed millions for decades. Considering also how many people turned out at 11am on a Saturday morning to see the Welsh rocker at Glastonbury, his status as a bona fide Eighties legend lives on.

101 Liza Minnelli
Losing My Mind

Released: 12 August 1989   **Epic ZEE1**
Highest UK Chart Position: #6

Liza May Minnelli - the daughter of Hollywood starlet Judy Garland and acclaimed film director Vincente Minnelli - remains one of the few remaining Hollywood legends; those stars whose sheer presence and celebrity significantly outweighs their critical output.

From her first appearance aged 17 (in the off Broadway musical *Best Foot Forward*) Minnelli was always destined to be a star. Although she won her first Tony award in 1965 (at the age of just nineteen), it was to be the 1970s that would be the most glittering decade of her career.

Having been nominated for an Academy Award for the 1969 movie *The Sterile Cuckoo*, Minnelli shot to superstardom thanks to her Oscar winning performance as Sally Bowles in the 1972 film musical *Cabaret*. The title song, *Life Is A Cabaret*, became one of Minnelli's signature tunes, as did the theme from her 1977 movie *New York, New York* in which she starred with Robert de Niro. A cover of the theme from *New York, New York* also became a favourite of friend Frank Sinatra and the pair would often appear on stage together to perform a song that has become a modern standard. Minnelli was also nominated for a Golden Globe for her performance as Linda Marolla in the comedy *Arthur*.

Minnelli had released countless albums by the late 1980s, most of which were collections of modern standards, soundtrack recordings or live recordings of shows (including the critically acclaimed *Liza With A Z*). In the summer of 1988, Minnelli met with the successful electropop duo the Pet Shop Boys at the London Mayfair hotel. The trio hit it off immediately and, after they had recorded a demo version of the band's own *Tonight*

Is Forever in New York, Chris Lowe and Neil Tennant sent a number of demos to Minnelli of songs they would like to include on a new album.

The collection of songs that would end up being the acclaimed 1989 *Results* album came from a variety of sources: as well as cover versions of existing Pet Shop Boys songs (including a beautiful orchestral version of their 1987 top Five single *Rent*), there were new Pet Shop Boys compositions (including singles *Don't Drop Bombs* and the stunning *So Sorry, I Said*), a cover of Tanita Tikaram's 1988 single *Twist In My Sobriety* and a version of the 1981 Yvonne Elliman song *Love Pains*.

The first single from the album, however, was a song from the 1971 Broadway musical *Follies*, written by legendary American lyricist and composer Stephen Sondheim. *Follies* is set in an old Broadway theatre scheduled for demolition, during a reunion for the old cast members of an inter-war revue show entitled *Weismann's Follies*. The show ran for over five hundred performances on Broadway and was also successful on its revival in London in the late 1980s, starring Diana Rigg, Julia McKenzie and, later, Eartha Kitt.

Originally sung in the Broadway production by Dorothy Collins, *Losing My Mind* appears towards the finale of the stage show. The Minnelli version had the recognisable and trademark Pet Shop Boys electronic backing and its upbeat and powerful production (by both the band and respected 80s producer Julian Mendelsohn) carried *Losing My Mind* to number Six in the UK singles chart. It remains Minnelli's only top Forty chart success in the UK as, despite the Pet Shop Boys production, follow-up singles *Love Pains*, *Don't Drop Bombs* and *So Sorry, I Said* failed to reach the top Forty. The terrific *Results* album from which the singles were taken reached number Six in the autumn of 1989.

Minnelli also performed *Losing My Mind* at the Grammy Awards in 1990 where she became one of an extremely select group to have won an Emmy, Tony, Oscar and Grammy award, joining the likes of Richard Rodgers, Audrey Hepburn and Mel Brooks.

Losing My Mind has become a favourite 'hit from a musical' and has been covered by the likes of Michael Ball and Shirley Bassey. The Pet Shop Boys also recorded a version of the song themselves and this appeared as the B-side of their 1991 hit *Jealousy*.

Minnelli's career stalled again after the *Results* album and it wasn't until an appearance in the 1997 Broadway musical *Victor/Victoria* and her 2002 concert tour *Liza's Back* that the she returned to the celebrity A-list. An unlikely appearance on My Chemical Romance's 2006 *The Black Parade* album followed before Minnelli finally returned to Broadway in her *Liza's At The Palace....!* show in December 2008.